LEVANA'S TABLE

LEVANA'S TABLE

Kosher Cooking for Everyone

LEVANA KIRSCHENBAUM

Photographs by Ann Stratton

STEWART, TABORI & CHANG

NEW YORK

Page 2: Artichoke Hearts and Carrots in Lemon Sauce; Pages 6–7: Gravlax; Miso, Shiitake, and Swiss Chard Soup; Wild Rice Salad on Sautéed Watercress; Lamb-filled Ravioli with Fresh Tomato Sauce; Olive-Lemon Chicken; and assorted desserts

Published in 2002 by
Stewart, Tabori & Chang
A Company of La Martinière Groupe
115 West 18th Street
New York, NY 10011

Export Sales to all countries except Canada, France,
and French-speaking Switzerland:
Thames and Hudson Ltd.
181A High Holborn
London WC1V 7QX
England

Canadian Distribution:
Canadian Manda Group
One Atlantic Avenue, Suite 105
Toronto, Ontario M6K 3E7
Canada

Library of Congress Cataloging-in-Publication Data is available. Please contact the Library of Congress, Washington, D.C., 20540-4320.

ISBN: 1-58479-273-6

Printed in Italy

10 9 8 7 6 5 4 3 2 1

First Printing

ACKNOWLEDGMENTS

I am blessed to move in a circle filled with a wonderful family, friends, and neighbors. Many people, too numerous to mention them all, have generously provided me with their time and insights, often for no other rewards than my gratitude, friendship, and loads of free tastes. (What do you know—many people still work for food!)

My mother will probably have to have this read—and translated—for her, but my gratitude will no doubt please her to no end. She is the original master, and not only in the kitchen. Her standards were high and her message was clear: Who cares what you can or cannot afford if you have a talent, a skill, and a vision. We were the best-fed and best-dressed kids on the block and beyond, and we owed it to nothing more than her ingenuity.

I met Rozanne Gold at a time when my lifework was a jumble of ideas, projects, dreams, and recipes. She took the time and the special interest that only special people take to help bring my ideas into focus, removing the clutter and giving a name and a face to this book. That is the way she goes about everything: with unerring flair, generosity, and grace. She wears many hats—mentor, advocate, friend, artisan—and I hope she is proud of them all. My sincere thanks to her!

My thanks to my agent, Gareth Esersky, and to Leslie Stoker, the publisher I wish every author could have. She is so practical and efficient, yet so gentle and supportive, and her devoted staff does her proud. Her text and recipe editors, Amy Wilensky, Julie Stillman, and Sarah Scheffel were indefatigable. (After all the hard work I put them through, I hope we are still friends!) Thanks also to the talented photographer Ann Stratton and to Amanda Wilson for her exquisite design.

I must express my heartfelt gratitude to all my wonderful friends: Judy Ross, who got the ball rolling, Ruth, Helen, Chana, Georganne, and so many more. They make me think that entering middle age is not so terrible if it means so much togetherness, so much laughter and sharing, and so much creativity.

To my husband Maurice—what a patient man! He must think that enjoying his wife's good food, parties, floral arrangements, clothing designs, jewelry, and all manner of crafts are reward enough, or else how does he put up with the constant bustle and a portion of the house always looking like a construction site? If he ever dreams of being married to the staid corporate type, he never lets on. Vive la différence, and thank you for the wonderful times.

Special thanks to my extended family of students, in my classroom and around the country, who make my work a pleasure, let me do what I love best, and remind me that cooking, like every worthwhile endeavor, is a perennial work-in-progress.

Thanks to my children, my most untoppable dishes: Maimon the food maven and his lovely wife, Ruthie; Yakov the food junkie, who doesn't seem to hold it against me that I never caved in to his pleas for hot dog and fish sticks dinners; and Bella, whom I adore even though she has largely ignored my culinary prowess and to this day favors a bowl of cereal over any other dish.

CONTENTS

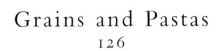

INTRODUCTION

Recently, I visited my friend Michael in the hospital. As usual, I brought along some of his favorite dishes. While there, I met another friend of Michael's who proudly explained that he was in charge of a major project for the relocation of Ethiopian Jews to Israel. "Oh," I breathed. "I don't know what I would give to adopt such a great cause, and be totally devoted to it." Michael cut in with a smile, saying, "Levana, darling, you *do* have a great cause. Your cause is to feed people delicious and beautiful food and make them happy. Your cause is to heal with food and love. Don't even *think* of looking for another cause!" I could have cried for joy, being described so gloriously with such kind words, and I realized that Michael was right, I do have a great cause.

I grew up in Casablanca, Morocco, observing my mother in the kitchen and learning the secrets of one of the world's great cuisines. In 1966, I went to France to study, a privilege usually reserved for the rich and well-connected (though I was neither) who did not have the "handicap" of being a woman. Upon beginning my studies, I had to take an aptitude test and, for fifteen years, was embarrassed by the results: *Arts Ménagers,* Home Economics. I had made so many sacrifices, had traveled so many miles from home, only to be told that I was best suited for precisely what I was running away from! So I ignored the computer printout, and four years later, received my master's degree in psychology.

However, by the time I settled in New York in the 1970s, I was able to put my international experiences and intimate knowledge of "home cooking" to work. Calling on my diverse culinary influences, I prepared elaborate dinners for family and friends and taught cooking classes on every theme imaginable: Moroccan, Mediterranean, Italian, Indian, Chinese, and vegetarian foods, holiday dishes, homemade desserts, hors d'oeuvres, soups, cooking with tofu, party planning, and holiday gifts. Opening my bakery, and later the upscale eponymous kosher Levana Restaurant, run by my brothers-in-law, were natural next steps. So was starting my own catering line—Table Classics—a few years later. As I devoted more time to my catering business, my philosophy emerged. Because I had experimented with so many different cuisines, and was interested in the visual aspects of cooking as well as the taste and quality of ingredients, my catering customers sensed that they would get much more than just food preparation from me. For each event I catered, I designed a menu and a setting in keeping with the client's expectations and vision, as well as his or her culinary and dietary preferences. The students who attended my cooking classes wanted to learn the widest possible array of dishes. No matter what we prepared, the guidelines remained the same: lean, simple, delicious, and nutritionally sound yet elegant, unusual, and beautifully presented dishes. The results were invariably an explosion of colors, textures, and fragrances, a melange of familiar and less frequently used spices, seasonings, and ingredients, which won me the unwavering allegiance of kosher and non-kosher diners alike. Friends would exclaim each time they enjoyed one of my edible gifts, "It smells just like Levana's house."

In my cooking classes I have had students from all over the world, many of whom were brought to me by enthusiastic relatives and didn't at first look "convertible," to say the least. For example, I have taught Hungarian grandmothers to make couscous, teriyaki, and boeuf bourguignon, for gatherings that had traditionally offered the same predictable fare—their families were pleasantly shocked. I believe (and hear from my students) that it is because I share with them so many anecdotes about cooking, dining, and entertaining that they fall in love with the history and culture of the countries where the dishes they learn to make were created. Add to that the simplicity and ease of preparation of each dish (no "Russian doll" or "recipes within a recipe") and the elegance of the finished products, and what do you get? Lots of delighted students who can't wait to try out their newly mastered creations on their own families and guests.

During my many years of working as a restaurateur, caterer, and cooking teacher, the question that I have been asked most frequently is "When are you writing your own cookbook?" My standard answer was always, "When I find the time." I now devote most of my working hours to cooking demonstrations, and with two of my three children grown and living on their own, it is time, finally, to gather my favorite recipes and share my culinary stories. I hope that my love for the dishes I have created comes through in every recipe and that you will be thoroughly engaged in my culinary and cultural odyssey. Without further ado, I welcome you into my kitchen!

KEEPING KOSHER

The word *kosher* means "good" and "proper" and so the kosher dietary laws offer us a diet to maintain our spiritual well-being, our moral and ethical fitness. The laws for keeping kosher govern everything related to food, including preparation, cooking, and serving. It is not my intention to give a crash course in the do's and don'ts of keeping kosher, but I would like to clear up a misconception that the sole reason for these laws is hygiene. First and foremost, the kosher diet is a spiritual diet. According to our Torah (the Bible), the only reason for following a kosher diet is "holiness." "For I am Hashem who elevates you from the land of Egypt to be a God unto you; you shall be holy for I am holy." (Leviticus, 11:44)

Although better health may be a beneficial by-product of observing many of the biblical decrees, certain foods are forbidden for a higher moral reason. For example, the Bible reiterates many times that blood may not be consumed. "Only be strong not to eat the blood—for the blood, it is the life—and you shall not eat the life with the meat." (Deuteronomy 12:23) Based on this decree, our sages concluded that when an animal is killed, care must be taken to drain off as much blood as possible before eating the meat. It has been found that the kosher method of ritual slaughter, severing the jugular vein, is not only designed to remove the optimum amount of blood, but it is also the most humane, causing the animal the least amount of pain. We are also commanded not to hunt, to emphasize that our only purpose for killing the animal is for sustenance, not enjoyment.

The koshering process is completed by the butcher or the cook, who soaks and then salts the meat to remove any remaining traces of blood. This method does not work on liver, which must be broiled on a grill for the blood to drain off. The animals we are permitted to eat are gentle and domesticated, and would not hurt another species. They are not carnivores, predators, or scavengers. Animals permitted for kosher consumption must have split hooves and regurgitate their cud. Fish must have both scales and fins. Hence, pork and shellfish are not part of the kosher diet.

Deuteronomy 14:21 says that "Thou shalt not seethe (cook) a kid in its mother's milk." From this commandment, scholars concluded that mixing meat and milk is a violation of kosher laws, therefore these ingredients must be kept separate in cooking and serving. Foods that are neither meat nor dairy are called *pareve,* meaning "neutral." Since pareve products include fish, foods that grow in the earth, and all food products made from them, they can be served with meat or dairy meals.

I believe it is remarkable that none of the animals that were decreed kosher in the Torah have become extinct; they are all still available to us thousands of years later, challenging the stigma that these laws were designed to be somehow punitive or obselete. They are divine commandments that the rabbis consider *chukim* or mandatory statutes, that must be obeyed because thousands of years ago when the Jews accepted the Torah on Mount Sinai, they accepted the whole package without question even though the ultimate reason for them is beyond our immediate comprehension.

Finally, as part of keeping kosher, before and after each meal we say a prayer to acknowledge that no matter how hard we work for our food, a Higher authority is ultimately responsible for providing it.

THE CONTEMPORARY CONNECTION

Some people mistakenly think that when they decide to keep kosher, they must give up good food. However, while keeping kosher involves many laws and restrictions, such as not mixing meat and dairy products, I want to stress that this does not mean sacrificing good taste. With the extraordinary array of ingredients available in today's marketplace, everyone can enjoy the most creative menus while satisfying their taste for gourmet cuisine. Keeping kosher today means you have access to the best wines, the finest ingredients, and the most creative recipes that cater to the sophisticated tastes of a younger generation.

Those readers who are contemplating a kosher lifestyle and have been accustomed to gourmet food will find my recipes especially appealing because you learn more than recipes, you also learn a philosophy of cooking dishes that are unusual as well as nutritious. And you discover that you can add a dash or two of your own personality without straying from my basic guidelines, preparing cuisine that is seasonal, fresh, lean, elegant, and fun.

MY MOTHER

I can't begin this book in earnest without properly introducing the master. My mother has recently relocated to New York from Morocco. It took nearly half my life to convince her to make this move, which she regarded as nothing short of an amputation. She loves Morocco and for years couldn't bring herself to leave, even after my father passed away thirteen years ago, and even though most of her family now lives in the New York area. As it became increasingly harder for her to travel, she finally decided to bite the bullet and settle near her numerous children and grandchildren.

When she is staying with us, most Friday mornings she is in my kitchen by six to help me cook dinner for our Shabbos guests. We are an unlikely team: I like to work quickly and quietly, using every amenity the kitchen has to offer, with soft background music. She asks a thousand questions, fast and furious, and uses anyone in her line of vision as her assistant, to reach something high—she's very short but terrified of the step stool—or something low—as "I can't bend because of my back." She is always calling out to my children, husband, and housekeeper, "Bella, *ma poupée;* Flora, *por favor!* Yakov, *chéri;* Maurice, please!" and finally, her war cry, "*La passoire! La passoire* (the colander)!" Every ingredient must always be completely dry before we can even think of going ahead with preparing any dish, "to prevent water damage." In her (and my) opinion, this is one of the secrets of good cooking!

With the exception of the colander, my mother, who has been cooking all her life, scorns appliances, even low-tech ones, that were created to help the harried homemaker. All she believes in is brute force. My state of the art "Magic Mill" dough mixer is supplanted by her furious kneading. In response to my plea, "Maman, it has a very powerful motor!" she dismissively replies, "I know, I know, but it doesn't have a heart!" I have won two major victories, though. The first is, we do *not* carry the carpets onto the balcony and beat them with sticks to air them out as is done in Morocco (fortunately, we have no balcony). We use a vacuum cleaner, much to my mother's dismay. The other is that, all protests aside, we buy our chickens dead and plucked. Period.

Quirks aside, my mother has made me the cook that I am. Her skills in the kitchen are nothing short of acrobatic. If the litmus test for a cook is to get fabulous results from ordinary ingredients, then she passes with flying colors. Her cooking always reminds me of the lyrics of the old French song "L'Auvergnat" that translates approximately as follows, "It was nothing but a piece of bread, but it warmed my body all over, and in my soul it is still burning like a big feast." As soon as she enters the kitchen, my mother forgets her daily grievances (cholesterol, high blood pressure, arthritis), much like a frail elderly couple who seems as nimble on a dance floor as in their courting days. I watch her with an undiminished thrill each time she balances a peeled onion on her fingertips and, using a sharp knife, minces the onion in seconds. Carrots get peeled with the sharp side of a knife on a slight bias, a little like a man shaving, in the wink of an eye. Her bread, fragrant with fennel and light as a feather, barely has time to be sliced. Her recipe for almond apricot tart must be shared with the world; it is guaranteed to make every tongue smile. And her chocolates! To think a human hand has shaped them so flawlessly! They taste even more sublime than they look. Godiva, eat your heart out!

My mother needs half the kitchen's arsenal to make soup. Everything must be just so. "So what?" she says. "We will clean. I know you people don't like to work hard!" (She's right, we don't, not if we can help it!) She is almost brought to tears as she watches the culinary fiasco of the day: A wonderful dish of striped bass with baby carrots, preserved lemons, and Niçoise olives must be thrown out because the addition of three tiny peppers (habanero, that's who!) that looked so innocent at the market made the dish too hot for human consumption. At the dinner table, she begs me to explain to our guests why we are serving ordinary gefilte fish as a first course, ignoring the fact that this is what they have at home every week and that it suits them just fine.

When my mother is at our home, my guests thank *her* on their way out for their dining experience. They have all learned, for her sake, to kiss her on both cheeks and say a few words in French, which pleases her no end. Her presence conjures up vivid images of my youth. I can still see her sitting on a low stool wearing a huge apron in our old tiled kitchen where a carton full of mint has just been unloaded, waiting to get stripped of its tough stems. Or seeding a vat of raisins for jam, soaking olives in salt water and vinegar for pickling, or standing by the sink where a dozen chickens who have just met their fate wait to get plucked with her deft hands. I recently saw my mother do something I used to watch her do when I was a child but had dismissed as a trick of my imagination. She boned birds, sometimes as small as pigeons (in Morocco, they are not the pesky creatures who create a nuisance on your windowsill: they are perfectly domesticated and comestible) without making one single incision into them, and with nothing more than an ordinary knife to assist her in loosening up the flesh from the bones. After a few minutes, she would turn the whole boned bird inside out like a glove and stuff it. Having grown up so close to such prestidigitation, how could I help but be a cook?

ABOUT THE RECIPES

Throughout the book, you will note that there are no hidden meat or dairy ingredients in any recipe, items eschewed by many modern diners for various reasons. Every dish that does not expressly feature chicken, meat, or cheese is vegetarian and pareve (nonmeat and nondairy). For example, the only soups that contain meat are Matzoh Ball Soup; beef borscht (a variation of Hot Russian Borscht); and Lamb, Spinach, and Lima Bean Soup. Likewise, only decidedly dairy dishes such as cheese blintzes or cheesecake contain dairy ingredients.

Note that when I call for flour in a recipe, I am referring to all-purpose white flour unless otherwise noted. Eggs are always large eggs.

Finally, a note about the number of servings. You'll find that the majority of recipes in the book make at least eight servings. That's because I entertain a lot and like to have a lot of leftovers—soups freeze beautifully and a big batch is just about as easy to make as a small batch; salad dressings and condiments will keep in the refrigerator for several weeks; and some dishes are decidedly "party dishes" (such as poached salmon, gravlax, couscous, brisket, turkey), suitable for large groups. But many of the main course recipes are great for everyday cooking, so those make four to six servings. Of course, if you want to make those dishes for a larger group, they can be doubled very easily.

THE HOST'S SURVIVAL GUIDE

For some reason, my mother, who cooked up a storm every day of her life when her children were living at home, could not reconcile herself to my choosing catering as a profession. "*Tu vieilliras avant l'age* (You will be old before your time)," she would tell me each time she would visit me in my catering kitchen. I am happy to report that after all these years her dire prediction has not come true: not yet!

Cooking and entertaining are among my greatest personal pleasures and, since opening my catering business and starting my bakery and restaurant, they have also been my profession. But you don't have to make cooking your life or your livelihood to enjoy delicious dishes or serve them graciously and elegantly at home. If you are an experienced host, many of the following tips will be second nature to you, but they represent my commonsense philosophy of entertaining, and I hope they will be helpful to you.

REMEMBER THAT YOUR GUESTS TAKE YOUR INVITATION SERIOUSLY

My mother always says, "Don't invite them: they might *come*!" In other words, don't invite guests unless you intend to provide them with a wonderful experience. My sister, whose family used to summer with us in the mountains, once invited my son Yakov, then nine years old, to lunch on Saturday after services. As we all walked home from Temple, my son waved good-bye to me and followed his favorite aunt, sauntering eagerly behind her and her children. When

my sister arrived at her door, she told him cheerfully, "Okay, Yakov. Have a good Shabbos," and turned to go inside. But Yakov didn't move. Shifting uncomfortably from one foot to the other, his hands digging self-consciously into his pockets, he finally managed to say in a voice barely above a whisper, "Have a good Shabbos too, but you invited me!" Keep in mind that your guests are setting aside time to devote to you in honor of the gathering. Make their evening worthwhile: Good food, good mood, good treatment, and more!

Above all else, remember a host must always enjoy the occasion. There is nothing a guest senses faster than the host's lack of generosity, effort, or spirit.

PLAN REALISTICALLY

Determine a realistic budget and timetable. If you have both money and time at your disposal (lucky you!), you can prepare as many dishes as you want to on your own and hire a caterer to do the rest of the cooking, along with all the serving and cleaning up. For those occasions when you must go all out, call the florist (and any rental companies) well in advance. Describe your preferences for flowers, china, linens, and glassware as specifically as you can. For a big party, you can hire a party planner to coordinate every aspect of the event: location, food, linens, china, flowers, wine and liquor, staff, party favors, room layout, and invitations.

However, you don't need endless hours and an unlimited budget to entertain in style. If you have little money but lots of time and energy and an honest desire to please your guests, there are great menus for you in this book. If you have a more generous budget but a less flexible schedule, I've included time-saving menus. (See pages 197–198 for both.) You don't have to prepare for days to have a successful party.

CHOOSE YOUR MENU CAREFULLY

Create a reasonable and not overly complicated menu, reflecting your own personal style and creativity rather than the latest food fads. Then you will appear to be a competent not pompous host and avoid having dinner conversation focus on the food. Do not answer the question "May I have the recipe for this dish?" by saying "Let me see, four eggs, two cups of sugar," and so on, but with a gentle and firm "Call me during the week." Likewise, if a guest grabs you and tries to share a recipe for her latest creation, politely steer her away from the topic. Food, no matter how delicious, should be an unobtrusive vehicle for the event.

Do not try too many new dishes at one meal. If you are creative, a dinner party is a good time to try one (just one!)

new dish. If you are a novice, or unadventurous, remember that you can never go wrong with the classics. Who can accuse you of being repetitious or dull if you serve the juiciest roast, the tiniest roasted baby potatoes, the freshest asparagus, the tenderest corn, the ripest tomatoes, the crispest salad greens, the most fragrant fruit, the meanest chocolate cake? Such dishes are as safe, timeless, and fool-proof as a Chanel suit (and much more affordable!). Incidentally, let me confess that after all my years of cooking and hosting, a meal of classic favorites is the one that gets me the most hugs from my family.

When planning your menu, look for seasonal items at the peak of quality and flavor. This enables you not only to prepare a delicious meal at considerable savings but also to pay a personal tribute, which will not escape your guests, to what nature has to offer at different times of the year. Baked baby pumpkins are wonderful at Thanksgiving but an anomaly at Passover. The best doesn't mean rare or hard to get. On exceptional occasions, we must make sacrifices and buy out-of-season strawberries or artichokes at exorbitant prices. But for the most part, there's no need to go crazy: Guests can eat asparagus when asparagus comes to town.

Do not duplicate textures or tastes within the same meal. For example, don't serve lemon chicken followed by a lemon tart, or a fruit-stuffed turkey followed by fruit salad, or quiche followed by pumpkin pie. One of my good friends makes the best gefilte fish, the best matzoh ball chicken soup, the best potato kugel, the best stuffed cabbage, the best chopped liver. So what's the problem? She serves them all at the same meal! A delicious, but monochromatic, homogenized meal. Also, make sure that most items on your menu are recognizable. For example, if you are serving a first course that is minced or ground, do not serve a stuffed or "en croûte" main course. You are having a dinner, not a camouflage party. Likewise, don't serve more than a couple of unfamiliar or very spicy dishes. You will only turn a guest who is full of anticipation into a wary diner. No one should have to ask more than once or twice during the course of a meal, "What exactly am I eating?"

If your guests include people you do not know intimately, don't risk serving an organ meat or a very pungent dish as a main course. Serve unusual cuts only as accessories to the meal, and spicy items only as condiments, that is, on the side. You should also avoid serving an assortment of very rich foods at the same meal. Even if you are bored by diet obsessions, for your guests' sake, if not your own, have a heart! Naturally, the opposite holds true: Don't serve a spartan, steamed dinner under the lame premise that "it's good for you." Your guests did not save this evening to be treated like convalescents and be reminded of recipes, calories, cholesterol, blood pressure, and all those dreadful things they read about every day, thank you very much!

MISE EN PLACE—PLAN AHEAD

So many things can be done in advance: setting the table, polishing the silver, chilling the wine, chopping parsley and other herbs for garnishes, and lining up all the platters and serving pieces you will need over the course of the meal. *La mise en place* is every bit as important as the meal itself and very easily accomplished.

Avoid making too many dishes that require your last-minute attention (soufflés, stir-fries, tempura). And don't attempt to do everything yourself. Help is a bargain at any price, and a competent kitchen assistant can make a world of difference, allowing the host to be, well, a host. Who among us doesn't have dismal memories of a dinner party during which the hostess disappeared into the kitchen, whisking away her husband to boot, to engage in a mighty struggle with slicing, unmolding, or carving, while the hapless guests tried their hardest to be gracious and converse with unknown dining companions? A perfectly charming evening with good food and lively talk can easily turn into a strained and tedious gathering. The impression you create with your cooking prowess will never compensate for the offense of leaving your guests to their own devices while you are voluntarily "stranded" in the kitchen.

SERVE BEAUTIFULLY

In Arabic we say, "The eye eats first." Whatever your budget or artistic ability, you can create an atmosphere of plenty. Pile food generously on beautiful serving plates. These don't have to be luxurious china or crystal; visit flea markets for unusual and inexpensive serving dishes. Luckily, Mediterranean food presentation does not require sculptural talents. You will not see radish roses or zucchini boats "gracing" a traditional Mediterranean serving dish, just beautiful food served on beautiful dishes, simply and elegantly.

Start your meal on a high note. If the meal is composed of several courses, and one of them is giving you some grief, do not start with it. Likewise, do not replicate the "restaurant look" by plating and decorating more than the first course and perhaps the dessert. When your guests want to eat as in a restaurant, they will go to a restaurant. In my own catering business, I always tried to replicate the "home" look, never the other way around. This may well have been my trademark. A happy customer wrote me about a party I catered for him, "It was as if you were entertaining us in your own home. You were not just attending to Rebecca's party, you were having one right along with us." So, show them what you've got!

SERVE GRACIOUSLY

Do absolutely everything you can before your guests arrive, and resist the temptation to let on how hard you have worked, or worse, how much money you have spent, even if you're asked directly. I had a literature teacher who used to say, "A good writer is a writer who sweats blood to make us believe he didn't sweat." The same can be said of the talented host. So, not a word about that fallen soufflé, or those frozen berries you had to substitute for fresh ones, or purchased cake you (and your guests) had to settle for because things got backed up and you couldn't find the time to bake.

It's perfectly acceptable to take your guests up on their offer to help for small tasks, but if you get overcome by all the work that your menu requires, pick something simpler in the future or supplement your dinner with some good gourmet store-bought items. Just a word about the friend who offers to come before dinner so that he or she can help while at the same time catching up on your life a bit. I learned a long time ago, and mostly at my own expense, that not everyone has the good housewife's knack, or rather genius, for peeling, chopping, or frying at lightning speed while she talks and laughs with matching intensity. If your friend's hands can keep up with her storytelling, you are a team. But if her hands are frozen in the air, a potato in one hand and a motionless peeler in the other, make a mental note to save this friend's charms for the dinner table next time, and surround yourself in the kitchen with helpers who can do two things at the same time.

A LITTLE DECORUM

It is fine to have a friend clear plates and bring them to the kitchen. It is most decidedly not okay to accept the friend's offer to do the dishes, no matter how close the friend or compelling the offer. It is nice to pass your adorable baby around for hellos. It is not okay to "forget" him on a guest's lap for the remainder of the evening. You may ask a guest who calls on his way to your home to pick up the ice. It is not okay to ask him to pick up the cake or the Champagne. It is acceptable to share psychiatrist jokes with a guest who is a psychiatrist. It is not okay to ask a guest for "informal"

advice about the course of action he recommends with your rebellious son, your mother's surgery, or your unreliable contractor. Why not? Because no matter how assertive your guests might be ordinarily, while they are your guests they are in your debt, and saying no to you will be next to impossible for them, unless they don't mind appearing like boors. Do not exploit your position or theirs and turn innocent guests into unsuspecting babysitters, errand boys, consultants, or dishwashers.

Finally, be sure every guest receives the attention he or she deserves. Do not slight a shy, single, unglamorous guest by seating her next to a frivolous or snooty guest who will ignore her and turn her into a wallflower for the evening. Try your best to seat most guests near someone they have already met, so they might forgo the boring openings and proceed with the fun stuff.

ENJOY YOURSELF AND THE REST WILL FOLLOW

So, what makes an evening a great evening? The food is unquestionably important, but it is not, by far, the only factor. Everyone has his or her own style, and it cannot be denied that some people are more talented than others at entertaining. But if you invite people you like or want to get to know better (and learn to cope graciously with less appealing obligations), have good food and good humor, plus a real desire to please your guests rather than just impress them, why shouldn't it be a great evening? Before your guests arrive, remind yourself that you have done your best. Look forward to an enjoyable evening, but be prepared to laugh off a couple of inevitable mishaps. Take a shower, have a cup of coffee, compose yourself, and when the guests arrive, look and feel ready and in control. Most important, relax and have a good time. You deserve it! Remember that it is worrying, not cooking or entertaining, that will age you before your time.

The Pantry
Preserves, Pickles, and Condiments

There are times when we do not have the leisure or desire to fuss in the kitchen. It is in anticipation of such times that we should stock our pantries. A well-stocked pantry, replete with simple-to-store spices, grains, and condiments, will enable you to whip up hundreds of dishes in minutes. The following condiments will dress up a steak, a bowl of pasta, poached chicken breasts, broiled fish fillets, and much, much more. Broil your steak, grill your fish, or poach your chicken breasts, then take out your jar of onion marmalade, harissa or chutney and add a dollop on top or on the side. Voilà—an easy and elegant main course in no time.

Homemade condiments are vastly superior in flavor and are a fraction of the cost of anything you might find on the shelves of specialty food stores. Also, a batch of any condiment you prepare at home will yield enough for months, plus extra for your friends. Think of these preparations as small culinary investments with delicious dividends, your accomplices in the kitchen, an integral component of your secrets.

Do not throw away glass jars from purchased products. Wash them thoroughly and scrape off their original labels. They are airtight, sanitary, and easy to use, as you can immediately identify the contents though the clear glass (you can always relabel the jar). When serving a condiment, always be sure to use a clean utensil. Unless you are planning on making large batches of condiments and storing them for more than a couple of months, you do not have to sterilize or seal the jars. Wash them with hot soapy water, rinse them well, and screw on the tops immediately after pouring in the condiment.

The single most important factor in promoting the longevity of a condiment, or any other prepared food, is to never use the same utensil twice. Don't be afraid to say "No double-dipping, please!"

Opposite: Preserved Lemons

PRESERVED LEMONS

8–10 large lemons

Kosher salt

MAKES 1 QUART

There is no Moroccan cooking without preserved lemons, and the store-bought variety doesn't even begin to compare with homemade. They take about ten minutes to prepare and two weeks to "incubate," and the result is a few months' supply of the single element that will convert many of your dishes from plain to glorious. This is a pure lemon quintessence for lemon lovers only.

When lemons are plentiful, buy a dozen or two, a box of kosher salt, and a couple of glass jars. That is all you need, along with some elbow grease to cram the lemons into the jar and force the juices out. That is the secret of their swelling and pickling, as well as their heady aroma. Do not let the amount of salt daunt you. Most of it gets washed away, and you can reduce or eliminate salt from the dish you are preparing with the preserved lemons.

Wash and dry the lemons thoroughly. Remove any green points attached to the ends of the lemons. Cut them in quarters almost all the way through, leaving them attached at one end (see photo, page 14). Enlarge the openings with your fingers, and cram them full of kosher salt. Close the lemons and place them in a clean, wide-mouth, quart-sized glass jar, pressing down hard on the lemons as you go to draw out the juice. Don't worry if the juices don't appear immediately; they will soon with all that salt. Repeat with all the lemons, forcing them into the jar. The lemons should be totally submerged in their own juices. Top with an extra layer of kosher salt to ensure that no lemon skin is exposed.

Place the jar in a dark cool place (I keep mine under the sink). The lemons will be ready in 2 weeks, at which point they should be refrigerated. To use, take out a quarter of a lemon at a time. Discard the pulp, rinse the skin thoroughly, and mince. Add to fish and chicken dishes, bean soups, salads, and salsas.

ONION MARMALADE

5 pounds onions

½ cup olive oil

1¼ cups sugar

3 tablespoons red wine vinegar

1¼ cups dry sherry

¼ cup grenadine (available at supermarkets)

2 cups dry red wine

4 sprigs fresh thyme, leaves only

Salt and freshly ground pepper

MAKES 1 QUART

You start with a mountain of ingredients and end up with barely more than a jarful of marmalade. But what a jarful! Delicious with turkey, roast chicken or beef, and grilled fish, this is so good you might even want to spread it on toast instead of jam. Grenadine adds a fruity tang and a pretty ruby tint.

Slice the onions very thin, by hand or in a food processor fitted with a thin slicing blade. Heat the oil in a large heavy pot over high heat. Add the onions, reduce the heat to medium, and cook, stirring occasionally to prevent sticking, until they are dark brown and greatly reduced in volume. This will take about 30 minutes.

Stir in the sugar and vinegar. Let the mixture caramelize; this will take about 3 minutes. Add the sherry, grenadine, wine, thyme, and salt and pepper to taste. Reduce the heat to medium-low and cook, covered, for about 30 minutes. Cool completely (the marmalade will thicken as it cools), and spoon into a clean, wide-mouth, quart-sized glass jar. Keep refrigerated.

CHINESE PICKLED CABBAGE

FOR THE MARINADE

½ cup cider vinegar

½ cup sugar

2 tablespoons grated
fresh ginger

1 tablespoon plus 1 teaspoon salt

1 tablespoon wasabi powder

2 cups water

FOR THE CABBAGE

½ small head green cabbage

2 large carrots, peeled

1 medium purple onion

4 Kirby cucumbers, or one long
seedless cucumber, unpeeled

MAKES ABOUT 2 QUARTS

Besides being delicious, with a clean taste and crisp bite, pickled cabbage is good for you. This version is prepared in minutes and is much less salty than its commercial counterpart. It can be served on its own or in a salad assortment, and is especially good with grilled fish or chicken. Pickled cabbage will keep for two to three weeks in the refrigerator, but I doubt it will last that long.

To make the marinade: Combine the vinegar, sugar, ginger, salt, wasabi, and water in a heavy pot and bring to a boil. Remove from the heat and let the mixture return to room temperature.

To prepare the cabbage: Slice all the vegetables, by hand or in a food processor fitted with a slicing blade. Transfer the vegetables to a glass bowl, pour the marinade over them, and toss. Pack the mixture into clean, wide-mouth glass jars, liquid and all. Refrigerate and let the cabbage pickle for 2 days before serving.

APRICOT-PEACH CHUTNEY

2¾ cups cider vinegar

2 cups sugar

Grated zest of 2 lemons

1 tablespoon cayenne

1 tablespoon plus 1 teaspoon
curry powder

1 tablespoon salt

7 cups water

2 medium onions, quartered

2 cups dried apricots, packed

2 cups dried peaches, packed

One 3-inch piece ginger, peeled

MAKES ABOUT 2 QUARTS

Here's a chutney that looks like a jam, but the resemblance stops there. It has a sharp bite, and a dollop will greatly enhance a fruit salad, roast duck, or cheese sandwich.

Combine the vinegar, sugar, lemon zest, cayenne, curry, salt, and water in a heavy pot and bring to a boil.

Combine the onions, dried fruit, and ginger in a food processor and pulse until coarsely chopped. Stir this mixture into the pot and bring to a boil again. Reduce the heat to medium-low and cook, covered, for about 30 minutes. Cool completely (the chutney will thicken as it cools), and spoon into clean, wide-mouth glass jars. Keep refrigerated.

CHUTNEY: AN ANCIENT ADDITION TO THE MODERN KITCHEN

Chutneys—from the Hindi "to be licked" (an inspired derivation, if you have ever tasted a good one)—are relishes that originated in India as a way of preserving fruits and vegetables. Sweet, tart, chunky, and with a bit of fire, a good chutney is complex and intriguing. Chutney preparation is always based on the same principle: Fruits and vegetables are simmered in a hot liquid containing vinegar, sugar, and spices until the mixture is reduced and thickened. Chutney is easy to make and to modify. After a few batches, you will learn to adjust the amounts of spices to your own taste. Chutney is incredibly versatile. Serve it with curries, roasts, or cold cuts; mix it with a little honey and add to fruit salads; stir it into low-fat mayonnaise or creamed tofu and serve as a dip.

APPLE-TOMATO CHUTNEY

¾ cup mustard seeds

3½ cups sugar

2 cups cider vinegar

2 cups diced tomatoes, fresh
or canned

2 tablespoons salt

1 tablespoon cayenne

1 tablespoon turmeric

1 tablespoon cardamom

2 tablespoons curry powder

2½ cups water

2 cups dark raisins

2 Granny Smith apples, peeled,
cored, and quartered

2 medium onions, quartered

2 celery ribs, peeled and cut
into thirds

One 2-inch piece ginger, peeled

MAKES ABOUT 2 QUARTS

Pungent and crunchy, the mustard seeds enhance the texture of this chutney. Their appealing and distinctive taste offsets the tartness of the apples and tomatoes.

Combine the mustard seeds, sugar, vinegar, tomatoes, salt, cayenne, turmeric, cardamom, curry, and water in a heavy pot and bring to a boil.

Combine the raisins, apples, onions, celery, and ginger in the food processor and pulse until coarsely chopped. Stir this mixture into the boiling liquid and bring to a boil again. Reduce the heat to medium-low and cook, covered, for about 30 minutes. Cool completely (the chutney will thicken as it cools), and spoon into clean, wide-mouth glass jars. Keep refrigerated.

HERB-MARINATED OLIVES

4 cups cracked purple or green olives (no liquid)

2 lemons, halved lengthwise, then thinly sliced

6 large cloves garlic, cut into slivers

¼ cup packed flat-leaf parsley leaves, chopped

2 tablespoons crushed red pepper flakes (or less, to taste)

1 tablespoon fennel seeds

1 tablespoon dried oregano

½ cup extra virgin olive oil

¼ cup red wine vinegar

MAKES 1 QUART

Do not use canned olives for this dish, as they are tasteless and watery. I prefer cracked purple or green olives, which absorb seasonings readily, but many other kinds work well alone or in combination: Niçoise, picholine, kalamata. Do not discard the liquid after you remove the olives and their flavorings. Throw in more olives, or some chunks of mozarella or feta cheese.

Combine all the ingredients in a glass jar. Marinate in the refrigerator overnight or for up to 2 weeks. To serve, drain off all the liquid and reserve for another use.

SUN-DRIED TOMATO PESTO

2 cups sun-dried tomatoes, soaked briefly in warm water and squeezed thoroughly dry

1 large bunch basil, all tough stems removed (about 2 cups packed)

1 large bunch flat-leaf parsley, leaves and stems (about 1 cup packed)

1 head garlic, all cloves peeled

1 cup extra virgin olive oil

Freshly ground pepper

MAKES ABOUT 3 CUPS

This pesto is a cousin to classic basil pesto but gets its kick from sun-dried tomatoes rather than nuts or cheese. Refrigerated, it keeps for three to four weeks, so when you are in a rush, boil some pasta and toss it with some pesto, with or without grated cheese. Add salad, and you have a dinner fit for a king. This pesto is also delicious on chicken or grilled fish. Please note that I have left salt out of this recipe, as the tomatoes are salty enough to season it. When choosing sun-dried tomatoes, pick the bright red ones rather than the dark red ones; they are softer and less salty.

In a food processor, combine the tomatoes, basil, parsley, and garlic. Process, adding the oil gradually through the feed tube. Add pepper to taste.

Transfer the pesto to clean, wide-mouth glass jars and refrigerate.

SQUEEZING VEGETABLES DRY

In many of my recipes, I direct you to squeeze a vegetable—such as spinach or, here, sun-dried tomatoes—thoroughly dry. I don't mean drained, I really mean squeezing with both hands until not a drop of liquid remains. Leaving any moisture will throw off the chemical balance of the ingredients and result in a soggy dish.

HARISSA

¾ cup crushed red pepper flakes, (use up to 1 cup hot pepper flakes, if you want it extra hot)

2 cups boiling water

1 large bunch cilantro, stems cut off (about 1 cup tightly packed)

1 head garlic, cloves separated and peeled

1 cup olive oil

1¼ cups paprika

3 tablespoons cumin

Salt and pepper

MAKES ABOUT 4 CUPS

Harissa is a fiery pepper relish that originated in North Africa. Although connoisseurs (including this one) insist that authentic harissa is made with water-reconstituted dried red hot peppers, they are not readily available, so I devised this fabulous recipe using dried hot pepper flakes, with identical results.

Few condiments suffer from commercial processing as much as harissa. I think I have an idea why this is so: garlic powder. In my book, garlic powder gets the grand prize for ruining a dish. Why use it at all? Fresh garlic is ubiquitous and costs pennies, and you will be rewarded with a far superior end product.

Harissa is the classic accompaniment to couscous and is also delicious served with fried fish and grilled chicken. Diluted with a little water and lemon juice, it is a superb marinade for beef, fish, or chicken, even vegetables. (In marinade form, it is called chermoula.*)*

In a bowl, stir together the pepper flakes and boiling water and set aside. Combine the cilantro and garlic in a food processor and pulse until coarsely chopped. With the motor running, gradually add the oil through the feed tube. Add the paprika, cumin, salt and pepper to taste, and the reserved red pepper flake mixture and process for a few more seconds. Some of the pepper seeds will stay whole. Transfer the relish to clean, wide-mouth glass jars and refrigerate for up to a few months.

Appetizers

This course marks your entrance on the scene as the cook and, as we all know, you never get a second chance to make a first impression. If you like clever garnishes, this course can stand some extra decoration, but don't let the details eclipse the substance of the dish. I have suggested here (and throughout the book) what, if anything, I would do to decorate, keeping in mind, as always, that less is more.

GRAVLAX

2 sides of whole salmon (3 pounds each), all bones removed, skin on, tail ends cut off

½ cup kosher salt

½ cup sugar

¼ cup peppercorns, coarsely crushed with a rolling pin

¼ cup coriander seeds, coarsely crushed with a rolling pin

3 large bunches fresh dill, fronds and stems (reserve some for garnish)

Thinly sliced pumpernickel squares

Lemon wedges, for garnish

Capers, for garnish

MAKES 16 AMPLE SERVINGS

I own six bricks, which I use only for the preparation of gravlax. Once while passing a construction site, I asked one of the workers if I could have some of his bricks. He eyed me suspiciously and asked what I intended to do with them. When I told him I wanted to use them as weights on a salmon dish, he looked totally baffled and asked, "Lady, can't you just buy lox, like we all do?" But he did give me the bricks, although I heard him chuckle with his working pals as I hobbled away with two massive bags, praying for a cab. Some time later, I spotted bricks at my neighborhood lumber store, selling for ninety-nine cents each. Because they are dense and compact and have such a flat, steady surface, bricks compress the salmon perfectly and cure it effortlessly. If you are serving a smaller group, you can very easily cut this recipe in half.

Rinse the salmon thoroughly and dry thoroughly with paper towels.

In a small bowl, combine the salt, sugar, peppercorns, and coriander seeds. Rub this mixture on the flesh side of each piece of salmon, using all of the mixture. Place one piece of salmon, skin-side down, on your work surface, pile the dill on top of it, and cover with the second piece of salmon, making sure the flesh side is next to the dill. Wrap the salmon very tightly in plastic wrap and set it on a big tray that will trap any juices. Place the bricks on top of the salmon and refrigerate.

Turn the salmon over every 12 hours for 2 days, or up to 3 days, always putting the bricks back on. Unwrap the salmon and remove the dill, taking care not to scrape off the spice mixture. Using a long sharp knife, cut the salmon on the bias into very thin slices, discarding the skin. Serve on the pumpernickel squares topped with the lemon wedges, capers, and extra dill.

TRIMMING SALMON

You will notice on the outside edge of each salmon half a flat, opaque strip, which runs the whole length of the fish. This part is very fatty and not meaty, and contributes nothing but a greasy, fishy taste. Be sure to have no mercy—cut every bit of this strip off and discard it.

SALMON TARTARE

1¼ pounds salmon fillet, skin and bones removed, minced

4 scallions, thinly sliced

2 tablespoons bottled hot sauce

2 tablespoons vodka

2 tablespoons toasted sesame oil

2 tablespoons olive oil

1 tablespoon coarsely ground pepper

3–4 tablespoons soy sauce

¼ cup fresh lime or lemon juice

1 tablespoon finely grated fresh ginger

MAKES 6 SERVINGS

The term "tartare" is used loosely here. It only suggests that the fish is not cooked, in the strictest sense of the word. But in reality, the lime juice, oil, and vodka do "cook" the shredded fish. You can make the marinade a day or two ahead of time, then shred the salmon and add it to the mixture one to four hours before serving the dish. Fresh tuna can be substituted for the salmon with equally good results.

The salmon can be served over grated daikon and celery root, or spread on daikon or cucumber slices or small rounds of pumpernickel bread.

Mix all the ingredients together in a stainless steel or glass bowl. Marinate in the refrigerator for 1 to 4 hours. Drain thoroughly before serving.

WILD MUSHROOM DUXELLES IN PUFF PASTRY

FOR THE DUXELLES

¼ cup olive oil

6 medium shallots, chopped

2 pounds shiitake mushrooms, caps only, coarsely chopped

½ cup sherry

1 teaspoon dried thyme

1 tablespoon bottled green peppercorns, crushed

Salt

FOR THE PASTRY

16 squares frozen puff pastry, thawed and kept chilled

1 egg, beaten with a little cold water

MAKES 32 TRIANGLES

Duxelles is a lovely mixture of mushrooms, shallots, and dry sherry. Not only is it great in stuffings or as a base for sauces, it also makes a delicious spread for bread, crackers, or sliced vegetables. Duxelles can be made up several days in advance. All you will have left to do is fill the puff pastry triangles and pop them in the oven. The trick with puff pastry is to keep it chilled at all times: It is the impact of the hot temperature on the chilled dough that causes it to puff.

Preheat the oven to 400°F.

To make the duxelles: Heat the olive oil in a skillet over high heat. Add the shallots and sauté until soft, about 3 minutes. Add the mushrooms and sauté until all the liquid evaporates, about 4 minutes. Add the sherry, thyme, green peppercorns, and salt to taste and cook until all the liquid evaporates, about 3 minutes.

To prepare the pastry: Cut each puff pastry square into 2 triangles. Place 1 heaping teaspoon of filling on one corner of each triangle. Fold the pastry over the filling and press all edges closed with the tines of a fork. Place on an ungreased cookie sheet. Repeat with the remaining pastry and filling. (If you are preparing the pastries in advance, keep them chilled until ready to bake.)

Brush the pastries with the egg wash. Bake the pastries for about 20 minutes, until puffed and golden. Serve hot.

NORI-WRAPPED FISH SAUSAGES WITH WATERCRESS-WASABI SAUCE

FOR THE SAUSAGES

3 scallions, minced

4–5 chives, minced

1 small carrot, grated

4 shiitake mushrooms, caps only, minced

½ red bell pepper, julienned

1 pound sole, salmon, or flounder fillet

1 egg

3 tablespoons olive oil

½ medium onion, cut into chunks

Salt and pepper
❈
4 sheets nori

1 bamboo mat
❈
FOR THE SAUCE

1 bunch watercress, including stems

1½ tablespoons wasabi powder

½ cup low-fat mayonnaise

1 tablespoon green peppercorns in brine

2 teaspoons sugar

Salt

MAKES 6 SERVINGS

My love for sushi and the difficulty of keeping it fresh were the inspiration for this invention. It looks as gorgeous and tastes as delicious as traditional sushi, but it is all fish and no rice, and is lightly poached and chilled, making it suitable for advance preparation. Don't let the number of steps scare you! This dish will be ready in no more than twenty minutes, and guests will be sure you slaved over it for hours.

To prepare the sausages: In a small bowl, stir together the vegetables. Set aside.

Bring a large pot of water to a boil. In a food processor, combine the fish, egg, oil, onion, and salt and pepper to taste. Process into a smooth paste.

Divide the vegetable and fish mixtures into 4 portions. Place 1 sheet of nori on a bamboo mat and spread 1 portion of the fish mixture neatly on its surface, leaving a ½-inch border along the top side. Place 1 portion of the vegetable mixture on top of the fish mixture to cover the bottom third of the nori only. Roll tightly, jelly-roll style, into a log, guiding the process with the bamboo mat. One complete turn should encase the vegetable filling completely. Wrap the finished roll tightly in plastic wrap and secure with a twist tie

at each end. Repeat with the remaining nori, fish mixture, and vegetable mixture.

Lower the logs gently into the boiling water. Let the water come back to a boil, reduce the heat to medium, and poach for about 10 minutes. Remove the logs with a slotted spoon and let them cool.

To make the sauce: Bring a medium-size pot of water to a boil. Blanch the watercress in boiling water. Immediately rinse it in very cold water. Squeeze thoroughly dry. Place the watercress in a food processor with the remaining sauce ingredients and process until smooth.

To serve: Unwrap the cooled logs, and using a sharp knife, cut each log into 6 pieces. Serve at room temperature, with the sauce on the side.

INDIVIDUAL PASTILLAS

FOR THE FILLING

4 medium onions, quartered

1 large bunch flat-leaf parsley

1 whole chicken (about 3½ pounds), cut into 8 pieces

2 pinches of saffron threads

1 teaspoon freshly ground pepper

2 cinnamon sticks

½ teaspoon ground turmeric

1 tablespoon grated fresh ginger

½ teaspoon ground cloves

2 teaspoons ground cinnamon

3 tablespoons sugar

4 sprigs cilantro, minced

4 eggs

1 cup blanched almonds, lightly toasted and coarsely ground (see Blanching Almonds, page 181)

1 cup vegetable oil

1 pound frozen phyllo dough, thawed

Confectioners' sugar and cinnamon for dusting, optional

MAKES ABOUT 36

Pastilla—a phyllo pie made with chicken and layered with almonds, onions, and herbs— is one of the world's great dishes, and it takes just one delightful bite to understand why. It epitomizes Moroccan cuisine, spicy and sweet, delicate and intriguing. I admit I toast the almonds instead of frying them as is traditional, because I avoid frying at almost all costs, both for health reasons and ease of preparation.

These individual hors d'oeuvres are smaller versions of the traditional pastilla. The ingredients are the same, but here they are arranged differently. Perfect for a first course or as part of a buffet, this dish is also ideal for parties and receptions.

To make the filling: Combine the onions and parsley in a food processor and pulse until coarsely chopped. Transfer the mixture to a heavy pot and add the chicken, saffron, pepper, cinnamon sticks, turmeric, and ginger. Bring to a boil. Reduce the heat to medium, cover, and cook for 1 hour or until the chicken is tender, stirring occasionally to prevent sticking.

Uncover, and add the cloves, cinnamon, sugar, and cilantro. Increase the heat to high, stirring constantly until all of the liquid evaporates (this is the secret of a good pastilla; any remaining liquid will make the phyllo dough soggy). Remove the chicken from the pot and set aside. Remove and discard the cinnamon sticks. Add the eggs to the pot and stir until the eggs look set and the mixture thickens.

Remove the skin, bones, and any gristle from the chicken pieces. Place the chicken in a food processor and pulse until it is coarsely ground. Transfer the chicken to a bowl, add the egg mixture and the almonds, and mix thoroughly.

The filling is now ready. (The filling can be prepared up to 3 months ahead and frozen, or up to 2 days ahead and refrigerated. Add the almonds only when ready to bake, though, or they will lose their crunch.)

Preheat the oven to 375°F.

To assemble: Place the vegetable oil in a bowl and have a pastry brush handy. Cut the pile of phyllo leaves crosswise into thirds. Take out 2 leaves and place on a board with the narrow side facing you. Brush the top leaf lightly with oil. Place 1 heaping tablespoon of filling down the center. Roll the phyllo over the stuffing, partway up, jelly-roll style. Fold the sides toward the center and roll tightly all the way up. Place seam-side down on a greased cookie sheet. Repeat with the remaining leaves and filling, always working with 2 leaves at a time.

Bake for about 35 minutes, or until the pastry is golden brown and very crisp. Dust with confectioners' sugar and cinnamon, if using, and serve hot. Allow 2 to 3 pastillas per person.

LIVER PÂTÉ WITH BRANDY AND GREEN PEPPERCORNS

1 pound chicken livers

¼ cup olive oil

1 medium onion, quartered

4 medium shallots

2 large cloves garlic

3 tablespoons brandy

¼ cup soy milk

2 tablespoons soy milk powder (available at health food stores)

2 tablespoons green peppercorns in brine

1 teaspoon allspice

½ teaspoon dried thyme

Salt

MAKES ABOUT 3 CUPS;
8 AMPLE SERVINGS

One of my gastronomic dilemmas is that I adore liver, yet I am a nutrition nut. So I have devised a way to quell my cravings, which I wouldn't presume to recommend to anyone. Three to four times a year, I laugh in the ugly face of the cholesterol dragon, settle in comfortably at my table, and quietly polish off a pint of chopped liver, complete with a good baguette, a glass of red wine, and some gherkins.

This pâté is chopped liver with a wonderful twist. The addition of brandy and green peppercorns makes it a delicacy. Don't buy precooked livers as they tend to have an "off" flavor and are often overcooked. Be careful to broil the livers just until they lose their raw pink color inside, so that they retain the lovely creaminess they are so prized for.

Preheat the broiler.

Broil the chicken livers until they are no longer pink but are still soft, about 3 minutes per side, checking to be sure they don't overcook.

Heat the oil in a heavy pan. Combine the onion, shallots, and garlic in a food processor and pulse until coarsely chopped. Add this mixture to the oil and sauté until well browned, about 10 minutes. Return to the food processor, add the brandy, soy milk, soy milk powder, peppercorns, allspice, thyme, livers, and salt to taste and process until smooth.

Transfer the mixture to a serving bowl, seal tightly, and refrigerate for about 2 hours. The pâté will firm up as it cools. Serve with bread or crackers.

WORKING WITH PHYLLO

Many people are intimidated at the thought of working with phyllo. It's really quite easy if you follow these tips.

◆ Have everything ready before you open the package: the oven, the board, the bowl filled with oil, the pastry brush, and the greased cookie sheet.

◆ Make sure your phyllo is good and fresh, not brittle, and that the leaves are whole and separate easily.

◆ Do not waste time on recalcitrant leaves. Discard them and keep going!

◆ Rather than wrap the phyllo in a damp cloth, work quickly with a third of the leaves at a time, tightly wrapping and refrigerating the rest until you are done with the pile you are working with.

◆ Brush with oil lightly, not heavily, or your dish will be too greasy and messy to eat.

◆ Work quickly!

LAMB-FILLED RAVIOLI WITH FRESH TOMATO SAUCE

FOR THE SAUCE

8 plum tomatoes

1 tablespoon tomato paste

2 large cloves garlic

¼ cup olive oil

½ cup dry white wine

1 tablespoon sugar

Salt and pepper

FOR THE RAVIOLI

2 tablespoons olive oil

1 medium onion, chopped

1 pound lean ground lamb

¼ cup chopped mint

1 teaspoon allspice

½ teaspoon turmeric

⅓ cup raisins

¼ cup toasted pine nuts

Salt and pepper

3 quarts water

1 package (1 pound) frozen wonton skins, thawed

FOR THE GARNISH

¼ cup chopped flat-leaf parsley

3 tablespoons chopped chives

MAKES 6–8 SERVINGS

I admit I make these fabulous ravioli with store-bought wonton skins, not because I am lazy but because I find them ideally suited for the job. Once filled, sealed, and lowered into boiling water to poach, they behave themselves and retain their shapes. Wonton skins come in many shapes and sizes. You can also cut them with cookie cutters. Whatever the shape of the ravioli, lamb and mint are a classic and delicious combination.

To make the sauce: Briefly plunge the tomatoes into boiling water, then peel, quarter, and seed them. Combine all the sauce ingredients in a food processor and process until smooth. Transfer to a saucepan over low heat to keep the sauce warm.

To prepare the ravioli: Heat the oil in a heavy skillet over high heat. Add the onion and sauté until translucent, about 3 minutes. Add the lamb and sauté until it is no longer pink. Add the mint, allspice, turmeric, raisins, pine nuts, and salt and pepper to taste and mix thoroughly.

In a large pot, bring the water and a few drops of oil to a boil. Place some filling in the center of a wonton skin (about 1 teaspoon for small wonton skins, 1 tablespoon for large) and brush the edges with water. Top with another skin and press the edges tightly. Repeat with remaining skins and filling.

Drop the ravioli gently into the boiling water, making sure you do not crowd the pot; cook in two batches if necessary. Cook for 7 to 10 minutes; the ravioli are done when the skins start to look translucent. Remove the ravioli from the water with a slotted spoon and transfer to a platter in one layer so they do not get stuck together.

To serve: Divide the sauce among 6 to 8 individual plates. Arrange 4 to 5 ravioli on top of the sauce. Sprinkle with the parsley and chives.

TOASTING NUTS

To toast pine nuts or slivered almonds, place them in one layer on a cookie sheet and bake in a preheated 300°F oven for 10 to 12 minutes, until they are fragrant and golden brown. To toast walnuts, pecans, cashews, or pistachios, preheat the oven to 325°F. Always be sure to watch the nuts carefully: They burn quickly.

CURRIED CHICKEN SALAD IN TINY CRÊPES

FOR THE CHICKEN SALAD

4 chicken cutlets

1 cup coconut milk

1 tablespoon curry powder

1 teaspoon cumin

¼ cup chopped cilantro

½ pound smoked chicken breast, cut into big chunks

2 ribs celery, peeled and cut into big chunks

½ small red onion

1 Granny Smith apple, peeled, cored, and quartered

½ cup low-fat mayonnaise

Salt and pepper

FOR THE CRÊPE BATTER

4 eggs (8 egg whites if watching your cholesterol)

2 cups flour

1½ cups soy milk

1 cup cold water or seltzer

2 tablespoons vegetable oil

Pinch of salt

MAKES 6 SERVINGS; 18 CRÊPES

You won't think of chicken salad as an old standby after you have tried this wonderful version. Poaching the chicken breasts in coconut milk makes them succulent and tender. The crêpe batter takes just a minute to whip up. Soy milk works beautifully and allows you to serve this dish with a meat meal. I am giving you three different presentations to play with. If you can't decide on one, try mixing and matching! If you don't want to bother with the crêpes, you can serve the salad on lettuce leaves or make sandwiches.

To make the chicken salad: Place the chicken cutlets, coconut milk, curry, cumin, and cilantro in a pot just big enough to contain them. Bring to a boil. Reduce the heat to medium and cook, covered, for 20 minutes. Remove the chicken and pat it dry, reserving the poaching liquid. Cut the chicken into big chunks and transfer them to a food processor. Add the smoked chicken breast, celery, onion, and apple and process until coarsely chopped, in batches if necessary.

Transfer the mixture to a bowl, add the mayonnaise and salt and pepper to taste, and mix thoroughly. If needed, moisten with 2 to 3 tablespoons of the poaching liquid.

To make the crêpes: Blend all the batter ingredients in a blender or food processor until smooth.

Spray a small nonstick skillet (about 7 inches in diameter) with cooking spray and heat over high heat. Using a very small ladle, add just enough batter to coat the bottom of the pan. Swirl the batter in

the pan to ensure that the pan is evenly coated. After a few seconds, the edges will start pulling away from the bottom of the pan, and the top will look dry. Turn the crêpe over with a spatula, cook for a few more seconds, and transfer to a plate. Repeat with the remaining batter, spraying the pan each time.

To serve—three variations

◆ Fill one quarter of the crêpe with a heaping tablespoon of the filling and fold the crêpe over the filling.

◆ Fill the center of the crêpe with a heaping tablespoon of filling and bring all the sides up around the filling, enclosing it like a little purse. Tie the purse with a chive.

◆ Cut the crêpe into a square. Form a little log of filling the length of the crêpe and ½ inch in diameter. Roll the crêpe tightly around the filling all the way up to form a "cigar." Roll a ½-inch wide strip of nori around the center of the cigar. Moisten the end of the nori strip with a drop of water to secure the closing.

TRICOLOR VEGETABLE TERRINE WITH BASIL-LEEK COULIS

FOR THE TERRINE

3 leeks, white parts only, cut into 2-inch pieces

2 large baking potatoes, peeled and cut into large chunks

3 small turnips, peeled and cut into large chunks

3 medium parsnips, peeled and cut into large chunks

1 medium celery root, peeled and cut into large chunks

¼ cup olive oil

Pinch of nutmeg

2 eggs

¼ cup flour

Salt and pepper

One 10-ounce box frozen spinach, thawed and squeezed thoroughly dry

¼ cup basil leaves, packed

1 cup sun-dried tomatoes, soaked in cold water for ½ hour and squeezed thoroughly dry

FOR THE COULIS

3 tablespoons olive oil

3 leeks, white parts only, sliced

¼ cup basil leaves, packed

¼ cup soy milk

Salt and pepper

MAKES 12 SERVINGS

In some Berber parts of Morocco, turnips grow huge. A popular Moroccan anecdote tells of a simple-minded man and his son who were passing through the town of Zagora, where they were fed lavishly by a local family. "Please," the family would beg, "just one turnip, in honor of our father Abraham." But no sooner had the simple-minded man finished eating than the family started in again. "Please have just one more turnip, in honor of our father Isaac." He was reeling, but hospitality is sacred in Morocco, and he forced down the turnip. "One last turnip, please," they begged, "in honor of our father Yaacov." Finally, the simple-minded man whispered, "Son, remind me again. How many fathers are there in the Bible?" "Three," replied the son. "Thank goodness!" the father cried. "If there had been just one more, this father would have dropped dead tonight!"

This dish featuring the lowly turnip is no joke, though. It is elegant enough to serve to your most honored guests. Vegetable terrine makes a nice accompaniment to a menu featuring fish or meat, because it is light and very colorful. It's a good dish to serve plated as a first course, but it makes a beautiful presentation in a buffet as well.

To make the terrine: Place the leeks, potatoes, turnips, parsnips, and celery root in a heavy pot with water to barely cover and bring to a boil. Reduce the heat to medium, cover, and cook for 20 to 30 minutes, or until all the vegetables are tender. Drain thoroughly; the mixture must be absolutely dry.

Transfer the vegetables to a food processor. Add the oil, nutmeg, eggs, flour, and salt and pepper to taste and process, in batches if necessary, until the mixture is perfectly smooth.

Preheat the oven to 375°F.

Grease a 1½-quart loaf pan and line it with plastic wrap, letting the excess hang over.

Divide the mixture into thirds, in three bowls. Place one third in the food processor with the spinach and basil and process until smooth. Transfer the mix-ture to the mold and pack it tightly. Rinse and dry the bowl of the food processor. Pack the second (white) third on top of the green layer in the mold. Place the last third in the food processor with the sun-dried tomatoes and process until smooth. Transfer to the mold and pack tightly on top of the white layer.

Fold the overhanging plastic on top of the mold. Place the mold in a pan two-thirds full of hot water. Bake the terrine for 1 hour or until the top is firm. Refrigerate the terrine after it has cooled.

To make the coulis: Heat the oil in a skillet over high heat. Add the leeks and sauté until translucent, about 3 minutes. Transfer the leeks to a food processor, along with the basil, soy milk, and salt and pepper to taste, and process until smooth.

To serve, cut the chilled terrine into 12 slices, and serve it with the coulis.

Soups

I develop all my recipes with the home cook in mind, and I have come to the conclusion that most cooks find making home-made soup stock before proceeding with a recipe a real imposition, maybe even a deterrent. Almost all cookbooks use stock as the essential ingredient for a good soup, which at the outset excludes the ambitious but busy cook. The good news is that you can make a delicious soup from scratch using water as "stock." Until recently, I used to trick my mother and tell her a soup she liked was made with stock, and she would invariably say, "See what a difference it makes?" Trust me. If I could make a convert out of her, you should be no problem at all. You will never miss homemade stock in these recipes.

Making soup is the ultimate showcase for a cook. You have much freedom and flexibility and room for creativity, provided that you keep a few basic principles in mind.

CHOOSE FULL-FLAVORED VEGETABLES AND GRAINS. Your choice of ingredients matters. For example, a vegetarian cream of broccoli soup will be wonderful, whereas a cream of zucchini is apt to be ordinary. The reason is quite simple: Broccoli has flavor that stands on its own, while zucchini tends to be bland. The best vegetarian soups use intensely flavored vegetables such as celery root, cabbage, turnips, parsnips, carrots, watercress, spinach, mushrooms, and tomatoes. Avoid mild vegetables such as zucchini unless you are combining them with more assertive ingredients such as tomatoes, garlic, and basil.

COMBINE INGREDIENTS EFFECTIVELY. Resist the temptation to make soup with a very long list of ingredients. First of all, you do not want all your soups to taste and look the same. Second, you should always give a particular ingredient and/or seasoning the chance to be the "star." A short, well-chosen selection of ingredients will produce infinitely better results than an enormous indistinguishable medley.

EXERCISE CAUTION WITH COOKING TIMES. Al dente does not work for soup. Vegetables must be tender yet not mushy. Beans must be soft enough to release their starch yet retain their character. In a pinch, use canned beans rather than end up with tough, undercooked beans. All root vegetables require long cooking times to fully release their flavors and fragrances. Add delicate vegetables, such as zucchini and bell peppers, halfway through the cooking process, so they don't get mushy or discolored or—worse—tasteless.

Opposite: Moroccan Fish Soup

Add very delicate leafy vegetables, such as spinach, watercress, lettuce, and scallions, at the very end of the cooking process. A minute or two is all they need to wilt yet retain their bright color.

MODULATE THE TEXTURE OF THE SOUP. In order to avoid thin, watery soup, start with less water and err on the side of thickness. All the recipes in this chapter result in soup you might have to thin, so before serving adjust the texture by adding a little liquid if you need to. A great tool for simplifying the soup-making process is the immersion blender. This nifty little hand-held blender gets immersed in a pot and blends up to eight quarts of soup in one shot, eliminating the mess involved in transferring soup to a blender or food processor. It is very inexpensive and takes up very little space in the kitchen. I hope you get one!

SAUTÉ IN OLIVE OIL. Leeks, onions, celery, and garlic, properly sautéed in very good olive oil, guarantee a delicious soup. I allow about ⅓ cup olive oil for three to four quarts of soup, which gives the soup the richness and smoothness it needs without making it too caloric. Do not try to reduce this amount of oil further, as it will result in an undistinguished "boiled" soup with no texture to speak of.

SEASON THE SOUP. Think about all the wonderful herbs and spices at your disposal when making soup: thyme, sage, oregano, tarragon, basil, bay leaves, and lemongrass, to name but a few. Add herbs toward the end of cooking so their flavor does not diminish. To enrich a soup, a cup of wine or coconut milk, a tablespoon of miso paste, a strip of kombu (kelp), or a few drops of soy sauce, mirin, or toasted sesame oil will do wonders. Experiment, and get different results each time. Because it is hard to determine just how your soup will respond to seasoning, be sure to taste before serving, and adjust the seasonings. You will notice that in all my soup recipes I add ground pepper at the very end of the cooking process. That's because I find that ground pepper added to a large amount of liquid for an extended cooking time tends to give the soup an acrid taste.

THICKEN THE SOUP APPROPRIATELY. If you want a clear soup, make a concentrated chicken, beef, or vegetable broth that you will serve as is, or to which you will add garnishes, such as dumplings, croutons, noodles, or shredded greens. If you are making a creamed soup, include one or two of the following starchy vegetables: potatoes, sweet potatoes, corn, parsnips, or peas. When blended with other ingredients, they will create a thick, rich soup. If you are making a chunky soup, just a handful of barley, rice, split peas, or lentils will add the necessary starch and impart wonderful taste. Grains such as bulghur, oats, or farina will disperse in the liquid and produce a delicious soup with a somewhat less starchy texture. Each grain produces different results, so try different combinations. Another mixture used to thicken soup without making it starchy is *sofrito*, which is widely used in Latin cooking. It is a marvelous mixture of sautéed minced onions, garlic, celery, peppers, cilantro, and parsley. The mixture cooks until very reduced and serves as a base or thickener for soups and other dishes that include tomatoes.

USE ONLY THE BEST. Notice I didn't say the most expensive or the fanciest, just the best. It is perfectly all right to use leftover vegetables or beans in soup, but it is not acceptable to use wilted greens or blemished vegetables. Your soup will reflect the standards you apply in selecting your ingredients, so use seasonal vegetables at the peak of their perfection whenever possible.

WHITE GAZPACHO

2 long seedless cucumbers, peeled

1 medium onion, quartered

2 slices white bread or challah, crusts removed

1 avocado, peeled and quartered

2 ribs celery, peeled

Juice of 2 limes or lemons

Grated zest of 1 lemon

¼ cup extra virgin olive oil

⅔ cup toasted sliced almonds, plus more for garnish

4 cups (32 ounces) plain low-fat yogurt

¼ cup mint leaves

¼ cup dill

Salt and pepper

Mint sprigs, for garnish

Lime slices, for garnish

MAKES 10–12 SERVINGS

This is a dazzling, refreshing summer soup, not white exactly, but the color designers call celery. A little couture in the kitchen can't hurt! This is also the only one of my soup recipes that won't freeze well. Make it the day it will be served.

Combine all the ingredients in a blender or food processor and blend until smooth. If the soup seems to thick, thin it with a little cold water. Serve chilled, topped with sliced toasted almonds, mint, and lime.

MOROCCAN FISH SOUP

Heads and tails of 2 salmon, tilefish, or any other big fish, quartered

⅓ cup extra virgin olive oil

2 medium onions, quartered

2 large leeks, white part and most of green part, cut into large chunks

4 ribs celery, peeled and cut into thirds

4 large cloves garlic

1 bunch flat-leaf parsley

1 small bunch cilantro

1 red bell pepper, seeded and cut into chunks

4 cups canned crushed tomatoes

2 large potatoes, peeled and cut into ½-inch cubes

1 cup dry white wine

½–1 teaspoon cayenne

Good pinch of ground cloves

3 bay leaves

1 tablespoon paprika

2 good pinches saffron

2½ quarts (10 cups) water

Salt

2 tablespoons anisette or arrack

4 pounds boneless, skinless fish, such as salmon, tilefish, or snapper, cut into 1-inch cubes

Freshly ground pepper

MAKES 12–14 SERVINGS

I eliminate the broth-making step by wrapping the heads and tails of the fish loosely in cheesecloth, cooking them with the soup, and then discarding them without any mess. Cooking the soup with the heads intensifies its flavor and imparts a light gelatinous texture. Moroccan fish soup (see photo, page 36) is every bit as interesting as traditional French soups containing shellfish.

Wrap the fish heads and tails loosely but securely in cheesecloth and set aside.

Heat the oil in a large heavy pot over high heat. Combine the onions, leeks, celery, garlic, parsley, cilantro, and bell pepper in a food processor and pulse until coarsely chopped. Add these vegetables to the oil and sauté until they are soft, about 3 minutes. Add the cheesecloth packet, tomatoes, potatoes, wine, cayenne, cloves, bay leaves, paprika, saffron, water, and salt to taste. Bring to a boil. Reduce the heat to medium and cook, covered, for 45 minutes.

Add the anisette, fish chunks, and pepper to taste and cook for another few minutes, just until the fish is cooked through. Press on the cheesecloth packet to release as much liquid as you can, then remove it and discard. Serve hot.

SAFFRON BASICS

Saffron is an essential spice in Mediterranean cooking. It is the stamen of crocus flowers, which can be harvested only by hand, hence its infamous reputation for being as expensive as gold. But in my book, the delicate color and flavor it imparts to a dish makes it more valuable than gold. Besides, a little goes a very long way. Ignore the expensive vials sold at produce stores, and get a one-ounce box at an Indian or Italian grocery store—it will last for months and costs a small fraction of the price.

CURRIED BUTTERNUT SQUASH SOUP

⅓ cup olive oil

2 large onions, cut into large chunks

⅓ cup brown sugar

3 quarts (12 cups) water

1 butternut squash (about 3 pounds), peeled, seeded, and cut into large chunks

2 large sweet potatoes, peeled and cut into large chunks

2 large carrots, peeled and cut into large chunks

1–2 tablespoons curry powder

1 teaspoon allspice

1 stalk lemongrass, center part only, minced

One 1-inch piece fresh ginger, peeled and minced

2 cinnamon sticks

Salt

One 12-ounce can coconut milk

Freshly ground pepper

MAKES 12 SERVINGS

The caramelized onions and sweet vegetables in this soup contrast beautifully with the sharpness of the curry and tang of the lemongrass. The coconut milk provides the crowning touch. This soup has enough flavor to be served either iced or hot.

Note that coconut milk is not a dairy product. It is so called because of its "milky" appearance. It is obtained by mixing grated coconut pulp with water, then straining the mixture. It is delicious but quite rich, so feel free to substitute low-fat coconut milk.

Heat the oil in a heavy pot over medium heat. Place the onions in a food processor and pulse until coarsely chopped. Add the onions to the oil and sauté, stirring occasionally, until they are dark brown, about 20 minutes.

Add the brown sugar to the onions and cook, stirring, for 2 more minutes. Add the water, squash, sweet potatoes, carrots, curry, allspice, lemongrass, ginger, cinnamon sticks, and salt to taste. Bring to a boil. Reduce the heat to medium and cook, covered, for 1 hour.

Add the coconut milk and heat through. Puree the soup with an immersion blender or transfer it to a food processor and process until smooth. Add pepper to taste before serving.

ONION SOUP

12 slices baguette, cut on the bias

⅓ cup olive oil

2 large onions, cut into large chunks

4 large shallots

2 large leeks, white parts only, sliced

6 large cloves garlic

3 tablespoons sugar

2 cups dry red wine

⅓ cup brown hatcho miso paste

3 sprigs fresh thyme, leaves only, or 1 teaspoon dried

2½ quarts (10 cups) water

1 cup grated Swiss cheese

8 ounces smoked Provolone cheese, cut into small chunks

1 cup grated Parmesan cheese

Good pinch of nutmeg

Salt and freshly ground pepper

MAKES 12 AMPLE SERVINGS

This soup posed a unique challenge for me, which I was determined to beat. The two trademarks of a perfect onion soup (besides the onions, of course) are the rich beef broth that serves as its base, and the cheese that melts into it, making it taboo in kosher kitchens! I was not about to stand defeated, so I experimented endlessly, and bingo: A mixture of brown miso paste and dry red wine was my answer. I obtained a deep-flavored, luxurious-tasting and richly colored broth, a perfect foil for those caramelized onions and smoked cheeses. When you try this, you will understand my feeling of triumph. My food spies from the non-kosher world have issued a unanimous verdict: "I can't believe this is a meatless soup!" I have included several members of the onion family to make it even more glorious.

Preheat the oven to 375°F.

Toast the baguette slices until they are light brown and crisp.

Heat the oil in a heavy pot over medium heat. Combine the onions, shallots, leeks, and garlic in a food processor and pulse until coarsely chopped. Transfer this mixture to the pot and sauté, stirring occasionally, until the vegetables are dark brown, about 30 minutes.

Add the sugar to the pot and cook for 2 more minutes until caramelized. Add the wine, miso, thyme, and water and cook for 30 minutes. Add the cheeses, nutmeg, and salt and pepper to taste (use the salt sparingly, if at all; the cheeses and the miso are already salty). Cook for 1 more minute, until the cheese is melted.

To serve, pour into soup bowls and float 1 slice of toasted baguette in each bowl.

Variation: Baked onion soup. If you own individual ovenproof crocks, proceed exactly as above through the cooking of the soup, but do not add the cheeses. Pour the soup into individual crocks, float a slice of baguette in each crock, top with the grated cheese, add a few grinds of black pepper, and put the crocks under the broiler for just a minute or two, until the cheese is melted and bubbly.

HARIRA (MOROCCAN LENTIL SOUP)

1 pound brown lentils

6 cups water

3 medium onions, quartered

1 large bunch flat-leaf parsley

1 small bunch cilantro

6 ribs celery, peeled and cut into 2-inch sticks

4 cups canned crushed tomatoes

⅓ cup vegetable oil

1 teaspoon turmeric

Salt

3 quarts (12 cups) water

3 tablespoons lemon juice

1 tablespoon ground cumin

Freshly ground pepper

MAKES 12 SERVINGS

This soup is indelibly engraved in my memory as part of my childhood, and its name alone conjures up lovely scenes. The streets of Morocco are flooded with its aroma during the whole month of Ramadan (the Islamic holy month), and it is a delight to see everybody hurrying home to the dinner that awaits them after those long fast days. Every year I make a batch of harira for one of our waiters at Levana Restaurant. Seeing his eyes light up at the sight of the beloved brew is proof, every time, that being far from home is not so hard to bear if one can be reunited, however occasionally, with one's comfort foods.

Sephardic Jews like to make this soup during the week of Tish'a B'av, the commemoration of the Temple's destruction. I have streamlined the recipe and made it meatless. The lentils have such a rich, robust flavor, you will never miss the meat.

In a heavy pot, bring the lentils and the 6 cups water to a boil. Reduce the heat and simmer until the lentils are soft, about 1 hour.

Place the onions, parsley, cilantro, celery, tomatoes, oil, turmeric, salt to taste, and the 3 quarts water in a second heavy pot. Bring to a boil, reduce the heat to medium, and cook, covered, for 1 hour.

Puree the mixture with an immersion blender or transfer to a food processor and process until smooth. Add the cooked lentils, lemon juice, and cumin to the puree in the pot and stir. Bring to a boil and add pepper to taste. Serve hot.

WILD MUSHROOM SOUP

⅓ cup extra virgin olive oil

1½ pounds shiitake mushrooms, stems discarded, caps sliced

2 medium onions, chopped

6 shallots, minced

1½ pounds domestic mushrooms, sliced

⅓ cup flour

2 quarts (8 cups) boiling water

1 cup dry sherry

3 sprigs fresh thyme, leaves only

Good pinch of saffron threads

4 bay leaves

Salt

3 cups soy milk

Freshly ground pepper

MAKES 12 SERVINGS

A recipe that showcases the glorious mushroom. Years ago I made the unforgivable mistake of serving this soup at a dinner to all my guests except one, my then eight-year-old nephew Doveed who was visiting. I simply thought the taste would be totally over his head and served him a tamer chicken soup instead. We still laugh when we remember him, fists on hips, teeth clenched, waiting for me to straighten out my mistake, which took me years to live down. What do you know, kids do love mushrooms; mine do, always have.

For a special occasion, make a bigger dent in your budget and sauté a few sliced morels along with the shiitake mushrooms. If you can find porcini powder, you can also add a teaspoon of that to your soup (or you can grind dried porcini into a powder in a food processor). Porcini powder is available at specialty food stores, and although it is very expensive, a little goes a long way. For this recipe and every recipe calling for dry sherry or wine, I beg you: Do not use the dreadful supermarket compound labeled "cooking wine." Choose a bottle of wine that is reasonably priced but good enough to drink.

Heat the olive oil in a heavy pot over high heat. Add the shiitake mushroom caps and sauté until all the liquid evaporates, about 5 minutes. Remove the mushrooms with a slotted spoon and set aside.

Add the onions and shallots to the pot and sauté until translucent, about 3 minutes. Add the domestic mushrooms and sauté until the liquid evaporates. Reduce the heat to low, add the flour, and cook for 2 to 3 minutes. Raise the heat again and slowly whisk in the boiling water. Add the sherry, thyme, saffron, bay leaves, and salt to taste and cook, covered, over medium heat for about 30 minutes.

Puree the mixture with an immersion blender or transfer to a food processor and process until smooth. Return the puree to the pot, add the reserved shiitake slices, soy milk, and pepper to taste, and heat through. Do not let the soup boil or it will curdle. Serve hot or cold.

CREAM OF BROCCOLI AND WATERCRESS SOUP

⅓ cup olive oil

2 leeks, white parts and 2 inches of the green parts, sliced

2 medium onions, quartered

4 medium shallots

4 large cloves garlic

3 ribs celery, peeled and cut into thirds

2 large potatoes, peeled and cut into large chunks

1 bunch broccoli, stems peeled, heads separated into big florets (about 6 cups)

2½ quarts (10 cups) water

8 cups watercress, packed, including stems

4 tablespoons fresh chives

3 tablespoons fresh tarragon leaves, chopped, or 1 tablespoon dried

¼ teaspoon nutmeg

Salt and pepper

MAKES 12 SERVINGS

This is a perfect example of a soup that needs no stock, as each of its ingredients is so full of flavor. You can chop the leeks, onions, shallots, garlic, and celery in the food processor, in batches, but don't let the mixture get watery. Make sure you add the watercress to the soup at the very end so it retains its clean taste and lovely bright green color. Reheated leftovers will be delicious but discolored.

Heat the olive oil in a heavy pot over high heat. Combine the leeks, onions, shallots, garlic, and celery in a food processor and pulse until coarsely chopped. Add these vegetables to the oil and sauté until they are translucent, about 3 minutes. Add the potatoes, broccoli, and water and bring to a boil. Reduce the heat to medium and cook, covered, for 30 minutes.

Add the watercress, chives, tarragon, nutmeg, and salt and pepper to taste and cook until the watercress wilts, about 2 to 3 minutes. Do not let the watercress cook longer, or it will get discolored.

Puree the soup with an immersion blender, or transfer it to a blender or food processor and process until smooth, in batches if necessary. Strain the soup through a medium strainer. Serve hot or cold.

PEELING CELERY

Always peel the rounded side of a rib of celery. Use a vegetable peeler. You will be surprised at how much more pleasant the celery will be to cook with, especially in recipes where you have to cream a soup, as peeling the celery rids it of all its fibrous, bitter, tough threads. This step will also make your salads much more palatable, and scooping dips and spreads with celery sticks a real treat.

CHILI SANS CARNE

⅓ cup extra virgin olive oil

4 large cloves garlic

1 large onion, cut into large chunks

1 large red bell pepper, seeded and cut into large chunks

1 small bunch cilantro

1 large bunch flat-leaf parsley

3 ribs celery, peeled and halved

1 large carrot, grated

One 28-ounce can crushed tomatoes

2 cups dry red wine

2 cups red beans, soaked overnight, rinsed, and drained,

½ cup pearl barley

¼ cup chili powder

2 tablespoons oregano

2 tablespoons cumin

⅔ cup chopped semisweet chocolate

3 tablespoons sugar

2½ quarts (10 cups) water

Salt and pepper

MAKES 12 SERVINGS

Vegetarian chili is not an oxymoron. The fact that almost all versions of chili we encounter are made with ground beef doesn't mean it is indispensable: beans, chili powder, and peppers, not meat, are the trademarks of the dish. Okay, no meat, but chocolate? Those of you who have seen the delightful movie Chocolat know that pairing chocolate with chili is an ancient Incan formula that does wonders for both your taste buds and your love life.

This is also a perfect crockpot dish. After you sauté the first set of ingredients, you can simply transfer everything to a crockpot and leave it on the lowest setting all day: Your home will be permeated with the heady aromas of the dish. Serve the chili with white or brown rice. You can also set up bowls of guacamole, corn chips, and grated cheddar and let guests choose their own garnishes.

Heat the oil in a heavy pot over high heat. Combine the garlic, onion, red pepper, cilantro, parsley, and celery in a food processor and pulse until coarsely chopped. Add these vegetables to the oil and sauté until they look translucent and the liquid has cooked off, 3 to 4 minutes. Add the carrot, tomatoes, wine, beans, barley, chili powder, oregano, cumin, chocolate, sugar, water, and salt and pepper to taste. Bring the mixture to a boil. Reduce the heat to medium-low and cook, covered, for 3 hours. The chili should be thin but thicker than a soup. Serve hot.

LAMB, SPINACH, AND LIMA BEAN SOUP

3 quarts (12 cups) water

3 pounds lean lamb: necks, shanks, or 1-inch cubes of lean stew meat

8 cups spinach leaves (1 pound)

3 tablespoons olive oil

2 medium onions, quartered

4 cloves garlic

4 ribs celery, peeled and cut into large chunks

1½ cups canned crushed tomatoes

2 cups large lima beans (no soaking needed)

2 large potatoes, peeled and cut into ½-inch cubes

1 bunch flat-leaf parsley, chopped

½ bunch cilantro, finely chopped

1 teaspoon turmeric

2 pinches of saffron

2 teaspoons ground cumin

1 teaspoon ground cinnamon

Juice of 2 lemons

Salt and pepper

MAKES 8 MAIN-COURSE SERVINGS

When I made this soup at a cooking demonstration, a large group of people who were taking a Bible class in a room next to my kitchen lined up at my door at the end of their class, telling me how terribly hard it had been to concentrate on what their poor teacher was saying because the smell of the soup was driving them crazy. The teacher later told me that he found teaching on Monday nights exquisite torture. I could have told them what I had known all along: Man does not live by spirituality alone! This soup could easily be a complete meal, with the addition of some good bread and a green salad.

Bring the water to a boil in a large heavy pot. Add the lamb and cook over medium-high heat, covered, for 1½ hours.

Meanwhile, cut the spinach leaves into ribbons: Pile a few leaves together, roll them into a tight ball, and slice into the ball with a sharp knife, making thin strips. Repeat with the remaining leaves. (This is what is called a chiffonade.)

Heat the olive oil in a skillet over high heat. In a food processor, combine the onion, garlic, and celery and pulse until coarsely chopped. Add this mixture to the skillet and sauté until soft, about 5 minutes. Add the tomatoes and cook for 3 more minutes.

Add the vegetables to the reserved lamb mixture. Stir in the lima beans, potatoes, spinach, parsley, cilantro, turmeric, and saffron. Bring the mixture to a boil. Reduce the heat to medium and cook, covered, for 1½ hours.

Add the cumin, cinnamon, lemon juice, and salt and pepper to taste and cook for 15 more minutes. If desired, remove the lamb from the bones and return the meat to the soup. Serve hot.

TOFU AND OTHER SOY PRODUCTS

Since you will encounter recipes in this book containing tofu and other soy products, I would like to give you a quick primer. Until pretty recently, tofu and soy product users were easily identified, judged, and dismissed: They were on spartan diets and shopped only in health-food stores. They ate muddy-looking seaweed and other unidentifiable monochromatic mixtures with unpronounceable names. For the most part, they were the ones you would not ask to dinner at your home, for fear of culture shock on both sides. In the last few years, however, I don't know by what enchantment, soy products have entered the culinary mainstream. Which brings us to the question: Why bother with tofu—does it have any redeeming qualities, other than the fact that it is good for you? The answer is a resounding yes!

From a nutritional point of view, ounce for ounce, tofu has all the protein contained in meat, much less fat and sodium, and no cholesterol. Even if you are reluctant to eliminate meat from your diet, you can use a mixture of equal parts chicken or meat and tofu in stir-fried dishes, hamburgers, meat loaves, and lasagnas. Consider tofu a culinary chameleon. Sneak it into dishes that are intensely flavored and will impart their own flavor to it, which is pretty easy to do, since tofu has practically no taste of its own. In turn, tofu will impart its wonderful texture and all its nutritional benefits. A modern-day manna!

For those on dairy-restricted or kosher diets, tofu is a perfect substitute for cheese, milk, and cream. And because of its uncanny versatility and unctuousness, it is indispensable for texture in dishes such as mousses, salad dressings, and creamed soups.

And finally, tofu and other soy products are very economical. Although its price and appearance would suggest a humble, plebeian ingredient, once you are familiar with different ways to use it, you will find it a wonderful addition to so many dishes, with no downside. In my perennial quest for food with good nutrition and good taste, I have discovered a true ally in tofu. The range of possibilities with soy products is astounding.

Soy products come in all shapes and textures. Here is a quick overview of the most widely used forms.

MISO. A cultured, fermented paste made from soybeans, brown rice, or barley. Traditionally, the making of miso was much like wine making. Miso was left to age for years, and different grains yielded a wide range of colors, aromas, and flavors. Today the fermentation and coloration of miso is partly activated in plants with commercial ferments. A wonderful base for soups, it adds a mild, robust, and even meaty flavor according to what miso you choose (the darker, the meatier). Miso is also considered a great booster of the immune system.

SOY FLOUR. Made by grinding hulled and roasted soybeans. It has a robust taste and increases moisture and protein content in baking.

SOY GRITS. Used in soups and hot cereal dishes.

SOY MILK. Made by grinding soybeans with water, then cooking and straining the mixture. Ideal for all people who are lactose-intolerant, including babies, and for those who keep kosher and can't use dairy products in a meal that includes meat. In both cooking and baking, soy milk behaves just like milk, turning out perfectly creamed soups, custards, and much more!

SOY NUTS. Roasted soybean. They make for delicious healthy munching and have a high protein content and a much lower fat content than regular nuts.

SOYBEAN SPROUTS. Crunchy and distinctive, used in salads and in stir-fries.

TEMPEH. Cooked soybeans, to which a bacteria is added. The beans are then shaped into cakes and left to ferment in a warm place. Its delicious taste is guaranteed to make you forget its drab appearance. Tempeh is used in stir-fried dishes, or grilled just like hamburgers.

TEXTURED SOY PROTEIN (TVP). Soy flour heated and formed into clusters. I must admit, TVP bears an unfortunate resemblance to pet food, but I am certain it tastes much better. Great for meatless "sauce Bolognese," Sloppy Joes, and lasagna.

TOFU. Soy milk turned into a solid through the process of coagulation (using calcium sulfate, which further increases the calcium content in tofu) and heating. Silken tofu is the kind with the highest moisture content; it is perfect for salad dressings, custards, and other desserts. Extra-firm tofu is the densest tofu with the lowest water content, great for stir-frying and broiling. There are a number of textures that fall between silken and extra-firm, including soft (good for scrambling), and firm (for marinating or cutting in cubes in soups). Consider me a tofu missionary: I have turned hundreds of tofu skeptics into tofu enthusiasts, and I am always gaining converts!

MISO, SHIITAKE, AND SWISS CHARD SOUP

2 quarts (8 cups) water

1 pound shiitake mushrooms, caps only, thinly sliced

One 2-inch piece fresh ginger, peeled and minced

½ cup dark or light miso paste

2 ears of corn, cobs cut into 1-inch rounds

3–4 tablespoons soy sauce

3 tablespoons toasted sesame oil

1 tablespoon bottled hot sauce

1 pound firm or extra-firm tofu, cut into sticks

1 bunch (1 pound) Swiss chard, leaves only, cut into ribbons

4 scallions, thinly sliced

MAKES 8–10 SERVINGS

Although the flavors are rich and complex, this soup is ready in about fifteen minutes. Miso adds its intriguing fermented flavor and a bulky but not starchy texture to the broth. It is important to add the Swiss chard at the very end of the cooking process, so that it retains its brilliant color. The corn adds a wonderful flavor.

Combine the water, mushrooms, ginger, miso, and corn in a heavy pot and bring to a boil. Reduce the heat to medium and add the soy sauce, toasted sesame oil, hot sauce, and tofu. Bring to a boil again. Add the Swiss chard and scallions and cook for 1 more minute, until the Swiss chard is wilted. Serve hot.

THE HAMMER AS KITCHEN TOOL

To cut corn cobs, simply place a cleaver with the blade poised on the spots where you want to cut. Hit the cleaver with a hammer, with one clean strike. You may find the use of a hammer in the kitchen somewhat odd, but you will quickly change your mind when you see how many other thankless tasks it performs. In fact, used with a cleaver, a hammer makes short work of cutting all those monolithic items that usually cause us so much grief in the kitchen: butternut squash, chocolate blocks, big turnips, and more.

MATZOH BALL SOUP

FOR THE BROTH

5 pounds chicken or turkey necks, wings, meaty bones (sold at butcher shops)

4 large carrots, peeled and cut lengthwise into quarters

2 large onions, quartered

6 ribs celery, peeled and cut into thirds

4 large parsnips, peeled and cut lengthwise into quarters

1 large bunch dill

1 bunch parsley root, leaves and all, roots peeled

1 teaspoon turmeric

Salt and pepper

4 quarts (16 cups) water

FOR THE MATZOH BALLS

1 cup matzoh meal

¼ cup ice water or seltzer

¼ cup vegetable or olive oil

4 large eggs (if watching your cholesterol, use 8 egg whites)

Salt and pepper

MAKES 8 SERVINGS; 8 LARGE OR 16 SMALL MATZOH BALLS

An elderly friend of mine had avoided matzoh balls his whole life because the ones his mother made had the density and flavor of tennis balls. I told him I would treat him to lunch if he tasted mine. He took the first bite grudgingly, then wolfed down the rest and said with a delighted grin, "That lunch will have to be my treat, not yours, for curing an old man of one of his oldest phobias." So, what's my secret? A very thin, fluffy batter that firms up in an hour or so in the refrigerator. The batter takes only seconds to mix, so by all means make it ahead of time. Do not use valuable chicken parts you could be using for a dish in its own right: Not only is that more costly, but the soup will not be as flavorful.

To make the broth: Place the broth ingredients in a large pot and bring to a boil. Reduce the heat to medium and cook, covered, for 2 hours. Strain the broth, pressing lightly on the solids. Chill. Skim the fat off the top while cold.

To make the matzoh balls: Mix the matzoh ball ingredients together in a bowl or in a food processor. The mixture will look thin; do *not* add extra matzoh meal in an attempt to thicken it. Chill for 1 hour.

Bring a large pot of water to a boil. With wet hands, form the matzoh balls—2 inches in diameter for small, or 3 inches for large. Place the matzoh balls in the boiling water. Cover the pot and cook for about 30 minutes. (The matzoh balls will rise up to the top after a few minutes.)

Using a slotted spoon, remove the matzoh balls and add them to the broth. Heat the soup through, adding a little water if it seems too much of the broth has cooked away (you want about 10 cups liquid).

HOT RUSSIAN BORSCHT

½ cup olive oil

2 medium onions, quartered

6 large cloves garlic

3 ribs celery, peeled and cut into thirds

2 medium carrots, grated

2 medium parsnips, grated

2 medium turnips, grated

1 small head white cabbage, shredded

4 medium beets, grated

2 medium potatoes, grated (put in a bowl of cold water until ready to use)

4 cups canned crushed tomatoes

1 cup finely chopped dill

4 quarts (16 cups) water

½ cup sugar

½ cup vinegar

Salt and pepper

MAKES 16 SERVINGS

My Russian mother-in-law shared this recipe with me, so I can assure you it's the real thing. Her repertoire is short but dazzling. Meeting her was my first step toward making my peace with what everyone in my family called, with a dismissive snort, "Ashkenazi cooking."

In America, beets don't get the recognition they deserve, and borscht is a good way to turn dinner guests into beet worshippers. Traditionally, borscht is made with beef and constitutes a whole meal. This is a faithful but meatless version, suitable as a first course or a vegetarian main course. You will save considerable time by grating the vegetables in a food processor.

Heat the oil in a heavy pot over high heat. Combine the onion, garlic, and celery in a food processor and pulse until coarsely chopped. Add this mixture to the hot oil and sauté until soft, about 5 minutes. Add the carrots, parsnips, turnips, cabbage, beets, potatoes, tomatoes, dill, and water and bring to a boil. Reduce the heat to medium and cook, covered, for about 1½ hours.

Add the sugar, vinegar, and salt and pepper to taste and cook for 30 minutes. Serve hot.

Variation: If you want to make a beef borscht, start by cooking beef chunks, flanken, or bones (or a combination) in water for about 1 hour, and then proceed with the recipe. Sauté the first ingredients as instructed, and then add the remaining ingredients, including the meat and its cooking liquid.

COLD FRUIT SOUP

1 large piece lemon peel

1 large piece orange peel

6 cloves

10 black peppercorns

2 Granny Smith apples, peeled, cored, and cut into small chunks

8 cups frozen strawberries, blueberries, peaches, plums, and cherries, in any combination

2 cups semi-dry white wine

2 cups cranberry juice

2 cups unfiltered apple cider

Juice of 2 lemons or limes

MAKES 12 SERVINGS

This summery, cool, ruby-red masterpiece can be assembled in just a few minutes. The Granny Smith apples give the soup tang and pectin that adds texture naturally. Do not misunderstand my choice of frozen fruit for a desire to cut corners or save money: Frozen berries are picked at the height of their sweetness, ripeness, color, and flavor. Since this soup is going to be pureed, I don't mind if the frozen fruit is not as pretty as the fresh. Of course, if you find some fabulous summer fruit, use it instead, alone or in combination. Avoid raspberries, as they will force you to add the extra step of straining the mixture to rid it of those annoying seeds.

Serve the soup as a first course, garnished with mint sprigs and lime slices, or as a dessert, topped with a little scoop of coconut or fruit sorbet and a mint sprig.

Place the lemon peel, orange peel, cloves, and peppercorns in a piece of cheesecloth and tie it together with a piece of kitchen string.

In a large heavy pot, bring all the ingredients to a boil. Reduce the heat to medium and cook, covered, for exactly 10 minutes. Remove the cheesecloth packet and discard.

Transfer three quarters of the soup to a food processor or blender and process until smooth. Transfer the puree to a bowl and stir in the remaining chunky fruit mixture. Chill completely before serving. If the soup thickens too much while it cools, thin it with a little juice.

Salads

Salads are a great showcase for cooks, even those who have neither the time nor the inclination for elaborate preparations. I have catered parties for hundreds of people featuring only a great selection of salads. As long as all of your ingredients are perfectly crisp, fresh, and beautiful, the possibilities are endless. Ingredients past their prime do not belong in any salad. If you cannot bear the thought of throwing away a handful of less-than-fresh vegetables, make a small batch of pureed vegetables that will be eaten at one seating, so that you might start fresh all over again. Do not think only in terms of leaves and salad dressings when making salads. Experiment with all the wonderful combinations of textures, colors, and seasonings you can come up with.

THINK SEASONAL. Fennel, baby spinach, lamb's lettuce, arugula, and edible flowers will appear at local farmers' markets and good grocery stores when they are in season. Treat yourself and your guests while the prices are reasonable.

THINK DRY. Nobody likes a soggy salad. Roll the greens in paper towels, lay them in a thin layer on a counter lined with paper towels, or dry them in a salad spinner. Perfectly dried greens will keep in the refrigerator for a couple of days. If a salad includes "wet" ingredients such as cut tomatoes, cucumbers, or mangoes, put them in a separate plastic bag and combine with the rest of the salad just before serving.

THINK COLORFUL. Romaine hearts look great with strips of radicchio and endive. A striking all-green salad can be made from mixed lettuce leaves, watercress, spinach, snow peas, and avocado. A dramatic all-white salad can be made from thinly shredded Chinese cabbage, fennel, endive, enoki mushrooms, and daikon.

THINK FRUITY. The tartness and juiciness of fruit makes it a wonderful contrast to peppery and pungent salad greens. Add mango, apple, papaya, or pear chunks or wedges to baby spinach, arugula, or watercress leaves, and sprinkle on dried cranberries for color and texture.

THINK NUTTY. Lightly toasted cashews, pumpkin seeds, sunflower seeds, poppy seeds, pistachios, or pecans will add wonderful taste and texture to your salad.

THINK CRUNCHY. Add grated raw vegetables (carrots, red cabbage, beets), croutons, or sprouts for appealing crunch. Sprouts don't just look and taste great, they are really good for you, and there are so many of them on the market today, including daikon, alfalfa, broccoli, sunflower, lentil, and mung bean sprouts.

THINK DRESSING. No item is less worth buying commercially than salad dressing. *Any dressing* you whip up at home in a few seconds will be vastly superior to the most elaborate store-bought dressing. Although you can't go wrong with a simple mixture of oil and lemon, if you are a frequent salad eater you will want to develop a repertoire of dressings. A salad is best served with a dressing that emphasizes the ingredients it was made with. For example, an all-leaf salad would be delicious tossed with an herb-based dressing, a salad including fruit would be great with a dressing containing orange juice or unfiltered apple juice, and a salad including nuts would be enhanced by a dressing made with walnut or hazelnut oil. My salad dressings usually veer from the time-honored tradition of three parts oil to one part vinegar or lemon juice, with excellent results. Don't get me wrong. I like French vinaigrette and use it quite often, but I really love dressings that have an interesting texture and less oil, relying for a good emulsion on "bulky" ingredients such as garlic, shallots, tofu, herbs, or mango thinned with juice or soy milk. These preparations result in delicious yet much less caloric dressings. And another bonus: The food processor is so powerful that any emulsion obtained using it is almost inseparable. Whatever dressing you choose, use it sparingly. When you have finished your salad, you shouldn't be left with a pool of dressing on your plate.

THINK MAIN COURSE. There are many ways to turn any salad into a satisfying entrée. You can add sliced grilled fish or poached chicken, combine mixed greens with grilled

Opposite: Arugula, Pear, and Walnut Salad with Walnut Vinaigrette

vegetables or steamed string beans or asparagus, or add a starch such as potatoes, lentils, beans, barley, or couscous. You might want to present a main course salad on a platter, with each item presented individually rather than tossed together. The dressing for a main course salad might not have the same high acid content as that for a first course salad.

I hesitate to give exact servings for salads. Let's just say that each of the following recipes will yield about eight ample first course servings. In my house, it will hardly serve three or four. On weekdays, we happily eat like rabbits! Please note that the dressing recipes make quite a bit more than you will need—leaving plenty to use on other salads.

ARUGULA, PEAR, AND WALNUT SALAD WITH WALNUT VINAIGRETTE

FOR THE DRESSING

⅓ cup toasted walnuts (see Toasting Nuts, page 33)

1 medium shallot, quartered

¼ cup walnut oil

¼ cup extra virgin olive oil

¼ cup red wine vinegar

⅓ cup dry sherry

Salt and pepper

FOR THE SALAD

3 bunches arugula, leaves only

1 pear, peeled, cored, cut into quarters, and sliced

½ small red onion, thinly sliced with a mandoline or the thin slicing blade of a food processor

⅓ cup blue cheese or goat cheese, crumbled

⅓ cup chopped toasted walnuts

MAKES 8 SERVINGS;
ABOUT 2 CUPS DRESSING

In France, dessert often consists of a platter of fruit, cheese, and nuts, with a little glass of wine or dry sherry. Combine these ingredients with peppery arugula, and you have this glorious salad (see photo, page 54). I make sure to get the most flavor from the nuts by toasting them.

I remember one balmy summer evening in Paris when a friend and I were dining at the outdoor terrace of a bistro. To conclude our meal, we were served an impressive array of French cheeses, simply but beautifully arranged on a wooden board with grapes and figs. The idea was to take a couple of slivers of what we liked best, and let the waiter pass the board on to the next customers. Now the homeless in Paris are no different from those in New York. Pretty soon half a dozen of them converged around our table, hands outstretched. Instead of the customary coin, we magnanimously handed each clochard (homeless person) one of the precious cheeses. While our waiter struggled to keep the amiable neutrality and unflappability proverbial in his profession, my friend and I struggled to withhold a hysterical fit of laughter. Oh, we were bad in those days!

To make the dressing: Combine all the ingredients in a blender or food processor and blend until smooth and emulsified. Store in a glass jar in the refrigerator. If the dressing thickens too much as it sits, thin it with a few drops of water.

To make the salad: Mix the arugula, pear, and onion in a salad bowl or on a platter. Add about 1 cup of the dressing, or just enough to barely coat the greens, and toss. Scatter the cheese and walnuts on top of the greens and serve immediately.

TRICOLOR RIBBON SALAD WITH CIDER-SHALLOT DRESSING

FOR THE DRESSING

4 medium shallots

½ cup extra virgin olive oil

¼ cup honey

⅓ cup balsamic vinegar

½ cup unfiltered apple cider

Salt and pepper

FOR THE SALAD

2 romaine hearts

2 heads endive

1 medium head radicchio

1 pint grape tomatoes

MAKES 8 SERVINGS;
2½ CUPS DRESSING

Romaine lettuce hearts are very tender and crisp. They cost a little more than whole heads of romaine, but they are worth it, especially because no leaves get discarded. This is the salad of choice in my home, and romaine hearts are the only salad greens I ever cut with a knife because it is the only way to get that lovely ribbon effect.

To make the dressing: Combine the shallots and oil in a food processor and pulse until the shallots are minced. Add the honey, vinegar, cider, and salt and pepper to taste and pulse a few more times. Store in a glass jar in the refrigerator.

To make the salad: Cut the romaine, endive, and radicchio into thin ribbons. Dry thoroughly. Place the lettuce and tomatoes in a large bowl. Add about 1 cup of the dressing, or just enough to barely coat the greens, and toss.

FOOD PROCESSOR FOLLIES

The food processor was invented around the time I got married, twenty-five years ago. In fact, you could say that the advent of this essential device played a major role in my decision to finally set up house! Recently I was invited to a spectacular home to do a food demonstration for about sixty students. I looked around the kitchen for a food processor and didn't see one anywhere. "Oh, I'll get it for you," the hostess said obligingly. She took off her shoes, found a ladder and climbed to the top shelf of a closet to retrieve the device and take it out of its original wrappings.

Surprised, I asked, "Did you just move to this house?" "No, we've been living here about twelve years," she replied sheepishly. I must have looked completely floored because laughter erupted throughout the room. At the end of my demonstration, which made extensive use of her machine, the host announced that she planned to sacrifice a square foot of her countertop to one of the most convenient and effective kitchen tools around: the food processor!

WILD RICE SALAD ON SAUTÉED WATERCRESS

1 cup dried cranberries

1 cup cranberry juice

2½ cups water

1 cup wild rice, rinsed and drained

2 ribs celery, peeled and minced

½ small red onion, minced

1 small bunch mint, finely chopped

1 small bunch flat-leaf parsley, finely chopped

¼ cup walnut oil

1 teaspoon allspice

1 tablespoon grated fresh ginger

1 tablespoon grated orange zest

½ cup toasted pine nuts, optional

Salt and pepper

3 tablespoons olive oil

3 bunches watercress, leaves only

MAKES 6–8 SERVINGS

This salad is almost too beautiful to serve as a first course. It could very easily be converted into a main course with the addition of some diced smoked turkey breast or poached chicken breast. Aside from being delicious, it is quite forgiving and maintains its crunch and color even if made the day before serving. In this case, fold in the pine nuts just before serving.

Combine the cranberries and the cranberry juice in a bowl and set aside. Bring the water to a boil in a saucepan. Lower the heat to medium, add the rice, and cook, covered, for about 40 minutes. The grains should be partially open, so that they are tender but not totally soft. You will have about 3 cups cooked rice.

Transfer the rice to a bowl and add the cranberry mixture, celery, onion, mint, parsley, oil, allspice, ginger, orange zest, pine nuts, and salt and pepper to taste. Toss until thoroughly combined.

Heat the olive oil in a skillet over high heat. Add the watercress and sauté until just wilted, a minute or so. To serve, place the rice salad on a platter and surround it with the watercress.

MINCING AND GRATING

For this recipe or any recipe calling for mincing ingredients that will be used raw, mince by hand, not in a food processor; you will get a better presentation. For grating ginger, the long, narrow Microplane zester is the best—no more bloody knuckles. It is so narrow it allows room only for the item you are grating, and it is razor-sharp. It will also grate cheese and citrus zest in a flash.

SALAD OF MESCLUN AND AVOCADO WITH BASIL-HONEY DRESSING

FOR THE DRESSING

1 cup basil leaves, packed

½ cup extra virgin olive oil

2 medium shallots

½ cup unfiltered apple cider

¼ cup honey

⅓ cup red wine vinegar

Salt and pepper

FOR THE SALAD

1 pound mesclun (about 8 cups)

1 avocado, peeled, pitted, and cut into ½-inch cubes

2 dozen edible flowers, if available

Makes 8 servings; 2½ cups dressing

Mesclun is delicious and pretty but perishable. Buy it at the peak of its freshness, and serve it right away. If you find edible flowers at your market such as pansies, marigolds, or nasturtiums, take some home for a garnish. And don't let the basil season pass you by. When it is plentiful, buy a big bunch, wash and dry the leaves and soft stems thoroughly, cram them into a glass jar, and fill the jar with olive oil. The leaves will lose their volume but none of their flavor or fragrance. Don't discard the gorgeous, emerald, basil-infused elixir: Dunk your bread in it, or use it in recipes calling for both olive oil and basil. It will keep a full two weeks in the refrigerator, although I doubt it will last that long!

To make the dressing: Combine the basil, oil, and shallots in a food processor and process until smooth. Add the cider, honey, vinegar, and salt and pepper to taste and process for 1 more minute. Store in a glass jar in the refrigerator for up to 2 weeks.

To make the salad: Combine the salad ingredients in a bowl or on a platter. Add 1 cup of the dressing, or just enough to barely coat the greens, and toss. Serve immediately.

HOMEGROWN BASIL

I did think of growing basil on my modest windowsill. I planted it in a small clay pot, and it throve for about two weeks, flooding my kitchen with its exuberant aromas and delighting us with its sunny flavors— and then it started wilting as fast as it blossomed from lack of adequate sun. When I mentioned this to my sister Lea, a home-owner, she poured her heart out to me about her unhappy love affair with basil. She said it grew so wild, she couldn't stamp out the basil plague, and she couldn't bear to let it go to waste, so she bought about fifty dollars' worth of pine nuts to make gallons of pesto, which she gave out to everyone on the block. Her verdict was irrevocable: Never again. Store-bought basil, she assured me, was cheaper at any price than homegrown, and no guilt feelings about letting all those bushes grow wild. We apartment-dwellers have no such problems!

SPINACH, CRANBERRY, AND MANGO SALAD WITH CURRIED MANGO DRESSING

FOR THE DRESSING

1 mango, peeled and cut into chunks

½ cup extra virgin olive oil

2 tablespoons mustard oil (if unavailable, use olive oil)

¼ cup orange juice

¼ cup lemon juice

1 tablespoon grated lemon zest

1 tablespoon curry powder

Salt and pepper

FOR THE SALAD

1 pound baby spinach leaves (about 8 cups)

1 cup dried cranberries

1 small red onion, sliced paper-thin with a mandoline or the thin slicing blade of a food processor

1 mango, peeled and neatly diced

MAKES 8 SERVINGS;
ABOUT 2 CUPS DRESSING

Salads with fruit are feasts not just for the eyes but for the palate. And so fragrant! The fruity salad dressing highlights the tartness of the fruit used in the salad. If you are not already acquainted with mustard oil, this dressing provides a perfect opportunity for you to get introduced to it. Mustard oil is easy to find at specialty food and Indian grocery stores, and a few drops go a long way. Don't add the mangoes to the greens until you are ready to serve the salad. If you want to save time, cut the fruit in advance and keep it in a plastic bag in the refrigerator until it's time to toss the salad. Baby spinach leaves are commercially washed and rewashed and already dry, so this means significant savings on preparation time.

To make the dressing: Place the mango in a food processor. With the motor running, add the oils in a slow stream, then add the orange juice, lemon juice, lemon zest, curry, and salt and pepper to taste. Store in a glass jar in the refrigerator for up to 2 weeks.

To make the salad: Place all the ingredients in a bowl or on a platter. Just before serving, add 1 cup of the dressing, or just enough to barely coat the greens, and toss.

FRESH CORN SALAD

6 ears white corn

½ red bell pepper, minced

4 whole scallions, thinly sliced

¼ cup finely chopped dill, packed

¼ cup extra virgin olive oil

2 teaspoons balsamic vinegar

Salt and pepper

<small>MAKES ABOUT 6 SERVINGS</small>

This dish is ideal for summer celebrations. White corn is plentiful then, as well as sweet and tender. Treat it gently and boil it only briefly. This salad looks like red, yellow, and green confetti and is very lightly seasoned, so the corn can be the star. If there are any leftovers, they will be good the next day, too.

Bring a large pot of water to a boil. Add the corn and boil for no more than 5 minutes. Remove with tongs and let sit until cool enough to handle. With a sharp knife, while holding an ear of corn upright on a plate, use a vertical motion to scrape off the corn kernels, cutting as close to the cob as you can.

Do not discard the milky sap that collects on the plate. Transfer the corn to a bowl and add the red pepper, scallions, and dill.

In a cup, whisk together the olive oil, vinegar, and salt and pepper to taste. Add the dressing to the corn mixture and toss to combine. Serve at room temperature.

MINTED TABBOULEH SALAD

1 cup bulghur wheat

1 cup boiling water

4 plum tomatoes, halved, seeded, and diced

4 whole scallions, thinly sliced

1 small bunch flat-leaf parsley, finely chopped

1 small bunch fresh mint (no substitutions), leaves only, finely chopped

¼ cup extra virgin olive oil

Juice of 2 lemons

2 teaspoons cumin

Salt and pepper

<small>MAKES ABOUT 6 SERVINGS</small>

I promise you will never go back to those half-pint containers at the supermarket, once you have tried this homemade version. There are two main rules for making this dish: Add the tomatoes just before serving, and ignore the cooking directions printed on ready-to-use boxes of bulghur. To make perfect bulghur, just remember: one part grain, one part boiling water, mix, cover, let rest for ten minutes. It is as easy as that.

Mix the bulghur and the boiling water in a stainless steel bowl or pot. Immediately cover very tightly to prevent any heat from escaping. Let rest for 10 minutes.

While the bulghur is resting, prepare the tomatoes, scallions, parsley, and mint and place them in a bowl. Add the oil, lemon juice, cumin, and salt and pepper to taste. Fluff the bulghur thoroughly with two forks and add it to the vegetable mixture. Serve at room temperature.

ROASTED BEET AND SWISS CHARD SALAD

1 bunch beets (about 3 large or 5 medium), with leaves attached

1 bunch Swiss chard

6 tablespoons olive oil

Juice of 1 lemon

1 tablespoon sugar

1 teaspoon cinnamon

2 tablespoons orange flower water

Salt and pepper

MAKES ABOUT 8 SERVINGS

In this country, beets are the butt of cooking jokes, much like prunes. This is unfortunate because they are absolutely delicious, as are beet greens. I once created quite a stir in the crowded line of a produce store as I lunged to restrain the cashier from severing perfect beet leaves from their roots with a huge knife she kept handy for this sacrilegious purpose. You too should treat beets and their leaves with respect. Orange flower water can be found at specialty food stores and most health food stores.

Preheat the oven to 425°F.

Separate the beet leaves and the Swiss chard from their stems, which run all the way up through the center of the leaves. Cut all the stems into thin slices. Separately, cut the leaves into very thin ribbons and set aside. Peel the beets and coarsely grate them. Place the sliced stems (not the leaves) and the grated beets on a cookie sheet, toss with 3 tablespoons of the oil, and roast for about 30 minutes or until greatly reduced, stirring once during the roasting.

Meanwhile, heat the remaining 3 tablespoons oil in a large skillet over high heat. Add the Swiss chard and beet leaves and sauté for about 5 minutes, stirring occasionally. Transfer the roasted beet mixture to a bowl. Add the sautéed leaves, lemon juice, sugar, cinnamon, orange flower water, and salt and pepper to taste and mix thoroughly. Serve at room temperature.

MOROCCAN TOMATO SALAD

6 plum tomatoes, seeds and juice discarded, diced

2 tablespoons minced purple onion

4 sprigs flat-leaf parsley, finely chopped

2 tablespoons capers, preferably tiny nonpareils

¼ cup minced dill pickle

6 pitted green olives, minced

2 pickled hot peppers, chopped (optional)

¼ of a preserved lemon, skin only, rinsed and finely chopped (see page 16)

¼ cup vegetable oil

¼ cup lemon juice

Salt and pepper

MAKES 6 SERVINGS

We Moroccans cook tomatoes, sun-dry tomatoes, pickle tomatoes, candy tomatoes—we prepare tomatoes in every way possible. In Mediterranean climates, they are spectacular year-round, inexpensive, and bursting with color and fragrance. Recently, it has become easier (although not cheaper) to get decent tomatoes throughout the year in the United States. This salad includes capers, gherkins, and preserved lemons; it is delightfully fragrant, colorful, and refreshing. If you do not have preserved lemons on hand, simply omit them and proceed with the recipe. If you must make this salad ahead of time, make it without the tomatoes (up to two days ahead), then add the tomatoes before serving.

Place all the ingredients in a glass bowl and mix well. Serve at room temperature.

SALADA MATBOOKHA (COOKED TOMATO SALAD)

1 whole head garlic

2 red bell peppers, seeded

2–3 jalapeño peppers

2 tablespoons olive oil

One 28-ounce can whole tomatoes, diced, with their juices (don't substitute crushed tomatoes)

½ cup olive oil

2 tablespoons paprika

3 garlic cloves, pressed

Salt and pepper

MAKES ABOUT 3½ CUPS

Moroccan Jews can't live without this dish, and they passed on the recipe to Jews around the world. It makes a great filling for tiny pies and can be served as an hors d'oeuvre, but it is best with good bread. Don't be alarmed by the amount of oil used, and do not try to reduce it—it gets discarded at serving time. Don't hesitate to double the recipe, as it keeps very well for a good two weeks.

Preheat the oven to 400°F.

Slice about ¼ inch off the pointed end of the head of garlic, leaving the cloves exposed. Place the head of garlic, bell peppers, and jalapeños on a cookie sheet. Drizzle the olive oil onto the vegetables and roast for 30 minutes, or until the garlic is soft and the peppers are charred (the peppers might be ready a few minutes before the garlic). Squeeze the garlic cloves out of their skins while still warm and mash with a fork. Peel the peppers and cut them into thin strips.

In a large heavy-bottomed pot, bring the tomatoes, oil, and paprika to a boil. Reduce the heat to medium, add the roasted garlic and peppers, and cook, covered, for about 30 minutes, stirring frequently. All of the moisture should evaporate, and the oil will resurface. (If you neglect this step, you will not get the desired look and texture but a glorified tomato sauce.) Add the pressed garlic and salt and pepper to taste.

Let the salad cool. Serve at room temperature using a slotted spoon. Store in a glass jar in the refrigerator for up to 2 weeks.

HOW TO ROAST PEPPERS

I have found a less messy, time-consuming alternative to broiling peppers. I roast them at a high temperature, rubbed with a little olive oil. First, I wash them thoroughly, because rinsing them after they are cooked lessens their luster and lovely smoky flavor. It is also important to get rid of all the seeds before roasting. Cut around the stems of the peppers, and the stems and seeds will come right out and can be discarded. Roast at 425°F for 30 to 40 minutes. In order to peel roasted peppers easily, put them in a brown paper or plastic bag for a few minutes as soon as they come out of the oven, and their skins will come right off. You might want to make extra and store them in the freezer for later use.

MARINATED TOMATO SALAD

3 firm ripe tomatoes, cut into wedges and seeded

1 cup sun-dried tomatoes, briefly soaked in lukewarm water and squeezed thoroughly dry

1 small head fennel, thinly sliced

½ small purple onion, thinly sliced

4 large cloves garlic, minced

½ cup fresh basil leaves, packed, cut into thin strips

2 tablespoons capers

½ cup Niçoise olives

¾ cup extra virgin olive oil

⅓ cup red wine vinegar

1 tablespoon coarsely ground pepper

Salt

2 bunches arugula, washed and spun dry

MAKES 8 SERVINGS

Another starring role for the summer tomato, although this salad can be made year-round. The best of Mediterranean spirit, flavors and colors come together in this glorious dish. When serving the salad at a dairy meal, you can add grated Parmesan or cubed goat cheese, if desired.

In a large bowl, combine all the ingredients, except the arugula. Gently mix so as not to bruise the tomatoes. Marinate in the refrigerator for up to 5 hours. Just before serving, add the arugula to the tomatoes and toss.

CELERY ROOT AND CABBAGE SALAD WITH RÉMOULADE

FOR THE RÉMOULADE

⅓ cup low-fat mayonnaise

⅓ cup soy milk

3 tablespoons cider vinegar

2 tablespoons prepared white horseradish

2 tablespoons Dijon mustard

1 tablespoon dried tarragon

1 teaspoon sugar

Salt and pepper

FOR THE SALAD

1 medium celery root

1 teaspoon fresh lemon juice

½ small head white cabbage, thinly shredded

3 McIntosh or Granny Smith apples, unpeeled, coarsely grated

3 medium shallots, minced

MAKES 8 SERVINGS;
ABOUT ¾ CUP SAUCE

Celery root is either ignored or used to flavor soup. The French, however, eat it quite often, and so can you. I tend to like the underdogs, so I bring these ugly roots home regularly. Under that homely, grimy, warty exterior, I know what I will find: a vegetable truly noble at heart. This is a celery root salad for beginners, as it is mixed with more familiar items such as cabbage and apples. After the taste grows on you, or simply as a variation, use two celery roots and no other vegetables. Soaking the celery root first in water and lemon juice will prevent its oxidation. Rémoulade sauce is very versatile. You can also use it on smoked fish or turkey.

To make the rémoulade: In a small bowl, whisk all the ingredients together until smooth.

To make the salad: Coarsely grate the celery root and soak it in cold water with a little lemon juice. Squeeze out all the water from the grated celery root and transfer it to a bowl. Add the cabbage, apples, and shallots. Pour the sauce over the vegetables and toss.

SALADE NIÇOISE WITH GRILLED TUNA

FOR THE DRESSING

6 anchovies, bones removed, rinsed

3 tablespoons capers

5 sprigs flat-leaf parsley

3 tablespoons Dijon mustard

4 large cloves garlic

½ cup extra virgin olive oil

¼ cup wine vinegar

1 tablespoon dried oregano

Salt and pepper

FOR THE SALAD

12 small red bliss potatoes

1 pound *haricots verts* (or perfect string beans)

2 tablespoons olive oil

1¼ pounds fresh tuna, 1-inch thick, all skin and black parts removed, cut into 4 pieces

Salt and freshly ground pepper

2 heads romaine lettuce, torn

4 plum tomatoes, seeded and cut into wedges

¼ medium red onion, cut into thin strips

2 roasted red bell peppers peeled and cut into strips (see How to Roast Peppers, page 66)

24 Niçoise olives

4 hard-boiled eggs, peeled and halved

MAKES 8 SERVINGS;
1½ CUPS DRESSING

Fresh seared tuna and haricots verts propel this casual French classic to new heights. White albacore tuna will do just as well as its much more expensive yellowfin counterpart. Likewise, if the string beans look perfect to you on your shopping day, do not spend the extra money on haricots verts unnecessarily. Don't hesitate to serve this salad to your guests: They will love it! The dressing will keep very well, so make a big batch. The tuna will taste best if it is rare.

To make the dressing: Place all the ingredients in a food processor and process until smooth and creamy.

To make the salad: Bring a pan of water to a boil and cook the potatoes until just tender, about 20 minutes. Drain and let cool. When cool, cut the potatoes in half.

Cook the *haricots verts* in boiling water until just tender, about 5 minutes. Rinse them in cold water, drain, and set aside.

Heat the oil in a nonstick skillet over high heat. Season the tuna with salt and pepper to taste. When the skillet is very hot, add the tuna. Cook for about 2 minutes on each side for rare, or 3 minutes per side for medium rare. Let the tuna cool for a few minutes, then cut it into thin slices.

Mix all the salad ingredients, except the tuna, on a platter. Arrange the tuna slices on top and drizzle some of the dressing over the salad.

CHINESE BEEF SALAD

2 tablespoons olive oil

1 medium Napa cabbage (about 3 pounds), thinly sliced

1 pound shiitake mushrooms, caps only, sliced

One 2-pound London broil (about 1⅓-inches thick)

FOR THE MARINADE

4 scallions, thinly sliced

2 large garlic cloves, minced

2 tablespoons minced cilantro

1-inch piece fresh ginger, minced or grated

3 tablespoons toasted sesame oil

¼ cup mirin or dry sherry

3 tablespoons soy sauce, or to taste

2 tablespoons bottled hot sauce

½ cup roasted peanuts or cashews, for garnish

Makes 8 first-course
or 4 main-course servings

A fabulous cold dish, terrific served on a bed of soba or cellophane noodles. Even if you don't usually like rare beef, don't cook this beyond medium rare; you will end up with tough meat and an uninspired dish. I love to use London broil, as it's lean, tender, and free of sinew and fat.

Preheat the broiler.

Heat the oil in a large skillet over high heat. Add the cabbage and sauté until wilted (it will greatly reduce). Transfer the cabbage to a large bowl. Add a few more drops of oil to the skillet if necessary and add the mushrooms. Sauté until all the liquid evaporates, 3 to 4 minutes.

Broil the meat until medium rare, about 5 minutes on each side. Let the meat cool and cut it into very thin slices. Add the meat and the mushrooms to the cabbage and mix together.

To make the marinade: In a bowl, mix all the marinade ingredients together and add to the beef mixture. Marinate in the refrigerator for up to 8 hours.

To serve: Transfer the salad to a platter. Sprinkle the nuts on just before serving.

Fish

Since I was born and raised in the port city of Casablanca, you might think I had no fish aversions whatsoever. Au contraire! I grew up eating fish every day, prepared in every way imaginable, even at breakfast. I intend to make a fish lover out of you, as I have done for hundreds of guests, students, and customers. Many home cooks have only recently (and timidly) started experimenting with fish. In the past, unsure of how to discern its freshness or prepare it, let alone how and where to buy it, most cooks avoided unfamiliar fish and stuck with the old standbys: salmon, sole, and flounder (or frozen fish fillets). They further limited themselves by cooking these few varieties in the same unexciting ways: poached salmon, broiled sole, fried flounder.

Although increasingly unusual types of fish are available at local grocery stores, the big change these days is in consumers' consciousness. Fish is delicious, nutritious, and low in fat, and it takes just a few minutes to prepare. Don't be afraid to branch out when shopping, and keep in mind these few important guidelines:

WHERE TO BUY FISH. Fish markets and good supermarkets regularly receive a wide variety of fresh fish. Fish is fresh when it is firm to the touch and its eyes are wide open. Fish should be resting on plenty of ice, with good drainage to eliminate stagnant melting ice. It should look bright, clear, unspotted, and unmarred. It should smell briny, not "fishy."

FRESH VERSUS FROZEN. If you have a fish market near you, or a good fish department at your supermarket, do not bother with frozen fish. However, if you can't buy fresh, there are a couple of facts you should know. Fish captured at the peak of its freshness and immediately frozen will be nearly perfect when thawed. Good frozen fish is packed tightly to prevent the icy air from causing freezer burns. It is frozen quickly, to prevent ice from accumulating on the flesh and draining away its moisture during the thawing process. When you buy frozen fish, use the same guidelines as when buying fresh fish: Look for firm, bright, unmarred fish that appears free of freezer burns or bruises. Above all, do not refreeze thawed fish.

HELP FROM YOUR FISHMONGER. Do you recoil at the sight of scales, guts, bones, gills, and heads, even if they are those of a dead fish? Ask your fishmonger to make salmon and striped bass steaks for you; clean and fillet whole sides of salmon, mahi mahi, bass, and tilefish; thoroughly bone fish such as shad and whitefish; remove the skin of delicate fillets such as sole, flounder, and tilapia; cut tuna steaks to the desired size and rid them of that unappealing and bitter-tasting black-red border (blood line). Once you establish a relationship with your fishmonger, you can make requests. Do not be afraid of being imposing—every honest merchant loves a polite, informed consumer!

HOW TO CLEAN FISH. Remove all gills and intestines and scale the fish thoroughly. Rinse it in plenty of cold water mixed with salt and lemon juice or vinegar; this will ensure perfectly cleaned fish.

HOW TO COOK FISH. Dark varieties, such as bluefish and mackerel, are best when broiled briefly so they remain moist and robust. Tuna, both the dark and the light albacore variety, should be quickly seared or grilled, leaving the inside barely cooked. Thick white fillets such as mahi mahi, grouper, bass, and halibut lend themselves well to pan-frying, steaming, baking, broiling, and even stewing. Salmon is delicious baked, seared, stuffed, poached, marinated, and grilled. Thin flatfish fillets such as sole and flounder are too delicate for prolonged cooking or marinating and are best pan-fried, grilled, or *en papillote,* with a sauce or lemon wedges on the side. Whole small fish such as whiting or trout can be broiled, baked, or stewed with quick-cooking vegetables such as onions, garlic, and tomatoes.

All fish share one crucial characteristic: They toughen and lose moisture when overcooked. So take out that fish just in time!

Opposite: Blackened Tuna with Black Bean Salsa

BLACKENED TUNA WITH BLACK BEAN SALSA

FOR THE SALSA

2 cups canned black beans, rinsed and drained

1 large tomato, halved, seeded, and diced

2 tablespoons finely chopped purple onion

1 large clove garlic, pressed

1 teaspoon cumin

1 tablespoon capers

2 tablespoons chopped flat-leaf parsley

2 tablespoons chopped cilantro

¼ cup olive oil

3 tablespoons fresh lemon juice

1 tablespoon bottled hot sauce

Salt and pepper to taste

FOR THE SPICE MIXTURE

4 large cloves garlic

1½ tablespoons paprika

¼–½ teaspoon cayenne

1 tablespoon cumin

1 tablespoon oregano

2 tablespoons cornmeal or flour

Salt and pepper to taste

FOR THE FISH

2 tablespoons olive oil

1½ pounds skinless, boneless tuna fillet, cut into 4 pieces (about 6 ounces each), black borders removed, thoroughly dried with paper towels

MAKES 4 SERVINGS

Although I prefer to use tuna for this dish (see photo, page 72), I have obtained excellent results with salmon, tilapia, and mahi mahi. The seasonings for the spice mixture can easily be modified to suit your taste. When you arrive at a winning combination, make a big batch and store it in an airtight jar in the refrigerator.

The black bean salsa is a perfect accompaniment and is easy to prepare. It is also one of the rare recipes in which I use canned beans. This recipe makes plenty of leftover salsa for other uses, such as with poached chicken breasts.

To make the salsa: Combine all the salsa ingredients in a bowl and mix thoroughly. Serve at room temperature.

To make the spice mixture: Combine the spice mixture ingredients in a food processor and process until blended. Transfer to a plate or shallow bowl.

To prepare the fish: Press the fish into the spice mixture to coat it on both sides.

Heat the oil in a heavy frying pan until it is very hot and smoking. Add the fish to the pan and fry it for about 2 minutes without lowering the heat. Turn the fish over and fry for another 2 minutes. The fish should remain rare on the inside. Serve hot or at room temperature, plain or with salsa.

HOW TO BLACKEN FISH

There are two sacred rules for making blackened fish. The first is to start with perfectly dry fish, as moisture left in the fish will not only mix with the oil, steaming it instead of frying it, it will also splatter all over your face and your kitchen. The second is to use very hot, even smoking, oil. Choose a heavy frying pan for this recipe; let it get so hot that the addition of the fish doesn't bring the temperature down for more than just a few seconds. This method of frying not only ensures a lovely crust, it also uses minimal amounts of oil. In fact, hardly any oil penetrates the fish. Open some windows before you start frying, so that the fumes do not overpower your kitchen. We don't like the smell nearly as much as the taste of blackened fish!

TUNA BURGERS WITH WATERCRESS-WASABI SAUCE

2 tablespoons vegetable oil
(if pan-frying)

2 pounds skinless, boneless tuna,
all black parts removed

1 small red onion, quartered

1 small bunch flat-leaf parsley

2 large cloves garlic

1 egg

3 tablespoons olive oil

Salt and pepper

Oregano, cumin, basil, bottled hot
sauce in any combination to taste

Hamburger buns or other rolls

MAKES 4–6 BURGERS

For those of you who do not eat red meat or would like to limit your intake, tuna is the closest you will get to a meaty taste. Do not use a substitute for the tuna; no other fish gives you the robust flavor and texture you need for this dish. The watercress-wasabi sauce is a perfect foil for the burgers, with its sharp clean taste. You will find it delightful with many other dishes as well, such as sliced steak, poached chicken breasts, and poached salmon.

To make the sauce: See the ingredients list and directions on page 28.

To make the burgers: Preheat the broiler (or heat 2 tablespoons of oil in a nonstick frying pan over high heat if you want to fry the burgers).

Combine all the burger ingredients in a food processor and pulse until finely minced. Form the mixture into 4 to 6 burgers about 1 inch thick. Broil or pan-fry the burgers for 2 to 3 minutes on each side for medium-rare. Serve on buns, plain, with the sauce, or with tomato slices, lettuce leaves, and lemon wedges, if desired.

SEA BASS STEW

2 large bunches Swiss chard, red or green or a combination, cut into 1-inch strips, stems and all

4 large cloves garlic, minced

1 head fennel, thinly sliced (optional)

2 cups diced tomatoes, fresh or canned

24 pitted green olives

3 large potatoes, peeled and cut into 1-inch thick slices

¼ cup olive oil

1 teaspoon turmeric

1 tablespoon paprika

2 cups water

3 pounds skinless, boneless sea bass, cut into 8 pieces (about 6 ounces each)

MAKES 8 SERVINGS

This is a fragrant, easy-to-prepare meal-in-a-pot. I have suggested sea bass, but halibut, salmon, mahi mahi, grouper, and ocean perch are all thick enough for this recipe. Although the fish is "steaming" over, not in, the vegetables and their liquids, a thin fish such as flounder or sole doesn't have the robust flavor and sturdy texture necessary for stew. Don't be concerned if your pot looks too full at first. The chard leaves will greatly reduce in volume in a matter of minutes.

Place all the ingredients except the fish in a large, heavy-bottomed pan. Mix thoroughly with two big spoons and bring to a boil. Place the fish pieces on top of the vegetables, reduce the heat to medium-low, and cook, covered, for 45 minutes.

Using a slotted spoon, carefully transfer the fish and all the vegetables to a platter. Check the cooking liquid that is left in the pot. If it is too thin, reduce it over high heat for just a few minutes, until thickened. Pour the thickened sauce over the fish. Serve hot or at room temperature.

TROUT STUFFED WITH GEFILTE FISH IN JELLIED BROTH

FOR THE STUFFING

1½ pounds whitefish, cod, or scrod fillet, thoroughly boned

1 large carrot, peeled and cut into large chunks

1 medium onion, quartered

2 ribs celery, peeled and cut into large chunks

2 eggs

⅓ cup olive oil

2 slices challah, or any white bread, crusts removed

Dash of nutmeg

Salt and pepper

FOR THE TROUT

1 large sea trout (about 3½ pounds after cleaning), butterflied, head cut into large pieces

2 lemons, sliced

2 tablespoons peppercorns

4 bay leaves

Salt and pepper

1 bunch flat-leaf parsley

3 cups water

Makes about 8 first-course servings

"Gefilte fish" literally means stuffed fish, but most people are only familiar with the stuffing part of the original dish. My family and I were served the complete dish at a wedding in Israel. The sight of the fish shimmering in its lightly jellied broth brought a nostalgic grin to my husband's face. "That's how my mother used to make it," he exclaimed with a little boy's delight.

With the food processor as your assistant, this previously time-consuming preparation is a snap. And so elegant! Your fishmonger will butterfly and debone the fish for you. He will also cut the heads into chunks so they can be immersed more completely in the cooking liquid, creating a lovely gelatinous broth. If you spot any remaining bones, remove them with tweezers or needle-nose pliers. You can also make this recipe with salmon, snapper, sea bass, carp, or striped bass.

Preheat the oven to 375°F.

To make the stuffing: Combine all the stuffing ingredients in a food processor and process into a smooth paste.

To prepare the fish: Rinse and dry the trout thoroughly inside and out. Fill the cavity evenly with the stuffing. Fold the fish closed. Place the fish in a pan just big enough to hold it snugly. To keep the stuffing in place, roll a large square of foil into a long, thick strip the length of the fish and "block" the open side of the fish

with it. I call this my "Honey, I shrunk the pan" trick.

Add the fish head pieces and all remaining ingredients to the pan, making sure the fish heads are immersed. Bake for 1 hour.

Transfer the fish to a platter and strain the liquid over it, discarding the solids. Chill. To serve, cut the fish into slices and spoon some of the thickened broth over each serving.

CURRIED PAN-FRIED TILAPIA

⅓ cup vegetable oil

1 cup fine cornmeal

½ cup coconut milk

2 eggs

1 tablespoon curry powder, or less to taste

3 tablespoons chopped flat-leaf parsley

Salt and pepper

6 tilapia fillets (about 6 ounces each), cut in half lengthwise, thoroughly dried with paper towels

Makes 6 main-course or 12 first-course servings

Dipping fish fillets in coconut milk makes for an incredibly moist and tender dish. I love to coat my fillets with cornmeal, as it makes a thin, crisp, golden crust, much more so than flour or matzoh meal does. St. Peter's fish, from the Kineret River in Israel, is also called tilapia when it is grown locally. It has firm flesh and sweet flavor and costs about half as much as flounder or sole. The fillets have a natural division along the center, with one thick side and one thinner side, so I suggest you cut each fillet in half lengthwise. The thin sides will take less time to cook than the thick sides, and you can take them out sooner. This recipe works equally well with sole or flounder fillets. The fish is delicious served plain, or with Harissa (page 23) or Curried Mango Dressing (page 61).

Heat the oil in a large nonstick frying pan over high heat. Place the cornmeal in a dish. In another dish, mix the coconut milk, eggs, curry, parsley, and salt and pepper to taste. Lightly roll each fillet first in the cornmeal, shaking off the excess, then in the coconut milk mixture, letting the excess liquid drip back onto the dish.

When the oil starts to sizzle, lower the heat slightly and add the coated fillets; avoid crowding them so as not to lower the temperature. Let the thin fillets cook for about 2 minutes on each side and the thick fillets for about 3 minutes on each side, until golden and crisp. Using a slotted spatula, transfer the fillets to a platter lined with layers of paper towels to absorb any excess oil. Serve hot or at room temperature.

FIVE-MINUTE FISH TIP

Want to have dinner ready in five minutes flat? Here is a delicious, foolproof fish recipe for when you are not in the mood for cookbooks. Take whole small fish or fish fillets, squeeze lots of lemon juice on them, drizzle on olive oil and soy sauce, and place under the broiler. Fillets will be ready in about five minutes; whole small fish should be cooked for about five minutes on each side.

SALMON POACHED IN BASIL-TOMATO SAUCE

FOR THE SAUCE

½ cup dry white wine

Salt

2 tablespoons olive oil

Juice of ½ lemon

1 tablespoon green bottled peppercorns

½ cup basil leaves, packed

1 cup canned crushed tomatoes

½ tablespoon bottled hot sauce

One half of a salmon fillet (about 1¾ pounds), skin and bones removed

Makes 4 main-course or 6 first-course servings

One of the best salmon dishes you will ever taste. There are two simple secrets (the first is hardly a secret by now, but I can't emphasize it enough): Do not cook the fish a second longer than instructed and use a wide skillet that will fit the fish snugly in one layer.

Cut off and discard the flat, opaque strip that runs the whole length of the salmon side.

Place everything but the fish in a wide skillet and bring to boil over high heat. Add the salmon to the skillet and bring the mixture to a boil again. Reduce the heat to medium-high, cover, and cook for 20 minutes.

Using two slotted spatulas, carefully transfer the salmon to a platter. Reduce the liquid in the skillet to about ½ cup and strain it over the fish. Cut the fish into 6 small pieces, or 4 larger pieces. Serve warm or at room temperature.

COLD POACHED SALMON WITH HORSERADISH-DILL SAUCE

FOR THE SALMON

1 whole salmon (about 6 pounds after cleaning), butterflied, rinsed, and dried thoroughly

½ cup olive oil

2 lemons, halved

Salt and coarsely ground pepper

2 very large bunches dill, fronds and stems

FOR THE SAUCE

1 large bunch dill, fronds and stems

1 cup low-fat mayonnaise

¼ cup prepared white horseradish

¼ cup Dijon mustard

2 tablespoons sugar

Salt and pepper

Makes about 16 servings;
about 2 cups sauce

I know this may sound like the tired workhorse of your familiar fish repertoire. But I think you will be happy to have a flawless recipe for a poached salmon that "poaches" in the oven. No fuss, no mess, and all the flavors are all sealed in, not lost in the poaching liquid—this produces a succulent moist fish. Don't overcook it for even a minute, or the flesh will toughen. If you like, the sauce can be made in advance and stored in the refrigerator.

Preheat the oven to 375°F.

To prepare the salmon: Cut off the flat, opaque strips that run the whole length of the salmon and discard. Rub the fish all over with the olive oil. Rub it again with the lemons, squeezing them as you go. Then rub with salt and pepper to taste. Pack the dill inside the cavity, close the fish, and wrap it very tightly in double layers of foil, sealing the fish completely.

Place the fish in a baking pan and bake for exactly 50 minutes. Remove from the oven and let it come to room temperature, still in its wrappings. Chill completely before unwrapping.

To prepare the sauce: While the fish is chilling, make the sauce. Combine all the sauce ingredients in a food processor and process until smooth.

To serve: Unwrap the fish and remove all the dill from the cavity and discard it. Place the fish on a platter and serve with the sauce.

SALMON TERIYAKI

FOR THE TERIYAKI SAUCE

1½ tablespoons toasted sesame oil

1 tablespoon olive oil

1 tablespoon minced fresh ginger

2 tablespoons fresh lime or lemon juice

2 tablespoons soy sauce or more, to taste

2 tablespoons dry sherry or mirin

½ teaspoon coarsely ground black pepper

1½ teaspoons bottled hot sauce, or to taste

2 whole cloves

1½ tablespoons honey

2 scallions, thinly sliced

1½ pounds salmon fillet, skin removed, wiped thoroughly dry, cut into 4 pieces (about 6 ounces each)

MAKES 4 MAIN-COURSE OR 6 FIRST-COURSE SERVINGS

You can't go wrong with this classic dish. Tuna, bass, or mahi mahi are all equally suitable. I have tried a dozen or more commercial teriyaki sauces, out of duty. None holds a candle to homemade, and all of them cost significantly more. Teriyaki sauce will keep for a good three weeks in your refrigerator and is delicious not only on fish but on chicken breasts and legs, beef, and tofu. Make a big batch and watch it disappear—the sauce recipe makes plenty of extra.

In a bowl, whisk together all the ingredients for the teriyaki sauce. Place the fish in a container just large enough to fit it snugly in one layer. Pour half the teriyaki sauce over the fish; refrigerate the rest for another use. Marinate the fish in the refrigerator for 2 to 3 hours (no more, or it will start breaking up).

Prepare a grill or preheat the broiler.

Remove the fish from the marinade and set the marinade aside. Grill or broil the fish for about 5 minutes on each side.

Avoid overcooking, or the fish will be dry. Transfer the fish to a serving platter.

Transfer the reserved marinade to a small saucepan and bring to a boil. Cook the sauce until it is reduced and thickened, 10 to 12 minutes. Skim off as much of the oil as you can. Pour the sauce over the fish. Serve hot or at room temperature.

Variation: Oven method: The fish can be baked in a preheated 400°F oven for 20 minutes. Proceed with the sauce as above.

MARINATING

The container in which you marinate the salmon (or anything else) makes all the difference. If your container is too big, you risk either having to use too much marinade to cover the food or leaving the food on top unmarinated. If the container is too small, the lower layers will not marinate properly, as they will be too constricted and not evenly exposed to the marinade. Use a container just big enough for your ingredients to fit snugly in one layer and be just barely immersed, not submerged, in the marinade liquids. Don't skip the step where you reduce the cooking liquids. It takes minutes and is the secret of a rich and wonderful sauce.

PICKLED SALMON

2 quarts (8 cups) water

2 pounds skinless, boneless salmon fillets, cut into 1-inch cubes

1 cup ketchup

1 cup cold water

½ cup cider vinegar

¼ cup olive oil

¼ cup sugar

4 bay leaves

12 whole black peppercorns

4 whole cloves

Kosher salt

1 medium onion, cut into paper-thin slices in a food processor or with a mandoline

MAKES 8 SERVINGS

Delicious on its own, with tiny boiled potatoes, or on top of mixed greens, this Russian favorite takes only minutes to prepare and keeps for up to a week in the refrigerator. Move over, pickled herring!

Bring the water to boil in a large pot. Add the salmon and boil for about 5 minutes. Drain and thoroughly dry the salmon pieces and transfer them to a large, wide-mouth glass jar.

In a saucepan, combine the ketchup, water, vinegar, oil, sugar, bay leaves, peppercorns, cloves, and kosher salt to taste, and bring to a boil. Pour the mixture over the salmon. Top with the onion slices, making sure they are submerged. Let the jar come to room temperature, then refrigerate for at least 2 days.

To serve, remove the salmon pieces with a slotted spoon, discarding all liquid, and top with the onions.

BAKED STRIPED BASS NIÇOISE

2 striped bass fillets, (3–3½ pounds total)

2 large tomatoes, thinly sliced

1 cup sun-dried tomatoes, rinsed, squeezed thoroughly dry, and halved

1 cup tiny Niçoise olives

6 large cloves garlic, minced

¼ cup olive oil

1 cup dry white wine

1 cup basil leaves, thinly sliced

Freshly ground pepper

MAKES 6–8 SERVINGS

A Niçoise preparation generally features tomatoes and olives. Other fish can be used in this flavorful dish, including black bass, snapper, sea trout, ocean perch, or Spanish mackerel. Serve hot as a main course with mashed potatoes or rice, or warm or at room temperature as a first course.

Preheat the oven to 400°F.

Place the fish fillets skin-side up in the center of a baking pan large enough to hold all the ingredients in a single layer. Arrange the tomatoes, sun-dried tomatoes, and olives around the fish. In a bowl, mix the garlic, olive oil, wine, basil, and pepper to taste; pour the mixture evenly over the fish and vegetables. Bake, uncovered, for 20 minutes or until the fish flakes easily.

Transfer the fish skin-side down to a serving platter. If the sauce left in the pan looks too thin, return it to the oven until it thickens. To serve, pour the sauce and vegetables over the fish.

BLACK SEA BASS EN PAPILLOTE WITH MISO SAUCE

4 black bass fillets (about 8 ounces each), thoroughly dried with paper towels

4 squares parchment paper or foil, about four times the size of the fillets

3 tablespoons miso paste

2 tablespoons toasted sesame oil

1 tablespoon rice vinegar

Freshly ground pepper

4 scallions, thinly sliced

½ cup shiitake mushrooms, caps only, sliced

Vegetable or olive oil for brushing

MAKES 4 SERVINGS

A meal in a package! Enclosing the fish and its toppings in foil or parchment paper seals in all its flavors. Papillote is a cute French word that means curl, flutter, or blink. In the food world it refers to the frill that tented paper forms around an enclosed ingredient, which remains moist and succulent throughout the cooking process. Try this recipe with any firm-fleshed fish such as snapper, striped bass, ocean perch, or mahi mahi.

You might want to top the fish with other quick-cooking fruits or vegetables such as lemon, zucchini, or tomatoes. Only make sure you slice them very thin so that they cook quickly and roast evenly; don't pile them too high on top of the fish. Season with olive oil and any herbs of your choice. The combination I use here is a surefire hit. The miso paste helps make a rich, thickened sauce, and the rice vinegar is very mild and delicate.

Preheat the oven to 425°F.

Place each fillet near the center of a paper square. In a small bowl, combine the miso paste, sesame oil, vinegar, and pepper to taste. Spread this mixture on top of the fillets. Scatter the scallions and mushrooms on top of the fillets. Fold the paper or foil squares to enclose the fish loosely but completely, crimping the paper as you go, forming packets. Leave enough room when shaping the packets to provide an outlet for steam. If you are using parchment paper, brush the top of each closed packet lightly with vegetable or olive oil.

Bake for 12 to 15 minutes. Transfer the packets to individual dishes. Let each guest open his or her own packet and eat out of it.

MOROCCAN FISH CAKES IN LEMON SAUCE

FOR THE FISH CAKES

¾ pound skinless, boneless fish fillets, such as cod, scrod, flounder, sole, tilapia, or salmon, cut into big chunks

½ small onion

4 sprigs flat-leaf parsley, stems removed

Half of 1 beaten egg

1 tablespoon vegetable oil

½ tablespoon grated lemon zest

Dash of nutmeg

Salt and pepper

¼ cup fresh bread crumbs

FOR THE SAUCE

1½ cups water

Pinch of saffron threads

¼ teaspoon turmeric

1½ tablespoons vegetable oil

1½ tablespoons lemon juice

1 tablespoon capers

1 tablespoon Dijon mustard

MAKES ABOUT 5 FIRST–COURSE SERVINGS

This dish is the Moroccan answer to gefilte fish. It can be served warm or at room temperature and can be made up to two days in advance, which makes it a convenient addition to extensive menus and buffets. It is often served at Shabbos meals, mainly, I think, because it is boneless, and on Shabbos we avoid serving items that entail sorting out or separating. It looks like French quenelles (a type of dumpling) but the absence of cream or wine makes it much lighter. Mustard is not indigenous to Moroccan cuisine, but our Arab neighbors have happily adopted this delicious dish (and many others you will find in this book) inspired by distinct Spanish-Jewish influences.

Don't hesitate to make your own bread crumbs; they will taste much better than store-bought. Put several pieces of stale bread in a food processor and grind for a few seconds.

To make the fish cakes: Combine the fish, onion, parsley, egg, oil, lemon zest, nutmeg, and salt and pepper to taste in a food processor, and process until perfectly smooth. Transfer the mixture to a mixing bowl, add the bread crumbs, and mix thoroughly. With wet hands, shape the fish mixture into 6 oval patties.

Combine the water, saffron, turmeric, oil, lemon juice, and capers and bring to a boil in a heavy saucepan over high heat. Add the fish patties to the pot and cook, uncovered, for about 20 minutes. Using a slotted spoon, transfer the patties to a platter. Reduce the liquid in the pot until thickened, 8 to 10 minutes. Add the mustard and stir until smooth. Pour the sauce over the patties. Serve warm or at room temperature.

CAPERS: THE BASICS

Capers are the buds of the caper bush that grows in Mediterranean regions. They vary in size from very tiny (nonpareils) to as big as tiny olives with stems about an inch long (caperberries). Capers are pickled in brine or a mixture of water, salt, and vinegar, or packed in coarse salt. They add tang and zip to salads and sauces, and the berries look delightful as a garnish for martinis.

ROASTED FISH AND VEGETABLES MOROCCAN STYLE

1 whole side striped bass
(2½–3 pounds), head off, gutted,
cleaned skin left on

1 medium onion, sliced paper-thin
in a food processor or with a
mandoline

2 large potatoes, peeled, and
sliced paper-thin in a food
processor or with a mandoline

2 large tomatoes, sliced paper-
thin (by hand)

1 lemon, sliced paper-thin in a
food processor or with a
mandoline

¼ cup olive oil

¼ cup dry white wine or water

½ tablespoon paprika

½ teaspoon cayenne, or to taste

2 large cloves garlic, minced

Pinch of saffron threads

¼ cup finely chopped flat-leaf
parsley

2 tablespoons finely chopped
cilantro

½ tablespoon ground cumin

Salt and pepper

Makes 4 main-course or
6 first-course servings

The trick with this dish is to make sure the vegetables are sliced paper-thin so they cook as fast as the fish. Make sure you don't pile the vegetables too high in the pan, or the bottom layer will steam and release too much moisture instead of roasting and reducing. If you have a mandoline, you can make slices so thin you can almost see through them. If not, most food processors come equipped with a very thin slicing blade that does an amazing job. While the tomatoes must be sliced by hand, the potatoes, lemons, and onions will be perfect sliced in this way. Many other types of fish fillets are suitable for this dish, including sea trout, salmon, bass, and mahi mahi.

Preheat the oven to 450°F.

Place the fish in a large baking dish, skin-side up. Arrange the onion, potatoes, tomatoes, and lemon around the fish. In a bowl, mix the oil, wine, paprika, cayenne, garlic, saffron, parsley, cilantro, cumin, and salt and pepper to taste. Pour this mixture over the fish and vegetables. Bake, uncovered, for about 30 minutes, or until the fish is golden and the vegetables are tender. The liquid in the pan will get thick.

Strip the skin off the fish with one quick, firm stroke. Check the vegetables, especially the potatoes; if they are not cooked through, transfer the fish carefully onto a platter and return the pan to the oven to cook for a few more minutes.

Cut the fish into serving portions and spoon the cooking juices and vegetables on top. Serve hot or at room temperature.

Poultry and Meat

Kosher meat and poultry are very tender because they are presalted during the koshering process, and that salting is sufficient to flavor any dish in which the meat or poultry is used. For that reason, none of my poultry and meat dishes list salt as an ingredient. Those of you using non-kosher poultry and meat should add salt to taste in all of the following dishes.

Unless you and your family love to gnaw on neck and carcass bones and are absolutely sure no one is watching (or listening), I don't consider those parts of the bird presentable for serving, except in whole or half small birds. Wings are acceptable when roasted or barbecued. Otherwise, save the necks, carcasses, giblets, and wings for chicken soup, where taste matters more than looks, and stick to legs, thighs, and breasts for serving (referred to as "chicken parts" in the ingredients). I consider one serving of chicken to be any two of the following: drumsticks, thighs, boneless breast halves. For those of you who cannot or would rather not use dark chicken meat, breasts are delicious but somewhat less moist and tender than dark meat, and white meat cooks faster, and can dry out easily. Make sure you add about ¼ cup olive oil to a dish using only boneless breasts, and reduce the cooking time of the chicken to no more than thirty minutes total.

Unless you have severe dietary restrictions, cook poultry with its skin on, as it imparts wonderful flavor and moisture, and a much better presentation. You can always remove it once cooked. Don't worry about the extra calories: None of the recipes calling for dark chicken meat, beef, or lamb contain any added fat.

In most of the following recipes, the vegetables and meat cook together, producing wonderful results and saving the extra step of preparing a side dish.

Opposite: Olive-Lemon Chicken

OLIVE-LEMON CHICKEN

2 pounds chicken parts, dark and white meat, or all dark

1 medium onion, thinly sliced

1 tablespoon grated fresh ginger

½ cup green pitted olives, thoroughly rinsed

¼ teaspoon turmeric

Pinch of saffron

1 cup water

¼ of a preserved lemon, skin only, rinsed and chopped very fine (see page 16)

2 tablespoons chopped flat-leaf parsley

1½ tablespoons chopped cilantro

Freshly ground pepper

MAKES 4 SERVINGS

The key ingredient in this recipe is the preserved lemon. Don't make this dish without it, or you will have a good but ordinary result. With the preserved lemon, you will be transported by the authentic Moroccan flavors and heavenly aromas of this dish (see photo, page 88).

Place the chicken, onions, ginger, olives, turmeric, saffron, and water in a heavy pot and bring to a boil. Reduce the heat to medium-high and cook, covered, for 1 hour. Add the lemon, parsley, cilantro, and pepper to taste, and cook for another 10 minutes.

Using a slotted spoon, transfer the chicken to a platter and check the cooking liquid. If it is too thin, cook it over high heat until it is reduced and thickened. Pour the sauce over the chicken. Serve hot.

CHICKEN BREASTS
IN GARLIC-LEMON SAUCE

¼ cup olive oil

8 boneless chicken breast halves, thoroughly dried

Flour for dredging

1 head garlic, all cloves peeled and chopped

Pinch of saffron

½ teaspoon turmeric

2 cups water

¼ cup fresh lemon juice

Freshly ground pepper

MAKES 4–6 SERVINGS

I have my son Maimon to thank for this quick chicken dish. After ten years at yeshiva (seminary) eating cafeteria-style with other kids, he came home for college a formidable food connoisseur. This mystery has never been solved. Every morning before he leaves for class, he brainstorms about what the day's "protein" should be and what would make each dish I am considering as good as it can be. Every night he returns to lift pot lids and sniff, making comments like, "I don't think you should use the bay leaves again in this dish. The lemon and garlic give it enough flavor." I love to cook for him, because I am rewarded not only with free consultations but countless hugs and kisses. I present you with the final, Maimon-approved, bay-leafless recipe. He just got married, so his lovely wife, Ruthie, will be his next willing victim.

The elegant look and taste of this dish belie its scant preparation time: It's ready in thirty minutes from start to finish. Make it even easier by using a skillet large enough to hold all the cutlets in one layer. Rolling the chicken in flour and searing it first ensures a thick, smooth sauce.

Heat the oil in a large heavy skillet over high heat. Roll the chicken pieces in flour and shake off the excess. Add the chicken to the skillet and sauté for about 2 minutes on each side. Add the garlic, saffron, turmeric, and water and bring to a boil. Reduce the heat to medium and cook, covered, for 20 minutes. Add the lemon juice and pepper to taste and cook for 2 more minutes. Serve hot.

CHICKEN MARENGO

2 pounds chicken parts, dark and white meat or all dark

1 cup dry red wine

1½ cups peeled diced tomatoes, fresh or canned

¾ pound portobello mushrooms, sliced

8 ounces frozen tiny onions

¼ cup basil leaves, packed, cut in ribbons

Freshly ground pepper

MAKES 4 SERVINGS

A twist on the classic French version, which was created for Napoleon after his victory at the Battle of Marengo. I use portobello mushrooms and tiny frozen cocktail onions: They are perfect in this recipe and save you a lot of peeling time. The tomatoes thicken this sauce naturally and deliciously. Noodles make a nice accompaniment to this dish.

Place the chicken, wine, tomatoes, mushrooms, and onions in a large heavy pot and bring to a boil. Reduce the heat to medium and cook, covered, for 45 minutes. Add the basil and pepper to taste and cook for 15 minutes more, or until the chicken is tender.

Using a slotted spoon, transfer the chicken and vegetables to a platter. If the liquid in the pot is too thin, reduce it over high heat for just a couple of minutes, until it thickens. Pour the sauce over the chicken. Serve hot.

TEA-AND-GINGER ROASTED CORNISH HENS

4 Cornish hens

FOR THE MARINADE

¾ cup very strong Lapsang souchong tea (let 1 tea bag steep a few minutes in ¾ cup boiling water)

¾ cup orange juice

2 tablespoons plus 1 teaspoon olive oil

3 tablespoons ketchup

2 teaspoons grated fresh ginger

2 tablespoons plus 1 teaspoon honey

3 tablespoons Dijon mustard

Freshly ground pepper

MAKES 4 SERVINGS

With kosher meat, the smaller the item you buy, the saltier it is likely to be. That's why I recommend soaking these tiny birds before cooking them to release any excess salt. When roasted, the birds turn a beautiful mahogany color. Lapsang souchong tea has an intriguing pungent, smoky, "tarry" taste. As a drink, you will either love it or hate it, but you will always love it in a marinade. As for the ketchup, I surprised even myself when I discovered, while experimenting with the ingredients, that it actually enhances this elegant dish! This marinade is suitable for whole chickens or chicken parts.

Soak the hens in cold water for about 1 hour. Dry them thoroughly with paper towels.

Whisk together all the marinade ingredients in a large bowl. Place the hens in a large resealable plastic bag, add the marinade, and marinate in the refrigerator for 8 hours or overnight.

Preheat the oven to 375°F.

Transfer the hens, breast-side down, to a baking pan just large enough to fit them snugly, with half of the marinade.

Roast for 45 minutes. Turn the birds breast-side up and roast for another 10 minutes, until the skin is dark amber. Transfer the birds to a platter with a slotted spoon.

While the hens are cooking, pour the remaining marinade into a small saucepan and reduce it until thickened, about 10 minutes. If any liquids have accumulated during the roasting, skim off the oil and add them to the sauce. Pour the sauce over the hens and serve hot.

ADDICTED TO KETCHUP

Yakov is my food-junkie child. When he was little, his biggest compliment regarding my food was, "Delicious beans, Mommy. Almost as good as the baked beans from Eagle Day Camp." (I couldn't resist asking them for their recipe, and they graciously shared it with me: Heinz cans!) Ketchup takes up almost as much room on his plate as all the food combined.

Years ago, our family was invited to our friends James and Georganne's wedding, which I catered. "Did you bring ketchup?" Yakov asked me as everyone left the dance floor and headed to the buffet. I hadn't. "Did you at least bring noodles?" he tried again. I hadn't. In the huge elevator that carried the guests down from the party hall after the wedding, Yakov asked, in earshot of all the guests: "Everything except the food was great at James's wedding, right, Mommy?" Now I take ketchup along wherever I go with Yakov, the way asthmatic people carry a nebulizer. For his Bar Mitzvah, my kitchen staff bought him a giant (six-foot-tall) ketchup bottle from a store called "Think Big."

STUFFED CHICKEN BREASTS WITH ORANGE SAUCE

FOR THE STUFFING

½ pound extra-lean ground beef

1 cup finely ground almonds

½ bunch flat-leaf parsley, including stems

1 egg

½ small onion

1 tablespoon cornstarch (during Passover, use potato starch)

Grated zest of ½ lemon

Dash of nutmeg

Freshly ground pepper

1 tablespoon olive oil

❊

4 skinless, boneless chicken breast halves, pounded flat

❊

FOR THE SAUCE

⅓ cup orange juice

3 tablespoons lemon juice

1 tablespoon plus 1 teaspoon olive oil

¾ cup dry white wine

Small pinch of saffron

⅓ teaspoon turmeric

MAKES 4 SERVINGS

Cooking with nuts is a Moroccan custom inherited from our Spanish neighbors. Save this preparation for an elegant occasion. Do not be deterred by the step where you have to roll each "log" in foil. It secures the tight shape, keeps the stuffing in place, and takes only a couple of minutes. This is a perfect dish for Passover.

To make the stuffing: Combine all the stuffing ingredients in the food processor and process until smooth. Transfer the stuffing to a bowl.

To prepare the chicken: Half fill a large pot with water and bring to a boil over high heat. Form 4 logs of stuffing that are as long as the chicken is wide. Place a stuffing log on a long side of a breast and roll the chicken up tightly, encasing the stuffing completely. Wrap tightly in foil, twisting the ends like candy wrappers. Repeat with the remaining logs and chicken breasts.

Drop the chicken packets into the boiling water and poach for about 20 minutes. Remove the packets from the water and unwrap them carefully.

To make the sauce: Stir all the ingredients into the boiling water and add the chicken breasts. Reduce the heat to medium and cook, covered, for 15 minutes until the sauce thickens, turning the chicken once midway through the cooking time. Transfer the chicken to a platter and pour the sauce over it. Serve hot.

CELERY CHICKEN

3 celery hearts (about 1 pound), peeled and cut into 3-inch sticks

1 celery root (about 1 pound), peeled and cut into 1-inch cubes

Dash of saffron

½ teaspoon (scant) turmeric

2 pounds chicken parts, dark and white meat, or all dark

1 cup water

MAKES 4 SERVINGS

You must try this one. It is a Sephardi favorite and a real snap to make. Celery is used here not as garnish but as a vegetable in its own right, and you won't believe the powers of seduction it possesses. The pairing with the earthy, humble celery root makes for a magical combination of tastes.

Place the celery hearts, celery root, saffron, and turmeric in the bottom of a wide heavy pot. Arrange the chicken pieces on top. Add the water and bring to a boil over high heat. Reduce the heat to medium and cook, covered, for 1¼ hours, checking the pot occasionally to make sure the liquid has not cooked off (if it has, just add a little water).

Using a slotted spoon, transfer the chicken to a platter. If the cooking liquid is too thin, turn up the heat and cook until the sauce is reduced and thickened. Pour the vegetables and sauce over the chicken and serve hot.

CHICKEN PAELLA

FOR THE SOFRITO

1 small onion, quartered

1 rib celery, peeled and cut into thirds

2 large cloves garlic

¼ cup flat-leaf parsley

2 tablespoons cilantro leaves

½ red bell pepper, seeded and cut into chunks

FOR THE PAELLA

1½ tablespoons olive oil

1 cup canned crushed tomatoes

2 tablespoons tiny capers

¼ cup sliced pitted green olives

¼ teaspoon cayenne, or more to taste

Dash of ground cloves

1½ bay leaves

½ tablespoon paprika

Good pinch of saffron

2 pounds chicken parts, dark and white meat, or all dark

½ cup dry white wine

3 cups water

Salt and pepper

1 cup basmati rice

½ cup frozen corn kernels, optional

MAKES 4 SERVINGS

I inherited the secret to this dish from the wonderful staff with whom I worked all my catering years, two of whom still serve as my assistants at my cooking workshops.

They have shared wonderful recipes with me and laughed with delight when I tried to repeat the Spanish names of the dishes they routinely prepare for all of us: arroz con gandules, chicharrones de pollo, albondigas de pescado, platanos fritos, torta de almendras. And paella, perfect paella. They assure me that the success of the dish does not depend on the simultaneous presence of fish and meat or poultry (a no-no in kosher cooking), but on a mixture called sofrito, *which gets sautéed in a little olive oil and disperses in the dish in lovely green and red specks. If you find nice lean sausages and want to include them in the dish, add them at the same time you add the rice.*

To make the sofrito: In a food processor, combine the onion, celery, garlic, parsley, cilantro, and red pepper and pulse until coarsely chopped; do not let mixture get watery.

To make the paella: Heat the oil in a large heavy pot over high heat. Add the *sofrito* and sauté until the vegetables are translucent, about 3 minutes. Add the tomatoes and cook until only ½ cup of liquid remains in the pot, about 3 minutes. Add the capers, olives, cayenne, cloves, bay leaves, paprika, saffron, chicken, wine, water, and salt and pepper to taste, and bring to a boil. Reduce the heat to medium and cook, covered, for 45 minutes.

Add the rice and cook for 15 more minutes. Add the corn, if using, and cook for 5 more minutes, until the rice and chicken are tender. Serve hot.

Note: If you want to, make a bigger batch of *sofrito*. Once it is cooked, *sofrito* can be frozen in small containers and used in small amounts as needed.

CHICKEN TAGINE
WITH PRUNES AND ALMONDS

1½ tablespoons vegetable oil

1 medium onion, chopped

1 tablespoon sugar

2 pounds chicken parts, dark and white meat, or all dark

Pinch of saffron

½ teaspoon (scant) turmeric

1½ cinnamon sticks

½ teaspoon freshly ground pepper

1 cup water

½ tablespoon ground cinnamon

½ pound pitted prunes (about 1 cup packed)

2 tablespoons sesame seeds, toasted

3 tablespoons slivered almonds, toasted

MAKES 4 SERVINGS

The original Moroccan tagine was the clay pot used to cook food over hot coals, but the term has evolved to mean a stew of meat, poultry, or fish cooked with vegetables until the liquids are reduced and thickened. A friendly warning: You will never be able to speak disparagingly about the lowly prune again after you have tasted this magnificent dish. You might want to make this a day, even two days, in advance. Just be sure to add the sesame seeds and almonds immediately before serving so that they retain their crunch.

Heat the oil in a heavy pot over medium heat. Add the onions and fry until they are dark brown, about 30 minutes. Add the sugar and cook for 1 more minute.

Add the chicken, saffron, turmeric, cinnamon sticks, ground pepper, and water and bring to a boil. Reduce the heat to medium-high and cook, covered, for 1 hour. Add the ground cinnamon and the prunes and cook for 15 more minutes.

Using a slotted spoon, gently transfer the chicken and prunes to a platter, taking care not to bruise the prunes. The liquid left in the pot should be thick and creamy. If it is too thin, reduce it over high heat for a minute or two. Pour the sauce over the chicken. Just before serving, sprinkle on the sesame seeds and almonds. Serve hot.

CHICKEN COUSCOUS

6 medium onions, quartered

1 cup chickpeas, soaked overnight and drained (see note)

½ teaspoon saffron threads

¾ teaspoon turmeric

1 teaspoon black pepper

Salt

4 pounds chicken parts (legs, thighs, boneless breasts)

1 medium butternut squash (about 3½ pounds) unpeeled, seeded, and cut into 2-inch chunks

2½ cups couscous (*not* instant)

3 cups cold water

¼ cup vegetable oil

Salt and pepper

MAKES 8 SERVINGS

This is one of my favorite combinations for couscous. I use butternut squash instead of pumpkin because, in addition to being sweet, plump, and wonderful, it is available all year. Unlike many varieties of pumpkin, it is not hit-or-miss when you open it. However, when pumpkin is available and of high quality (heavy for its size, firm-fleshed, and deep-colored), feel free to use it instead of the butternut squash. You might also decide to add lamb to this dish (2 to 3 pounds shanks and necks) or make just a lamb couscous (6 to 7 pounds shanks and necks). Simply add the lamb at the very beginning of the cooking process and proceed with the recipe. And finally, serve the harissa next to, not on top of, the couscous. Some don't like it hot!

Place the onions, chickpeas, saffron, turmeric, pepper, and salt to taste in a heavy pot with water barely to cover (about 2 cups). Bring to a boil, reduce the heat to medium, cover, and cook for 1 hour. Add the chicken and cook for 45 more minutes. Add the butternut squash, skin-side up and cook for 30 more minutes, or until the squash is tender.

While this is cooking, prepare the couscous. In a bowl, combine the couscous, 2 cups of the cold water, the oil, and salt and pepper to taste. Mix until the grains are separated and no lumps remain. Fill the bottom part of the steamer two-thirds full of water. Place the couscous in the steam insert of the pot and put the insert in the steamer (make sure the bottom of your top insert is not touching the water). *Never* cover the couscous, or you will get glue. Bring to a boil over high heat. Lower the heat to medium. Soon you will see steam coming out of the couscous. After 30 minutes, adjust the water level of the bottom pot to two thirds again, pour the couscous back into the mixing bowl, add the remaining 1 cup of cold water, and mix again until no lumps remain. Put the couscous back in the steamer and cook for another 30 minutes, fluffing the grains with two forks. (Total steaming time: 1 hour.)

To serve: Place the couscous on a platter. Pour some of the chicken cooking broth evenly over it, only as much as it will absorb. It is important that the couscous not look wet or soupy. Arrange the chicken and the vegetables decoratively on the couscous. Pass any remaining broth in a gravy boat. Serve with Harissa (page 23) on the side.

Note: If you don't have time to soak the chickpeas overnight, soak them in boiling water and let them stand covered for 1 hour. No canned chickpeas, please!

ALL ABOUT COUSCOUS

Couscous is native to Morocco, and the word refers to both the grain and the traditional dish made with the grain. It is semolina, or durum (the heart of the wheat kernel), ground to the consistency of coarse cornmeal and mixed with flour and just enough water to make small grains, about the size of millet grains. These plump grains are then dried, preferably in the hot sun. Occasionally, couscous is also made from millet and barley. Prepared couscous is very easy to find in bulk at most health food and grocery stores.

Couscous the dish can be drab and tasteless if it is made with undercooked vegetables or poor quality or "instant" grains, or if it is overcooked and mushy. Sometimes grain sold as couscous is actually a couscous-shaped (usually larger) pasta, affectionately called "Israeli couscous," which is not suitable in traditional couscous recipes.

Although the combinations of vegetables and meats vary greatly, the structure of the dish called *couscous* always remains the same. In Morocco, we make couscous in a special two-tiered pot called a *couscoussier*. The bottom part is an ordinary pot where all the ingredients cook in a broth, and the top part is pierced with holes all over its base: This is where the couscous grain is placed and gets steamed. In order to ensure that the steam comes up evenly to the top (not the sides) of the pot, we "lock" the two parts of the pot with a paste made quickly with flour and water.

Couscoussiers are quite easy to find, but you can also use a stainless steel steamer-spaghetti pot. Popular brands of couscoussiers, such as Leysee and Cuisinart, are reasonably priced and available at all major houseware stores. These have four parts that fit snugly together and don't take up any more room than a regular spaghetti pot. The first part is the bottom where the water goes, the second a top insert with small holes all over its base and sides that fits hermetically on top of the water container. For making couscous, these are the two parts we are interested in. (The third part is an insert with big holes all over that reaches almost all the way to the bottom of the pot for cooking pasta—pull the insert up, and the pasta drains instantly. The fourth part of this wonderful contraption is the lid, equipped with two small vents to allow steam to escape, and used when steaming vegetables or rice: Place the water in the water container, the vegetables or rice in the top insert, cover with the lid, and open the two vents.)

Traditionally, the vegetables and meat cook together in the bottom part of the couscoussier, while the grain cooks on top. But I find that when I make couscous this way, the vegetables often get overcooked and I cannot control the cooking as well as if I were preparing them in a separate pot. It means one more pot to wash, but it's worth the trouble.

You are in for a great treat: Please do not spoil it by using "instant" couscous, which would be to couscous what minute rice is to rice. Besides, you are not saving any time, since you must wait for the rest of the dish to cook anyway. Most important, since this dish constitutes a complete meal, you might end up finding, like all my students, that it is not the complicated dish it is so often thought to be, after all.

CIDER-ROASTED TURKEY
WITH DRIED-FRUIT STUFFING

FOR THE STUFFING

3 cups dried apricots

1 large onion, quartered

6 ribs celery, peeled and cut into thirds

4 Granny Smith apples, peeled, cored, and quartered

6 cups freshly ground bread crumbs (from challah or any white bread)

¼ cup olive oil

Salt and pepper

FOR THE TURKEY

½ gallon (8 cups) unfiltered apple cider

¼ cup juniper berries, slightly crushed with a rolling pin

1 tablespoon coarsely ground black pepper

4 sprigs rosemary, leaves only, or 1 tablespoon dried

6–8 bay leaves

8–10 whole cloves

One 12–14-pound turkey, preferably fresh, or frozen and completely thawed

Triple thickness of cheesecloth

MAKES 15 SERVINGS

I don't wait for Thanksgiving to make turkey. My family and I enjoy it all year round and I never have to worry about leftovers: They freeze beautifully and the bones and scraps of meat still attached make delicious turkey soup. In this recipe, the unfiltered apple cider, juniper berries, rosemary, bay leaves, and cloves each lend a unique note to the whole and produce an incredibly moist and tender bird. I am confident this recipe will make a frequent turkey eater out of you too. Juniper berries are easy to find at health and specialty food stores. They are responsible for the flavoring of gin and are great in marinades. Try your best not to use a disposable pan for this recipe: They are not stable enough, and you will be handling about twenty pounds of boiling hot merchandise!

To make the stuffing: Combine the apricots, onion, celery, and apples in a food processor and pulse until coarsely chopped. Transfer to a bowl and add the bread crumbs, olive oil, and salt and pepper to taste.

Preheat the oven to 325°F.

To prepare the turkey: Mix the cider, juniper berries, pepper, rosemary, bay leaves, and cloves in a bowl. Place the turkey breast-side down in a roasting pan large and deep enough to accommodate it and its liquids. Pour the cider mixture over the turkey.

Fill the turkey cavity with the stuffing. Soak the cheesecloth in the cider mixture and spread the cheesecloth over the turkey. Bake for about 2½ hours, basting the cheesecloth with the cider mixture and juices every 30 minutes. Turn the turkey over, breast-side up, discard the cheesecloth, and roast for about 1 hour more, until the breast is a deep amber color and the juices run clear.

Transfer the stuffing to a bowl and keep it warm. Skim off any oil that may have accumulated in the roasting pan. Pour the roasting liquids into a saucepan and cook over high heat until reduced to about 4 cups; this should take about 10 minutes. Slice the turkey and serve with the stuffing and gravy.

ROAST TURKEY ON TV

One of the most unlikely—and unforgettable—manifestations of maternal love was bestowed upon me a couple of years ago, on a Thanksgiving eve when I had to demonstrate the cooking of a turkey and all its trimmings at a television studio. The studio had ordered a car service to pick me and my cooked bird up that morning at 7:30. As I walked into the kitchen at 6:00 A.M., I was startled to find my mother, tweezers in hand, leaning over the turkey with the stealth of a burglar and the precision of a surgeon, plucking at the turkey. "I didn't want to wake you," she started defensively, in an agitated whisper. "I have been working on this turkey for an hour. I found at least a dozen hairs. Don't you know that the camera amplifies every little imperfection? It has to look soigné!"

Straining to see the almost transparent wisps, I caught a glimpse of the turkey: After this last makeover, it looked tan, rested, and beautiful. I couldn't help being reminded of my wedding day, when, by contrast, my preparation for the big night took me fifteen minutes flat. Where was my mother then? In her immense unconditional love, she must have found any rearranging superfluous.

BRISKET IN SWEET-AND-SOUR SAUCE

FOR THE SAUCE

1 medium onion, quartered

One 2-inch piece fresh ginger, peeled

6 large cloves garlic

¼ cup Dijon mustard (omit on Passover)

½ cup dry red wine

½ cup Coca-Cola or ginger ale

1 cup ketchup

¼ cup honey

¼ cup cider vinegar

¼ cup soy sauce (omit on Passover, or if you think your meat might be too salty)

½ cup olive oil

½ teaspoon ground cloves

1 tablespoon coarsely ground pepper

1 first-cut brisket, 6–7 pounds, rinsed and patted thoroughly dry

Makes 12 ample servings

Every year, the expert cooking staff at Levana Restaurant showcases Passover programs in four prestigious hotels, two in Puerto Rico, one in Aruba, and one in Scottsdale, Arizona. This year my son Maimon worked as one of the supervisors at the Scottsdale Resort. At one of the dinners, the guests were served brisket. One guest was heard to say, "This is delicious but not as good as Levana's." "That's my mother!" my son cried proudly, like a third-grader, terminating then and there his incognito status as a member of the staff. Anyway, this is guaranteed to be the best brisket you've ever had. Never mind the weird ingredients. They work! And don't worry if the brisket is too much for your guests to finish. It freezes beautifully.

Preheat the oven to 350°F.

To make the sauce: Combine all the sauce ingredients in a food processor and process until smooth.

To prepare the brisket: Place the brisket in a pan just big enough to fit it, and pour the sauce over it. Cover tightly with a double layer of foil and bake for 2 hours. Turn the brisket over and bake uncovered for 1 more hour or until very tender. A knife inserted in its center should go in without any resistance. Transfer the brisket to a cutting board and let it cool slightly.

Transfer the sauce from the roasting pan to a saucepan. Cook over high heat until it is reduced to about 2½ cups. Skim the oil off the top.

To serve, cut the brisket into thin slices against the grain (if the slices look too long, cut the brisket in half across its whole length before slicing). Pour the sauce on top and serve hot.

POT-AU-FEU

Peel of 1 lemon

6 bay leaves

2 tablespoons black peppercorns

3 sprigs thyme

6 cloves of garlic

1 square-cut chuck roast, about 4 pounds

1 package beef neck bones (3–4 bones)

5–6 beef marrow bones

12 very small onions, peeled and left whole

12 very thin carrots, peeled and left whole

6 ribs celery, peeled and halved crosswise

4 medium parsnips, peeled and halved lengthwise

4 medium turnips, peeled and quartered

1 small head green cabbage, cut in wedges (leave each wedge attached at the stem)

24 very small potatoes, scrubbed

Salt (optional)

4 quarts (16 cups) water

❖

Baguette slices, Dijon mustard, and gherkins for serving

MAKES 10 AMPLE SERVINGS

A couple of years ago, my husband Maurice and I were strolling on La Place des Vosges in Paris. At the outdoor terrace of one of those lovely restaurants under the arcades, a middle-aged couple sat in front of their meal: a pot-au-feu, steaming in a gleaming red enamel pot. She was pouring the broth, he was pouring the wine, their eyes and smiles quietly, serenely locked on each other. A perfect moment, for them as well as for those who happened to notice them. I had always known pot-au-feu as staid family fare. Now I considered it with renewed respect: It may well be lovers' food. Okay, older lovers' food— but that's my team, so don't knock it!

"Pot-au-feu" means pot on the fire, to illustrate the fact that the whole meal cooks unhurriedly in one pot, filling the house with its heavenly aromas. The traditional serving rituals that surround the serving of pot-au-feu are sure to be as satisfying as the taste of the finished dish—the broth is served first, then the meat and vegetables, then the marrow spread on bread, with mustard and gherkins on the side. It is also a perfect crockpot recipe.

Place the lemon peel, bay leaves, peppercorns, thyme, and garlic in a piece of cheesecloth and tie it with kitchen string.

Place the cheesecloth packet and all the remaining ingredients in a large pot with a wide bottom, in the order listed above, and bring to a boil over high heat. Reduce the heat to medium-low and cook for 3½ hours.

To serve, transfer the meat to a cutting board and let it cool. Transfer the vegetables, neck bones, and marrow to a platter. Discard the cheesecloth packet. Serve the broth alone as a first course, adding a little water if it has reduced too much during the cooking process. Slice the meat across the grain and transfer it to the platter. Serve with slices of baguette topped with slices of the marrow, Dijon mustard, and gherkins.

Variations

◆ *Crockpot:* Place all the ingredients in a crockpot in the order listed above, except bring the water to a boil before adding it to the crockpot. Set the crockpot to low in the morning and let cook until dinnertime.

◆ *Turkey pot-au-feu:* For those of you avoiding beef, simply replace it with turkey parts (thighs, wings, and necks) and add salt to taste, 2 cups red wine, and ¼ cup olive oil to the pot.

◆ *Lamb pot-au-feu:* Substitute 6 lamb shanks for the square-cut chuck roast.

GRILLED MINTED BEEF KABOBS

1 medium onion, quartered

4 large cloves garlic

1 small bunch flat-leaf parsley,
including stems

1 small bunch mint, leaves only

1 tablespoon cumin

1 tablespoon paprika

Good pinch of cayenne, or more,
to taste

2 pounds extra-lean ground beef,
or extra-lean ground lamb, or a
combination

Freshly ground pepper

MAKES ABOUT 6 SERVINGS

This is the stuff of the barbecues of my childhood: hamburgers with a Mediterranean twist. These are perfect with Moroccan Tomato Salad (page 65). If you are avoiding beef or lamb and decide to substitute ground turkey, increase the amounts of the seasonings to taste and add 3 tablespoons of olive oil to the mixture.

Prepare the grill or preheat the broiler.

Combine the onion, garlic, parsley, and mint in a food processor and pulse until finely chopped; do not let mixture get watery. Transfer to a bowl, and mix in the cumin, paprika, cayenne, beef, and pepper to taste.

Form about 18 logs approximately 1 inch in diameter and 4 inches long. Thread onto wet wooden or metal skewers. Broil for 2 to 3 minutes on each side. Serve hot. Allow 2 to 3 skewers per guest.

BEEF CHUNKS WITH LEMON-OREGANO SAUCE

4 cups water

2 pounds square-cut chuck roast, cut into 2-inch cubes

1 large onion, thinly sliced

Pinch of saffron

½ teaspoon (scant) turmeric

3 tablespoons lemon juice

1 tablespoon dried oregano and 3 sprigs fresh oregano, leaves only

MAKES 4 SERVINGS

Square-cut chuck roast is a squarish slab cut from the neck of the animal. In my opinion, it is one of the most tender cuts of meat. A stew made with this cut will be fork-tender. The adornments for this wonderful dish, lemon and oregano, are deceptively simple, as you will realize after you taste (and smell!) it. If you can't find fresh oregano, use 2 tablespoons of the dried.

Bring the water to a boil in a heavy pot. Add the beef cubes and bring to a boil again. Reduce the heat to medium and cook, covered, for 2 hours. Add the onion, saffron, and turmeric and cook, covered, for 45 more minutes. Add the lemon juice and oregano and cook for 15 more minutes.

Using a slotted spoon, transfer the beef to a platter. Check the liquid in the pot; if it is too thin, increase the heat to high and reduce the sauce until it thickens. Pour the sauce over the beef. Serve hot.

GRILLED MARINATED STEAK WITH GREEN PEPPERCORN SAUCE

FOR THE MARINADE

¼ cup bottled green peppercorns, slightly crushed with a rolling pin

3 tablespoons honey

¼ cup mirin or dry sherry

3 tablespoons soy sauce

¼ cup Dijon mustard

3 tablespoons toasted sesame oil

Good pinch of cayenne pepper

One 3-pound minute roast, butter-flied to make two 1-inch steaks, all sinew removed

MAKES 6 SERVINGS

Poor minute steak has such an unromantic, uninspiring name, but don't let that stop you from cooking with it. It is lean, tender, delicious, and ready in minutes. Have your butcher prepare the meat for you, and don't worry if the two halves come apart.

Whisk together all the marinade ingredients in a large bowl. Add the steak and mix thoroughly with the marinade. Marinate in the refrigerator for 2 hours or overnight.

Prepare the grill or preheat the broiler.

Remove the steak from the marinade.

Grill or broil it for 5 to 8 minutes on each side for medium rare. Meanwhile, transfer the marinade to a small saucepan and reduce it to 1 cup over high heat.

To serve, slice the steak against the grain, about ⅛-inch thick. Strain the sauce over the steak. Serve hot or at room temperature.

CHOLENT

3 pounds small potatoes, peeled

3 cups soft whole-wheat berries

2 lamb shanks or 2 pounds lamb necks

1 turkey thigh

2 pounds beef neck bones

Good pinch of saffron threads

1 teaspoon turmeric

10 cups water

MAKES 10 SERVINGS

Cholent (presumably from the French chaud-lent, *or "hot and slow")—a dish of meats, potatoes, and beans—was born of the necessity to serve something hot for lunch on Saturdays. Since Orthodox Jews do not cook on the Shabbos, they devised a dish that would cook very slowly the night before. The delicious aromas permeate the whole house. I have many Jewish friends who cannot take the Shabbos quite seriously unless they have their fill of cholent.*

There are endless variations on this dish. Ashkenazi Jews make cholent with a fatty meat (usually flanken), potatoes, and mixed beans. Sephardis make a much bigger production of it, sometimes adding calves' feet, beef tongue, eggs, and whole heads of garlic. I have streamlined the recipe and made it, shall we say, digestible, omitting the beans and using delicious wheat berries. With the exception of the time-consuming step of peeling the potatoes, this dish takes just a few minutes to throw together. Make sure you choose soft wheat berries, as the hard ones take forever to cook. They are quite easy to find at health food and ethnic grocery stores.

Place the ingredients in a crockpot or in another heavy pot, in the order listed above. Plug in the crockpot just before Shabbos (if you are using a regular pot, bring it to a boil just before Shabbos). Leave the cholent on a low temperature setting and let it cook all night. Transfer to a platter for serving.

Note: Some of you might prefer to cook cholent partially (two thirds) before Shabbos.

Variations

◆ If you want to use all turkey parts, use 2 to 3 turkey thighs, plus 3 tablespoons oil. Turkey parts are a much better choice than chicken parts, as they take better to the long, slow cooking. You can also use all lamb, or all beef in any combination you like (but no added oil).

◆ For a delicious gelatinous texture, throw in a calf's foot.

◆ Make a vegetable mixture (affectionately called *kishka*): 2 grated sweet potatoes, ½ cup raisins, 1 small chopped onion, 2 tablespoons oil, cinnamon, and salt and pepper to taste. Shape into a log, wrap in foil, and add to the pot.

◆ Add a few whole eggs, uncooked and unpeeled.

◆ Add a couple of heads of garlic. The cloves get incredibly sweet and tasty during cooking.

◆ Make a ground meat mixture: 1 pound lean ground beef, 6 large cloves of chopped garlic, 1 small bunch of minced parsley, ¼ cup of raw rice, 1 egg, freshly ground pepper to taste, and a pinch of nutmeg. Shape into a log, wrap in foil, and add to the pot.

◆ Omit the wheat and potatoes. Add 2 bunches of celery, ribs separated, peeled, and cut into 3-inch chunks. Place in the bottom of the pan with the meat and seasoning on top. Do not add any water.

◆ Add sweet potatoes and a few pitted dates.

Recycle leftover cholent, don't throw it away! Store it in the refrigerator or freezer and make a soup out of it on a weekday—add water, canned crushed tomatoes, chopped onion, oregano, even a little wine.

LAMB AND EGGPLANT CURRY

1½ tablespoons olive oil

1 medium onion, chopped

½ large bunch flat-leaf parsley, including stems

2 large cloves garlic

1 tablespoon curry, or more to taste

¼ teaspoon turmeric

1½ large tomatoes, blanched, peeled, and diced

3 lamb shanks, meatless ends cut off (let your butcher do this for you), rinsed

1 pound lamb necks, 3–4 total

2 cups water

1 medium eggplant (about 1½ pounds total), peeled and cut into 1-inch cubes

½ tablespoon cumin

1½ tablespoons chopped cilantro

1½ teaspoons sugar

3 cups cooked basmati rice (no salt added)

MAKES 4 SERVINGS

Lamb is one of my favorite kinds of meat. Even the more plebeian cuts are tender when cooked like this, maybe even more so than expensive ones. Paired with eggplant, lamb is simply glorious (see photo, page 196).

Heat the oil in a heavy pot over high heat. Combine the onion, parsley, and garlic in a food processor and pulse until coarsely chopped. Add this mixture to the hot oil, and sauté until translucent, about 3 minutes. Add the curry and the turmeric and sauté for 1 more minute, until fragrant. Add the tomatoes and sauté for 3 more minutes, until most of the liquid evaporates.

Add the lamb shanks, lamb necks, and water and bring to a boil. Reduce the heat to medium and cook, covered, for 2 hours. Add the eggplant, cumin, cilantro, and sugar and cook for 1 more hour. Cut the meat off the lamb bones and return the meat to the pot. Serve the curry hot, spooned over the rice.

THE KIDDUSH SYNDROME

I have always been intrigued about the "kiddush scene." Kiddush is the blessing on wine, but it is also what we call the spread we serve in synagogues after Saturday morning services. Traditionally, we are served the Old World standbys: gefilte fish, herring, kugel, cholent, chopped liver, liquor, and so forth. The whole gig lasts about thirty minutes, but the "morning after" look of the room and the tables suggests damage caused by the elements. I have never understood why whole, often prosperous, congregations, who are going home to a sumptuous meal, behave with such dire urgency when kiddush is served on Saturday noon. Is it a taste of exile, or atavism, that throws everyone together so heartily?

Vegetable Dishes

Vegetarians who eat bland, unrecognizable foods are creatures of the past. The vegetarians I cook for want colorful dishes, vibrant colors and fragrances, and unusual ingredients. Even if you are a diehard meat-and-potato type, you will appreciate the following recipes. These dishes are creations in their own right, and can be served as side dishes or entrees.

STIR-FRIED TOFU AND VEGETABLES ON SOBA NOODLES

1 pound soba noodles

FOR THE STIR-FRY

¼ cup olive oil

¼ cup toasted sesame oil

1 pound extra-firm tofu

2 leeks, white part only, cut into julienne strips

2 carrots, cut into julienne strips

2 parsnips, cut into julienne strips

2 cups snow peas

1 red bell pepper, cut into julienne strips

1 bunch scallions, cut into 1-inch pieces

1 cup sliced shiitake mushroom caps

1 bunch thin asparagus, tough ends discarded, cut into 2-inch pieces

FOR THE SAUCE

One 2-inch piece of ginger, minced

4 large cloves garlic, minced

⅓ cup dry sherry

Soy sauce

Crushed red pepper flakes

2 tablespoons cornstarch, dissolved in ½ cup cold water

Makes 8 side-dish or 4–6 main-course servings

Soba noodles are made of buckwheat flour. They are less starchy and more delicate than the wheat noodles we are used to, but you can also make this stir-fry with ordinary linguine or spaghetti, or rice. Choose from many vegetables—cauliflower, broccoli, zucchini, drained and thoroughly dried soybean sprouts, snow peas, bok choy, eggplant—whatever is in season and looks appealing. Don't use canned vegetables, though. They will turn this beautiful medley into a lackluster, tinny, soggy mess.

A big wok is ideal for preparing this dish. A wok is shaped in such a way (narrow center, large sloping sides) that it allows only a small amount of vegetables to be in the center, nearest the heat source, so large batches can be cooked without fear of overcooking any of the ingredients.

Bring a pot of water to a boil. Add the soba noodles and cook 12 minutes or until al dente. Drain the noodles.

To make the stir-fry: In a small bowl, stir together the olive oil and sesame oil. Cut the tofu into ½ x 2-inch strips, then drain thoroughly on paper towels. In a wok, heat 2 tablespoons of the oil mixture over high heat. Add the tofu strips in one layer and sauté until golden-brown, turning them once. Remove the tofu and reserve on a platter. Sauté all the vegetables in batches, adding a little oil as needed, about 2 minutes each batch. Transfer the vegetables to the platter after stir-frying.

To make the sauce: Heat a little oil mixture in a small saucepan over high heat.

Add the ginger and garlic and sauté just until fragrant. Reduce the heat to low, add the sherry, soy sauce and red pepper flakes to taste, and the cornstarch mixture, and cook until thickened, about 1 minute.

Pour the sauce over the tofu and vegetables and toss gently. Serve hot, over the cooked noodles.

Note: This dish simply cannot be reheated. If you must make it in advance, stir-fry and reserve the tofu, cut up all the vegetables, boil the noodles or rice and make the sauce. In other words, do everything ahead of time except stir-fry the vegetables. At mealtime, it will take about 5 minutes to stir-fry the vegetables and toss them with everything else.

HOT AND SWEET PARSNIPS

18 very thin parsnips, peeled and left whole (or 5 big ones, peeled and quartered lengthwise)

3 tablespoons olive oil

3 tablespoons brown sugar

1 tablespoon paprika

½ teaspoon turmeric

½ teaspoon cayenne pepper, or less to taste

1 teaspoon ground cinnamon

Salt and pepper

MAKES 6 SIDE-DISH SERVINGS

My brother Toby recently described a trip he took to a little mountain town south of Marrakesh called Agoim, during a Hillulah (a several-day-long communal celebration on a holy gravesite). After two days of festivities, the roads got cut off due to bad weather, and the trucks carrying the food supplies could not get to them. Instead the town natives supplied them with their local produce. The group was so amazed at the magnificent locally grown vegetables and fruit that they extended their stay by several days—the parsnips were particularly impressive.

This Moroccan-Jewish classic uses the homely roots to great advantage. Look for very thin parsnips.

Place all the ingredients in a heavy pot, with water barely to cover (about 1½ cups) and bring to a boil. Reduce the heat to medium, cover, and cook until the parsnips are tender and the liquid in the pot has thickened, about 20 minutes. Serve the parsnips hot or at room temperature, with the sauce poured over them.

HERBED SAUTÉED NEW POTATOES

2 pounds very small new potatoes, white or red (about 2 dozen)

3 tablespoons olive oil

1 tablespoon rosemary

2 large cloves garlic, minced

Salt and pepper

Makes 6 side-dish servings

French-fry lovers who don't want the extra calories will love these melt-in-your-mouth, ready-in-minutes gems. The only real work here is drying the potatoes thoroughly before sautéing.

Scrub the potatoes and dry them thoroughly. Cut each potato in half. Heat the oil in a large, heavy, preferably nonstick, skillet over high heat. When the oil is very hot, add the potatoes, cut-side down. Reduce the heat slightly, cover the skillet, and cook for a few minutes. Check the bottoms of the potatoes; they should be golden brown. Insert a knife in the center of a couple of potatoes. If they offer no resistance, they are cooked through. If they still feel a little hard, lower the heat and cook, covered, for a few more minutes. Add the rosemary, garlic, and salt and pepper to taste, and cook for just 1 minute more, until all the seasonings are fragrant. Serve hot.

MUSHROOM-CHESTNUT PÂTÉ WITH GREEN GODDESS SAUCE

FOR THE PÂTÉ

2 pounds fresh chestnuts

⅓ cup extra virgin olive oil

1 medium onion, finely chopped

4 medium shallots, finely chopped

1 pound domestic mushrooms, coarsely chopped

½ cup pistachios, lightly toasted in a 300°F oven for 10 minutes

½ cup flour

½ cup finely chopped flat-leaf parsley

1 egg

¼ cup brandy or bourbon

1 teaspoon dried thyme

½ teaspoon dried sage

1 teaspoon allspice

Salt and pepper

FOR THE SAUCE

1 small bunch flat-leaf parsley, including stems

1 bunch watercress, including stems

3 tablespoons capers

3 cloves garlic

Salt and pepper to taste

1 cup low-fat mayonnaise (or silken tofu, drained)

3 tablespoons Dijon mustard

Makes 12 first-course or 6 main-course servings; about 2 cups sauce

I created this dish for the vegetarians who want pâté that is not just a pallid imitation. Meat eaters, you will love it too! When fresh chestnuts are out of season, simply buy dried chestnuts—available at specialty food stores and most health food stores—and boil them until tender, proceeding exactly as described below.

To make the pâté: Bring a large pot of water to a boil. Slit the chestnut skins with a sharp knife, add the chestnuts to the boiling water, and cook until tender, about 30 minutes. (Alternatively you can boil 2 cups dried chestnuts until tender, about 45 minutes). Peel the chestnuts and thoroughly dry them on paper towels. In a food processor, pulse the chestnuts until coarsely chopped and set aside.

Preheat the oven to 375°F.

Heat the oil in a heavy skillet over high heat. Add the onion and shallots and sauté until translucent, about 3 minutes. Add the mushrooms and cook until all the liquids evaporate, 4 to 5 minutes. Transfer the mushroom mixture to a large bowl and add the chestnuts, pistachios, flour, parsley, egg, brandy, thyme, sage, allspice, and salt and pepper to taste. Mix thoroughly.

Grease a 1½ quart loaf pan and pour the batter into it. Set the pan in a bigger pan filled with hot water that comes two thirds up the sides of the loaf pan. Bake for 1 hour or until the top is firm and set. Cool the pâté completely and chill it before serving.

To make the sauce: While the pâté is cooking, make the sauce. Bring a pot of water to a boil. Blanch the parsley and watercress for just a few seconds, then rinse in very cold water and squeeze thoroughly dry. Transfer the parsley and watercress to a food processor, add the remaining sauce ingredients, and process until smooth. Chill before serving.

To serve: Unmold the pâté, cut it into slices (thin slices for a first course, thicker slices for a main course), and serve plain or with the sauce.

WILD MUSHROOM, ASPARAGUS, AND TOMATO RAGOUT

¼ cup extra virgin olive oil

4 medium shallots, minced

3 cloves garlic, minced

1½ pounds wild mushrooms, in any combination, sliced (if you are using shiitake, discard the stems)

1 large tomato, peeled, seeded, and diced

½ cup dry white wine

2 sprigs fresh tarragon, leaves only, chopped

½ cup water

Salt and pepper

1 pound asparagus, tough ends discarded, cut into 2-inch pieces

MAKES 8 SIDE-DISH SERVINGS

Pretty and luxurious yet a snap to make. Use whatever kinds of mushrooms look good at the market on the day you are preparing this dish, or mix ordinary mushrooms with a handful of morels, chanterelles, or hen-of-the-woods. Serve with your favorite roast, grilled tuna, or with pasta. Reheating this dish discolors the asparagus, so if you must make it in advance, leave out the asparagus and add it just before serving: it will take only about 4 minutes to cook through.

Heat the oil in a heavy skillet over high heat. Add the shallots and garlic and sauté until translucent, about 3 minutes. Add the mushrooms and sauté until most of the liquid evaporates, 4 to 5 minutes. Add the tomato, wine, tarragon, water, and salt and pepper to taste and bring to a boil. Reduce the heat to medium and cook, covered, for about 10 minutes.

Add the asparagus and cook just until tender but still brightly colored, 3 to 4 minutes. Serve hot or at room temperature.

CHESTNUT EXPLOSION

My first encounter with raw chestnuts was brutal. At seventeen, I was fresh out of my childhood home and living in a dorm on the university campus in Strasbourg, France. Looking out of my window one Sunday morning, I admired a chestnut tree growing right on the campus grounds. Until then, I had always enjoyed chestnuts roasted from the street stands. I had a sudden urge for the delicious nuts and decided to go down and get some. "How hard could it be to roast them?" I wondered. I put them in a pot, covered the pot and put it on the stove of the dorm kitchen. I decided they would be ready in about half an hour, ample time for a bath. After about fifteen minutes, I heard what sounded like a mob pounding at my door. Seized with panic, I managed to get dressed at lightning speed and opened the door with great trepidation. The mob was led by the custodian of the dorm, who appraised me with a scornful look. The chestnuts, I was told, had burst out of their shells and out of the pot. The whole dorm had heard the "explosions." "For crying out loud," the custodian said haughtily. "Don't you know you have to make a slit in the chestnuts before you cook them?" How would I know? No one had ever told me, at that tender age, about cooking chestnuts, and a slew of other valuable things in life. Now I know!

BRAISED RED CABBAGE AND APPLES

⅓ cup olive oil

1 medium onion, chopped

3 medium Granny Smith or McIntosh apples, peeled, cored, and cut into small chunks

½ cup cider vinegar

⅓ cup brown sugar, packed

3 bay leaves

⅓ teaspoon ground cloves

2 cups unfiltered apple cider

1 medium head red cabbage, thinly shredded in a food processor

Salt and pepper

Makes 8–10 side-dish servings

Cabbage and apples are a natural fit, both so rustic and unpretentious. This sweet-and-sour dish will become a classic in your kitchen. The cider underscores the apples' fruity tang. Watch the initial mountain of cabbage collapse into a scrumptious handful as it cooks. This is perfect as a side dish or a condiment with chicken or turkey, hot or at room temperature.

Heat the oil in a heavy pot over high heat. Add the onion and apples and sauté until soft, about 4 minutes. Add the remaining ingredients and bring to a boil. Reduce the heat to medium-low and cook, covered, stirring occasionally to prevent sticking, until the cabbage is very tender and reduced, and all liquid has evaporated. This will take about 1 hour or a little longer. Serve hot or at room temperature.

MIXED ROASTED VEGETABLES

4 pounds mixed vegetables

½ cup extra virgin olive oil

**1 bunch basil, leaves only
(about 1 cup packed)**

6 large cloves garlic

1 tablespoon balsamic vinegar

Sea salt and pepper

Makes 8 side-dish servings

Roasted vegetables are delightful hot or cold, or even in a sandwich. If you happen to be grilling outdoors, go ahead and make these on the grill. Sea salt permeates the vegetables slowly and evenly during the roasting process and makes them wonderfully moist and tender. You can use anything that is in season and in any combination: eggplant, shiitake mushrooms, zucchini, peppers, endive, red onions, asparagus, and fennel. If you are mixing vegetables, watch their cooking times—mushrooms and asparagus take less time than most other vegetables, so take them out sooner. Do not pile the vegetables in the pan, or you will boil them instead of roasting them. One layer and high heat—that is the secret of good roasting.

Preheat the oven to 450°F.

Cut all the vegetables into thick slices or sticks. Combine the oil, basil, garlic, vinegar, and salt and pepper to taste in a food processor and process until smooth. In a large bowl, toss the vegetables with the basil mixture.

Place the vegetables in a foil-lined pan in a single layer (you might have to use two pans). Roast one pan at a time, for about 20 minutes or until the vegetables look charred. Serve hot or at room temperature.

ROASTED ROOT VEGETABLES

12 medium shallots

**1 head garlic, all cloves separated
and peeled**

24 Brussels sprouts

**2 sweet potatoes, peeled and cut
into 2-inch cubes**

18–20 small new potatoes

**1 medium celery root, peeled
and cut into 2-inch chunks**

**2 medium parsnips, peeled
and cut into 2-inch chunks**

**2 large carrots, peeled and
cut into 2-inch chunks**

⅓ cup extra virgin olive oil

2 teaspoons dried rosemary

**Sea salt and freshly ground
pepper**

Makes 8 side-dish servings

This ingredient list is deceptively simple, considering the luxurious dish you end up with. You might want to simplify the selection of vegetables by using, for example, twice the amount of carrots and no sweet potatoes, or twice the amount of celery root and no parsnips and so on.

Preheat the oven to 450°F.

Mix all the ingredients together in a bowl. Transfer the vegetables to a foil-lined baking sheet and arrange in one layer. Bake for 45 minutes. Check the vegetables, take out whatever looks roasted and charred (garlic, shallots, Brussels sprouts), and let the harder vegetables (potatoes, parsnips, carrots) roast for a little longer if they need to. Serve hot.

TOFU-VEGETABLE CASSEROLE

2 tablespoons olive oil

3 tablespoons toasted sesame oil

1 medium onion, chopped

4 large cloves garlic, minced

One 2-inch piece ginger, minced

2 pounds shiitake mushrooms, caps only

2 medium zucchini, thinly sliced

½ cup mirin or dry sherry

½ cup soy sauce, or to taste

Pinch of cayenne

2 tablespoons cornstarch, mixed with a little cold water

3 pounds silken tofu, each cake cut across into 4 pieces

8 plum tomatoes, thinly sliced

MAKES 8 SIDE-DISH OR 4–6 MAIN-COURSE SERVINGS

For this dish, you want to use silken tofu. Soft and delicate, it will absorb all the other flavors and form a light custard. The tomatoes contrast with the more traditional Asian flavors, adding color and texture to the sauce. Mirin is a delightful mild Japanese rice wine.

Preheat the oven to 375°F.

Heat the oils in a heavy pot over high heat. Add the onion, garlic, and ginger and sauté until translucent and fragrant, about 3 minutes. Add the mushrooms and zucchini and sauté until all of the liquids evaporate, about 5 minutes. Lower the heat, then add the mirin, soy sauce, cayenne, and cornstarch mixture and cook just until thickened, no more than 2 minutes.

Place half of the tofu slices in a 9 x 13-inch pan. Cover the bottom of the pan completely with tofu, trimming it to fit when necessary. Cover the tofu with half of the vegetable mixture. Make a third layer with half the tomatoes. Repeat the layers of tofu, vegetables, and tomatoes. Bake for 40 minutes or until the casserole is bubbly. Serve hot, plain or with noodles or rice.

SPINACH, RED LENTIL, AND TOFU CURRY WITH CUCUMBER RAITA

FOR THE RAITA

2 cups plain yogurt

½ cup mint leaves, packed, minced

1 large cucumber, or 2 small, peeled and coarsely grated

2 teaspoons cumin

Curry powder

Salt and pepper

FOR THE CURRY

¼ cup olive oil

1 large onion, chopped

One 2-inch piece fresh ginger, peeled and minced

1 tablespoon curry powder, or more to taste

1 teaspoon ground cumin

1 jalapeño pepper, minced (if you don't like it too hot, seed it first)

2 large tomatoes, chopped (or 1½ cups canned crushed tomatoes)

One 2-inch piece lemongrass, minced

½ cup tiny red or yellow lentils

3 cups water

Salt

1 pound firm tofu, cut into 1-inch cubes

1 large bunch spinach, leaves only

3 tablespoons chopped cilantro

3 cups cooked basmati rice

⅓ cup roasted peanuts, optional

Apple-Tomato Chutney (page 19) or a good store-bought variety

Makes 8 side-dish or 4–6 main-course servings

I learned to love Indian food when I was introduced to it properly by Christine, a Trinidadian who worked with me in my catering kitchen for about ten years. Not only did she teach me how to cook her native dishes, she also showed me the proper way to serve them. This is one of my favorites. The red lentils disperse in the dish and thicken the sauce naturally. You will love the fragrance of lemongrass, easy to find at good grocery stores. Discard the outer leaves and mince the center "core." Put a whole meal together and serve this curry with a refreshing cucumber raita (mine is a streamlined but delicious version), basmati rice, and chutney.

To make the raita: In a bowl, mix the yogurt, mint, cucumber, cumin, and curry powder and salt and pepper to taste. Chill for an hour or two to let the flavors develop.

To make the curry: Heat the oil in a heavy, wide-bottomed pot over high heat. Add the onion and ginger and sauté until translucent, about 3 minutes. Add the curry, cumin, and jalapeño and sauté until fragrant, 1 more minute. Add the tomatoes, lemongrass, lentils, water, and salt to taste and bring to a boil. Reduce the heat to medium and cook, covered, for 20 minutes.

Add the tofu, spinach, and cilantro, stirring very gently so as not to break the tofu. Cook, covered, for 10 minutes. The tofu will have absorbed all the flavors, the spinach will be reduced, and the sauce should be thick but smooth. Serve hot, over rice, topped with peanuts if desired, with the chutney and raita on the side.

Note: If you are serving a nondairy meal, make the raita as follows: Mix 1 cup soy milk with 1 tablespoon vinegar and let it sit for 10 minutes to curdle. Puree ½ pound silken tofu in a food processor until perfectly smooth. Use the curdled soy milk and the creamed tofu instead of the yogurt, and proceed with the recipe as above.

ARTICHOKE HEARTS AND CARROTS IN LEMON SAUCE

8 large fresh artichokes

¼ cup olive oil

1 medium onion, finely chopped

½ teaspoon turmeric

Good pinch of saffron

2 pounds very thin carrots (about 16), peeled (not baby carrots)

18 pitted green olives

2 cups water

Salt and pepper

¼ cup finely chopped flat-leaf parsley

Juice of 2 lemons, or less to taste

MAKES 8 SIDE-DISH SERVINGS

Artichokes are a Sephardi favorite, and in Morocco they are a staple. I remember a variety I haven't seen anywhere else: tiny, with pointed leaves as sharp as thorns, which we used to eat by the dozen at the end of a meal as dessert, much as the Japanese eat pickles. Another novelty, which I've seen only a few times in the Italian markets of the United States, are the long fuzzy artichoke stalks, called cardoons, which have an intriguing, bitter flavor and taste delicious cooked with chicken or lamb.

I love to pickle or stuff artichoke hearts, or simply eat them boiled with a vinaigrette. From dozens of beloved artichoke recipes, I have chosen this memorable side dish: Artichoke and carrots are a natural pair. This dish can be served as a first course or a side dish with chicken or meat.

Prepare the artichoke hearts (see box). Heat the olive oil in a large heavy pot over high heat. Add the onion and sauté until translucent, about 3 minutes. Add the turmeric, saffron, carrots, artichoke hearts, olives, water, and salt and pepper to taste and bring to a boil. Reduce the heat to medium and cook, covered, until the vegetables are tender, about 20 minutes. Uncover, add the parsley and lemon juice, and cook for just a few more minutes, until the sauce is thick. Serve at room temperature.

HOW TO REMOVE ARTICHOKE HEARTS

Take an artichoke and cut off the leaves one by one with a knife, cutting them an inch away from the rounded bottom. When you get closer to the center leaves, cut through them with a knife to come level with the cut outer leaves. With a small spoon or melon baller, remove the hairy, fuzzy choke at the center. Using a paring knife, smooth out the exterior of the heart, and trim the stem to about two inches long, cutting off the very dark green parts and rounding the edges. Place the artichoke hearts in acidulated water (cold water with a few drops of lemon or vinegar added) to prevent discoloration. You might want to wear rubber gloves so your hands don't turn black.

BRAISED LEEKS, ENDIVE, AND FENNEL

3 medium leeks, white parts only, quartered lengthwise (make sure they stay attached at the stem)

6 heads endive, quartered lengthwise (make sure they stay attached at the stem)

3 medium heads fennel, quartered lengthwise (make sure they stay attached at the stems)

¼ cup brown sugar

⅓ cup cider vinegar

¼ cup olive oil

6 bay leaves

1 cup water

Salt and pepper

MAKES 6 SIDE-DISH SERVINGS

Bitter endive and sweet fennel complement each other beautifully in this French favorite. You could make this a main course by topping the finished dish with some grated Gruyère or cheddar and broiling until the cheese melts and is lightly browned.

Carefully place the leeks, endive, and fennel in a heavy, wide-bottomed pot. In a bowl, mix the brown sugar, vinegar, olive oil, bay leaves, water, and salt and pepper to taste. Pour this mixture over the vegetables and bring to a boil. Reduce the heat to medium-low and cook, covered, for about 30 minutes.

Uncover and, if necessary, continue to cook over high heat until the liquid is thickened. Transfer the vegetables to a platter and pour the thickened sauce over them. Serve hot.

TZIMMES LOAF

1 large sweet potato (about
1 pound), peeled and grated

1 pound carrots (4–5 medium),
peeled and grated

1 medium onion, peeled and grated

1 cup canned unsweetened
crushed pineapple with its juice

One 1-inch piece fresh ginger,
peeled and grated

1 cup pitted prunes, coarsely
chopped

1 teaspoon ground cinnamon

3 eggs

1 cup flour

½ cup olive oil

¼ cup light brown sugar

3 tablespoons rum or brandy

Salt and pepper

MAKES 10 SIDE-DISH SERVINGS

This dish is where the expression "making a big tzimmes" (much ado) comes from. Traditionally, tzimmes is a slow-cooked dish of meat and all the vegetables included in this recipe, but it evolved into this simpler (and no less delicious) easy-to-prepare meatless side dish. Serving it in slices makes for a dramatic presentation. I like to have this variation on Rosh Hashanah to usher in a sweet new year.

Preheat the oven to 375°F.

In a bowl, mix all the ingredients thoroughly, but don't squeeze the mixture or you will extract moisture, and the end product will be soggy. Pour into a greased 10-inch round cake pan or tube pan. Bake for 1 hour or until a knife inserted in the center comes out clean. Cut into slices. Serve warm.

POTATO LATKES

1 medium onion

Vegetable oil for frying

1 cup flour

4 eggs

Pinch of nutmeg

Salt and pepper

8 large Idaho or russet potatoes, peeled

Applesauce, yogurt, or sour cream for serving

MAKES 24 LATKES

I rarely fry anything, but there is no Chanukkah without latkes! In my catering career and for my friends and family at home, I have made thousands upon thousands of them and always watch them disappear at an alarming but flattering rate. There is no doubt about it: Latkes are a heavenly treat, and once we enter a house where the heavenly fragrance of fried foods wafts through the kitchen, even spartan dieters will sheepishly watch their noble resolution not to eat such things turn to dust.

You may have guessed it: I have nothing nice to say about frying. Long ago I got burned while fishing schnitzel out of a frying pan. The hot oil turned my hand into a human dumpling for days and left its ugly scar for many months, so I am not enamored of this method of cooking. But my love for latkes has not suffered at all, thank you.

In a food processor fitted with a grating blade, grate the onion. Heat ⅓ inch oil in a heavy frying pan until very hot. While the oil is heating, in a bowl, combine the flour, eggs, onion, nutmeg, and salt and pepper to taste and mix thoroughly. Grate the potatoes in the food processor or by hand and immediately stir them into the batter. Work very quickly so they do not have time to get discolored.

Form small patties, about 2½ inches in diameter, and lower them into the hot oil, or drop the batter into the oil by heaping tablespoons. Fry until golden, about 3 minutes on each side. Remove the latkes and drain them on paper towels. Serve with applesauce, yogurt, or sour cream.

Variations

◆ *Vegetable latkes:* Substitute a mixture of zucchini, carrots, and parsnips (about 3 pounds) for the potatoes. Add seasonings of your choice such as oregano, garlic, and basil.

◆ *Sweet potato latkes:* Substitute sweet potatoes for the regular potatoes and add brown sugar, cinnamon, and ginger to taste.

◆ *Potato kugel:* Add ⅓ cup vegetable oil to the potato latke batter. Pour the batter into a greased loaf or square pan, and bake uncovered in a preheated 375°F oven for 1 hour or until the top is golden brown.

GUIDELINES FOR FRYING

Frying is the nemesis of every health-conscious cook (stir-frying does not fall into this category, as it requires very little oil and minimal cooking). But because fried foods are irresistibly delicious, I am happy to provide a few guidelines for frying occasional treats efficiently and safely.

KEEP IT DRY. Too much moisture will steam food instead of frying it, yielding soggy results. Be sure to dry whatever you are frying thoroughly with paper towels.

KEEP IT THICK. With a firm (not runny) batter, you will be able to form thicker patties, which absorb much less oil than thinner ones. The outside will be crisp, and the center will be tender yet cooked through.

KEEP IT HOT. Less-than-hot oil will seep into your food, making it inedibly greasy. If you are adding oil to your pan while frying, chances are your oil was not hot enough to begin with. When your oil is good and hot, you need to add very little, if any, additional oil to finish frying an entire batch of food. How hot is hot enough? Drop a smidgen of batter into the oil. If it sizzles and rises to the surface, the oil is hot and ready for frying.

KEEP IT STEADY. Do not crowd the pan. First of all, it makes handling the food more difficult and lowers the temperature of the oil. Adding what you are frying at steady intervals ensures that the oil has time to return to the desired temperature.

KEEP IT LEAN. I have my mother to thank for this advice. Rather than using spatulas or slotted spoons, work with two forks when frying. Lift each fried item with a fork on each side, and hold it vertically for a second or two over the frying pan: You will be surprised by how much oil drips off it. Immediately place the items on a plate lined with several layers of paper towels, which will absorb any remaining unwanted grease.

KEEP IT WHITE. This applies only to potato dishes. Peeled potatoes oxidize when exposed to air and turn an unappealing gray color. So when making latkes, get everything ready and peel and grate the potatoes last, adding them immediately to the otherwise finished batter.

KEEP IT FRESH AND HOT. A word about freezing and reheating. If you are entertaining a large group, it won't be enormous fun spending the afternoon frying while everyone is having a good time. If you must fry in advance, follow all the above guidelines, but fry each item until it is 90 percent cooked through, no more. Store it in a shallow pan in one layer. (You can place latkes standing upright in the pan like a deck of cards; you will be able to fit quite a few latkes in a pan in this position). Cover tightly. Refrigerate or freeze, depending on how long in advance you are preparing the dish. Reheat the latkes, uncovered, at about 350°F for 15 to 20 minutes if they were frozen.

Grains and Pastas

The following recipes draw from a wide choice of grains, and can indeed be considered main courses as well as side dishes. All you will need to make a meal is a salad and, if you wish, plain grilled fish or chicken. Pasta is not the only game in town, although I love it. Pasta is the starch we feel most comfortable preparing, but I find that making too many pasta dishes preempts experimenting with other wonderful grains. All the following dishes are easy to make and beautiful.

SYRIAN RICE WITH APRICOTS AND ALMONDS

¼ cup olive oil

1 large onion, sliced very thin (about 2 cups)

2 cups jasmine rice

Good pinch of saffron

4 cups water

1 cup dried apricots, coarsely chopped

½ cup chopped flat-leaf parsley, packed

Salt and pepper

¾ cup slivered almonds, toasted (see Toasting Nuts, page 33)

MAKES 8–10 SIDE-DISH SERVINGS

This wonderful side dish has so much fragrance, flavor, and color that you will not have to work too hard on the main course—grilled fish or chicken are perfect with it. If you are making this dish in advance, mix in the almonds at serving time.

Heat the oil in a heavy pot over medium-high heat. Add the onions and sauté until they are dark brown, 20 to 30 minutes. Add the rice and saffron and stir for a minute or two, until fragrant. Add the water and bring to a boil. Reduce the heat to medium and cook, covered, for 15 minutes.

Stir the apricots and parsley into the rice, add salt and pepper to taste, and cook, covered, for 5 minutes. Turn off the heat and stir in the almonds. Serve hot or at room temperature.

VEGETABLE FRIED RICE

2 tablespoons toasted sesame oil

2 tablespoons olive oil

1 red bell pepper, finely diced

2 cups sliced shiitake mushroom caps

1 cup frozen corn kernels

3 cups cooked (and cooled) white or brown rice

3 eggs

¼ cup soy sauce or more, to taste

1 cup bean sprouts, thoroughly drained

4 scallions, thinly sliced

Bottled hot sauce

MAKES 8 SIDE-DISH
OR 4–6 MAIN-COURSE SERVINGS

This dish can be easily converted into a main course with the addition of whatever left-over cooked or smoked meat or chicken you might have in the refrigerator. Once the rice is cooked, the dish takes only a few minutes to prepare.

Heat the sesame and olive oils in a large skillet over high heat. Add the red pepper and sauté until just soft, about 3 minutes. Add the mushrooms and sauté until the liquid evaporates, about 3 minutes. Add the corn and rice and stir until heated through.

Make a well in the center of the pan and add the eggs, scrambling them rapidly in the center. Stir to combine, add the soy sauce, bean sprouts, scallions, and hot sauce to taste, and stir until heated through. Serve hot.

FETTUCCINE WITH ANCHOVY-DILL SAUCE

3 heads garlic, points cut off, leaving cloves exposed

2 tablespoons olive oil

2 very large heads dill, fronds and stems (about 2 cups packed)

1 pound fettuccine

36 canned anchovies, drained and thoroughly rinsed

½ cup extra virgin olive oil

Freshly ground pepper

MAKES 8 FIRST-COURSE OR 4 MAIN-COURSE SERVINGS

My Aunt Renée has an Italian next-door neighbor who regales her with charm, kindness, and the wonderful fragrances that emanate from her kitchen. (Alas, no samples, because my aunt keeps kosher. But it's not against the law to catch whiffs!) When her neighbor goes away on vacation, my aunt tells me how insipid life is without her presence nearby, proof that cooking plays a seductive role in our lives, even in those cases when tasting isn't a factor.

This is one of Aunt Renée's neighbor's innumerable pasta recipes. Don't mention the "A" word to your guests—although the notion of anchovies is objectionable to some people, the taste usually isn't. Don't add salt until you taste the finished dish; the salt in the anchovies seasons the whole dish.

Preheat the oven to 400°F.

Rub the garlic heads with the olive oil. Wrap the garlic in foil and roast until soft, about 40 minutes. Squeeze all the pulp out of the garlic while garlic is still warm and set it aside.

Meanwhile, bring a large pot of water equipped with a pasta insert to a boil. Add the dill and blanch for 2 minutes. Pull out the insert, remove the dill, and squeeze it thoroughly dry. Replace the insert in the pot, add the pasta, and cook until just tender, 12 to 15 minutes. Set aside ½ cup of the cooking liquid, then drain the pasta.

Combine the reserved garlic, dill, anchovies, extra virgin olive oil, reserved cooking liquid, and lots of pepper to taste in a food processor and process until smooth. In a large bowl, toss the sauce with the pasta. Serve hot.

PEARL BARLEY WITH SWISS CHARD, BUTTERNUT SQUASH, AND CASHEWS

3 cups water

1 cup pearl barley, preferably organic

1 butternut squash (about 3 pounds), peeled and cut into ½-inch cubes

¼ cup olive oil

3 tablespoons brown sugar

1 teaspoon cinnamon

1 large onion, chopped

1 large bunch Swiss chard or spinach, leaves only, cut into ribbons

3 tablespoons pomegranate juice

½ cup cashews, toasted and coarsely chopped (see Toasting Nuts, page 33)

Salt and pepper

MAKES 8 SIDE-DISH OR 4–6 MAIN-COURSE SERVINGS

I have found while experimenting with this dish that organic pearl barley yields better results than ordinary pearl barley: The organic barley kernels are larger and get very soft but never mushy when cooked. Organic barley is easy to find at health food stores. So is pomegranate juice: You will love the tang and color it adds to the dish, and it is so good for you! If you are making this in advance, add the cashews just before serving time.

Preheat the oven to 375°F.

Bring water to a boil in a pot. Add the barley and cook for about 40 minutes, until it is soft and all the water is absorbed. Set aside.

Meanwhile, in a bowl, mix the squash with 2 tablespoons of the oil, the brown sugar, and cinnamon. Place in one layer on a cookie sheet and bake for 30 minutes or until tender.

Heat the remaining 2 tablespoons oil in a skillet over high heat. Add the onion and sauté until golden. Add the Swiss chard and cook until the leaves are wilted, just a minute or two. In a large bowl, toss the barley with the squash mixture, Swiss chard mixture, pomegranate juice, cashews, and salt and pepper to taste. Serve warm or at room temperature.

BASMATI AND LENTIL PILAF WITH OKRA

¼ cup olive oil

1 large onion, chopped

1 tablespoon curry powder

2 teaspoons cumin

1 large tomato, chopped

5 cups water

2 cups basmati rice

⅔ cup tiny red lentils

1 pound fresh or frozen okra, sliced ½ inch thick

Salt and pepper

MAKES 8 SIDE-DISH OR 4–6 MAIN-COURSE SERVINGS

At Indian grocery stores, you will find an amazing array of grains, especially lentils. They come in all different colors—yellow, green, red, black, and white—and they cook so fast! I have chosen red lentils for this dish because they look so nice with the green okra and yellow corn. Okra gives the dish its slightly gelatinous texture. Frozen okra is perfectly acceptable here.

Heat the oil in a heavy pot over medium heat. Add the onion and sauté until golden brown, about 10 minutes. Stir in the curry and cumin and cook until just fragrant, 1 minute more. Stir in the tomato and sauté for 1 minute. Add the water and bring the mixture to a boil.

Add the rice and lentils and bring the mixture to a boil again. Reduce the heat to medium-low and cook, covered, for 20 minutes. Add the okra, stirring it gently into the rice, and cook, covered, for 10 more minutes. Add salt and pepper to taste. Serve hot.

KASHA WITH MUSHROOMS AND ONIONS

5 tablespoons olive oil

1 pound domestic mushrooms, sliced

1 large onion, chopped

2 cups kasha (buckwheat groats), whole granulation

1 egg or 2 egg whites

5 cups boiling water

Salt and pepper

MAKES 8 SIDE-DISH
OR 4–6 MAIN-COURSE SERVINGS

Kasha, known to much of the world as buckwheat, is a staple in many Eastern European countries. Toasting it gives it a delicious nutty taste, and rolling it in beaten egg keeps every kernel separated and plump. Do not skip either of these very quick steps, or you will get mush. If you are nostalgic for the traditional Russian-Jewish comfort food, skip the mushrooms and add two cups of cooked bow-tie noodles to the finished dish. If you are feeling both nostalgic and racy, leave the mushrooms in and add the noodles too.

Heat 2 tablespoons of the oil in a pot over high heat. Add the mushrooms and sauté until all the liquid evaporates, 4 to 5 minutes. Remove the mushrooms from the pot. Heat the remaining oil in the pot over medium heat. Add the onions and cook until they are dark brown, about 20 minutes. Remove the onions from the pot.

Place the kasha in the pot over medium heat and toast until fragrant and lightly colored, about 2 minutes. Add the egg and stir quickly until the grains are uniformly coated, about 1 minute more. Add the boiling water and salt and pepper to taste, reduce the heat to medium, and cook, covered, for about 15 minutes, until the grain is tender.

Stir the reserved mushrooms and onions into the pot and cook for 2 to 3 more minutes, until heated through. Serve hot.

CHAMPAGNE RISOTTO WITH ARUGULA, PEAS, AND ASPARAGUS

¼ cup plus 1 tablespoon olive oil

2 bunches arugula, leaves only, cut into thin ribbons

¼ cup flat-leaf parsley, finely chopped

12 thin asparagus spears, tough ends discarded, cut into 2-inch sections

1 cup shelled peas

1 large onion, chopped

4 medium shallots, chopped

2 cups Arborio rice

Good pinch of saffron

2 cups champagne (or dry white wine)

4 cups hot water

Salt and pepper

MAKES 8 SIDE-DISH OR 4–6 MAIN-COURSE SERVINGS

This dish takes a little time, but good risotto must be made slowly by adding hot liquid gradually, as each previous addition is absorbed. It is fun to make, though, and you will be rewarded with a delicious and elegant dish. Take the trouble to find fresh peas, otherwise skip them and add more spinach and asparagus. If you are serving this dish as a main course, add grated Parmesan for a dairy meal or cubed poached chicken breast or smoked turkey breast for a meat meal. Choose a dry champagne (it doesn't have to be expensive), or settle for dry white wine. You want the greens to retain their brilliant color, so if you make this dish in advance, prepare them as instructed below, but do not stir them into the rice until serving time.

Heat 1 tablespoon of the oil in a heavy pot over high heat. Add the arugula and parsley and sauté for just a minute or two, until wilted. Set aside. Bring a pot of water to a boil and blanch the asparagus and peas for about 2 minutes. Drain and immediately rinse them in ice water. Set aside.

Heat the ¼ cup oil in the same pot in which you sautéed the arugula. Add the onion and shallot and sauté until translucent, about 3 minutes Add the rice and sauté for 2 more minutes, until it is very lightly golden and fragrant. Add the saffron and champagne and stir until all the liquid is absorbed.

Add the hot water, 1 cup at a time, adding each cup only when the previous liquid has been absorbed. This process should take 15 to 20 minutes. When the rice is almost cooked through, add the reserved arugula mixture, asparagus, and peas and heat through, 1 minute more. Add salt and pepper to taste. Serve hot.

CAVATELLI WITH BASIL, SUN-DRIED TOMATOES, AND OLIVES

1 pound cavatelli or other non-hollow pasta, such as farfalle or gemelli

1 bunch basil, leaves only (1 cup packed)

6 large cloves garlic

1 small bunch flat-leaf parsley, including stems (½ cup packed)

½ cup extra virgin olive oil

1 cup sun-dried tomatoes, rinsed, squeezed thoroughly dry, and cut into thin slices

1 tablespoon dried oregano

½ cup Niçoise olives

1 pint grape tomatoes

Salt and freshly ground pepper

Makes 8 first-course or 4 main-course servings

Here is a quick and unusually attractive dish. While the pasta boils, prepare the rest of the ingredients. If you have any leftovers, don't bother reheating them: This is delicious at room temperature too.

Bring a large pot of water to a boil and cook the pasta until just tender. Set aside ½ cup of the cooking liquid, then drain the pasta.

Meanwhile, place the basil, garlic, and parsley in a food processor and process until smooth. With the motor running, add the olive oil slowly through the feed tube, and process until smooth.

Pour the cooked pasta into a large skillet. Stir in the reserved cooking liquid, the basil mixture, sun-dried tomatoes, oregano, olives, grape tomatoes, and salt and pepper to taste. Heat through over medium heat, about 2 minutes. Serve hot.

NOODLE (LUKSHEN) KUGEL

12 ounces very thin noodles, boiled until just al dente, thoroughly drained

1 medium onion, finely chopped

1 cup unsweetened applesauce

⅓ cup vegetable oil

¼ cup sugar

4 eggs

½ cup golden raisins, optional

1 teaspoon cinnamon

Salt and pepper

Makes 12 side-dish servings

This is one of my family's favorite comfort foods and a welcome import from my sister Rackel's house—my children request her dishes as often as her children request mine. I have found that what tastes best to children is always what they are served outside of their own home. Here, applesauce, besides being delicious, acts as an emollient and allows you to decrease the amount of oil in the recipe with no loss of flavor or texture.

Preheat the oven to 375°F.

Mix all the ingredients thoroughly in a bowl. Pour the batter into a greased 9 x 13-inch pan. Bake for about 1 hour or until golden brown and serve hot.

Variation: If you want to serve this for dessert at a dairy meal, omit the onion, add ⅓ cup sugar and 1 cup ricotta, and proceed with the recipe. Serve warm or at room temperature.

LINGUINE WITH WILD MUSHROOMS

1 pound linguine or fettuccine

¼ cup extra virgin olive oil

1½ pounds mixed wild mushrooms (shiitake mushroom caps, morels, chanterelles, porcini), sliced

1 canned or bottled truffle (available at specialty food stores), cut into small dice

Salt and freshly ground pepper

Chopped flat-leaf parsley or chives

MAKES 8 FIRST-COURSE
OR 4 MAIN-COURSE SERVINGS

Yes, this dish is expensive and decadent, but so good it's worth every penny. Let me assure you that you will make up in labor and time what you lose in cost—it can be prepared in minutes and is suitable for serving to your most distinguished guests. If you can't find truffle, substitute 2 teaspoons porcini powder.

Bring a large pot of water to a boil. Add the pasta and cook until just tender, 12 to 15 minutes. Set aside ½ cup of the cooking liquid, then drain the pasta.

Heat the oil in a large skillet over high heat. Add the mushrooms, in batches if necessary, and sauté until all the liquid evaporates, about 4 minutes. Add the reserved pasta and cooking liquid and heat through. Turn off the heat, add the truffle, salt and pepper to taste, parsley or chives, and toss. Serve hot.

Brunch and Dairy Dishes

During the holiday of Shavouot, it is customary to serve dairy dishes. Shavouot is the commemoration of the giving of the Torah to the Jewish people at Mount Sinai about 3,300 years ago. We are told that at that time Jews refrained from eating meat dishes because they were not yet knowledgeable enough about the laws of kosher meat processing. This confirms the French proverb, "Necessity is the mother of invention." As a result, during this holiday we indulge in preparing and serving wonderful dishes we would never serve on Shabbos or on all other holidays, when meat meals are de rigueur. Also, because the point of waiting six hours after a meat meal before eating dairy items becomes moot, Shavouot creates a liberating feeling all its own— brunch à toute heure.

The following cheese-and-egg-based dishes are unpretentious, inexpensive, and delicious and lend themselves perfectly to leisurely brunches throughout the year. In all of the recipes, you may substitute two egg whites for each whole egg if desired.

CHEESE BLINTZES

FOR THE CRÊPE BATTER

4 eggs

2 cups flour

1½ cups milk

1 cup cold water or seltzer

2 tablespoons vegetable oil

2 tablespoons sugar

Pinch of salt

Cooking spray for the pan

FOR THE FILLING

12 ounces farmer's cheese

1½ cups ricotta cheese

¼ cup sugar

2 tablespoons lemon juice

Grated zest of 1 lemon

1 tablespoon vanilla

1 egg

6 tablespoons butter for frying

Makes 18 blintzes;
6 servings

Another Jewish favorite. Put in secular terms, a blintz is a crêpe filled with a sweet or savory filling and fried very lightly in a little butter or oil. If you are trying to save time, make the crêpes in advance and stack them, separating the layers with wax paper. Wrap the stacks tightly with plastic wrap and refrigerate for up two days, or freeze for up to a month, and thaw before filling.

To make the crêpes: Combine all the crêpe batter ingredients in a blender or food processor and blend until smooth. Spray an 8-inch nonstick skillet with cooking spray and heat it over high heat. Using a very small ladle, add just enough batter to coat the bottom of the pan. Swirl the batter in the pan to ensure that it is evenly coated. After a few seconds, the edges will pull away from the bottom of the pan, and the top will look dry. Flip the crêpe and cook it for a few more seconds. Remove the crêpe from the pan. Repeat with the remaining batter, spraying the pan each time. Stack the crêpes, overlapping them slightly so that you can separate them easily. You should have 18 crêpes.

To make the filling: Combine all the filling ingredients in a food processor and process until smooth.

To assemble: Place 1 crêpe on a board. Shape about 2 tablespoons of the filling into a log that is about 3 inches long and 1 inch in diameter. Place the log on the lower half of the crêpe. Fold the sides in toward the center, and roll the crêpe tightly. Repeat with the remaining crêpes and filling.

Heat 1 tablespoon of the butter in a nonstick skillet over medium heat. Place 6 to 8 blintzes in the frying pan seam-side down; do not crowd them. Fry for about 2 minutes on each side or until golden, then drain on paper towels. Repeat with the remaining blintzes, adding butter to the pan as needed. Serve hot.

Note: You can freeze the finished blintzes. To reheat, place in a 300°F oven (uncovered) for about 20 minutes, until just heated through.

POTATO-LEEK FRITTATA

3 medium red potatoes (about 1½ pounds), peeled and cut into ½-inch cubes

⅓ cup olive oil

4 large leeks, white parts only, thinly sliced

8 eggs

½ cup milk (soy milk, if serving at a nondairy meal)

6 chives, minced

¼ cup chopped flat-leaf parsley

Good pinch of nutmeg

Salt and pepper

MAKES 8 SERVINGS

A frittata is a giant rustic Italian omelet that gets cut into wedges and is perfect for a crowd. This is my favorite frittata recipe.

Bring a pot of water to a boil. Add the potato cubes and boil until tender, about 15 minutes. Drain thoroughly and set aside. Meanwhile, heat the oil in a nonstick 12-inch skillet over high heat. Add the leeks and sauté until they are soft, about 10 minutes.

Beat the eggs together in a bowl. Add the reserved potatoes, leeks, milk, chives, parsley, nutmeg, salt and pepper to taste, and beat again.

Reheat the skillet over medium heat, adding a few drops of olive oil if it looks too dry. Pour the egg mixture into the skillet and cook for about 5 minutes, until the edges look set. Slide the frittata onto a round plate, turn it upside down onto another plate, and ease it back into the skillet on the other side. Cook for 5 more minutes. Cut the frittata into wedges and serve hot or at room temperature.

Note: If you don't trust that you can turn the frittata over without breaking it, finish cooking it in a 375°F oven for about 10 minutes.

SPINACH-RICOTTA PIE

⅓ cup olive oil

1 large onion, thinly sliced

2 large bunches spinach (about 1 pound) cut into ribbons and thoroughly dried

1½ cups ricotta cheese

4 eggs

1 cup feta cheese, crumbled

1 tablespoon dried oregano

Salt and pepper

MAKES 8 SERVINGS

The sharp taste of feta cheese offsets the mildness of ricotta and goes well with oregano. Incorporating feta into baked dishes allows you to capitalize on its versatility.

Preheat the oven to 375°F.

Heat the oil in a heavy pot over high heat. Add the onion and sauté until translucent, about 3 minutes. Add the spinach, in batches if necessary, and sauté until the ribbons are just wilted.

Lightly beat the ricotta and eggs together in a bowl. Add the spinach mixture, feta, oregano, and salt and pepper to taste and mix thoroughly. Pour the batter into a greased 9 x 13-inch pan. Bake for about 40 minutes, until the top is very lightly browned. Serve warm or at room temperature.

OMELETS AND CRÊPES WITH ASSORTED FILLINGS

FOR THE OMELETS

8 eggs

1 cup milk (soy milk if serving at a nondairy meal)

Salt and pepper

FOR THE CRÊPE BATTER

4 eggs

2 cups flour

1½ cups milk (soy milk if serving at a nondairy meal)

1 cup cold water or seltzer

2 tablespoons vegetable oil

Pinch of salt

Makes 4 small omelets; 14–16 eight-inch crêpes

Once a week, my family decides to have an omelet or a crêpe party, with a choice of two fillings. Everyone has fun flipping and filling, and we play musical pans, eating the hot omelet or crêpe while somebody else is preparing the next one. This is great food for a fun-loving crowd. The omelet and crêpe fillings are virtually interchangeable. I offer a basic omelet recipe, a basic crêpe recipe, and a number of very simple fillings for both. Have fun mixing and matching.

To make the omelets: In a bowl, beat together the eggs, milk, and salt and pepper to taste. Spray a nonstick pan with cooking spray or grease the pan with a little butter (or olive oil for a nondairy meal) and heat over high heat. When the pan is hot, add ½ cup of the egg mixture. Lower the heat to medium. The trick to a good omelet is to keep shifting the egg mixture to the bottom of the pan. To do this, gently lift the edges of the omelet with the point of a knife and tilt the pan, letting some of the runny mixture on top move to the bottom. Continue to do this until the omelet is just set, about 1 minute.

Remove the omelet from the pan and eat as is, or place one or more of the fillings in it and fold it over. Repeat with the rest of the egg mixture.

To make the crêpes: Blend all the batter ingredients in a blender or food processor until smooth. Spray a nonstick pan with cooking spray and heat it over high heat. Using a very small ladle, add just enough batter to coat the bottom of the pan. Swirl the batter in the pan to ensure that the pan is evenly coated. After a few seconds, the edges will start to pull away from the bottom of the pan and the top will look dry. Flip the crêpe and cook it for a few more seconds.

Remove the crêpe from the pan and fold it over the filling of your choice. Repeat with remaining batter, spraying the pan each time.

Fillings
- *Fines herbes:* Any chopped herbs of your choice, such as parsley, chives, chervil, basil, dill, or scallions. These can be folded directly into the batter.
- *Grated cheese:* Grated Parmesan or cheddar, or crumbled feta, and coarsely ground black pepper.
- Butter or cream cheese.
- *Sautéed vegetables*: Any combination of sliced mushrooms, broccoli cut into tiny florets, spinach leaves, red bell peppers, zucchini, tomatoes, onion, or garlic.
- Sour cream or yogurt, and caviar.
- Cream cheese and smoked salmon.
- *Dessert crêpes:* Add a little sugar and vanilla to the batter. Fill the crêpes with powdered sugar, jam, sautéed apple slices, vanilla, rum (ignite first for more drama), chopped nuts, and/or ice cream.

SPINACH AND BLUE CHEESE QUICHE

FOR THE CRUST

1½ cups flour

½ teaspoon salt

1 stick (8 tablespoons) cold butter, cut into small pieces

4 tablespoons ice water, slightly more if needed

FOR THE FILLING

3 tablespoons olive oil

1 medium onion, chopped

2 tablespoons flour

1½ cups milk

¼ cup dry sherry

Two 10-ounce boxes frozen chopped spinach, thawed and squeezed thoroughly dry

3 eggs, lightly beaten

1 cup blue cheese, crumbled (or ⅔ cup grated sharp cheddar plus ⅓ cup grated Parmesan)

Pinch of nutmeg

Salt and pepper

MAKES 6–8 SERVINGS

Serve this with a big salad and a good red wine, and you have a great meal. Do not try freezing it, as the crust will get soggy, eliminating the contrast of crust and filling in a good quiche. The trick to making perfect crust in a food processor is to pulse it very, very briefly, so it does not get overheated or tough: It is the combination of cold ingredients that ensures the layered flaky texture. Refrigerate the dough if you have the time, and handle it minimally.

To make the crust: Combine the flour, salt, and butter in a food processor and pulse briefly, until the mixture resembles coarse meal. Add the ice water and pulse again. Roll out the dough to a 14-inch circle on a barely floured board. Transfer the dough to an 11-inch springform fluted tart pan. Do not stretch the dough or it will shrink during baking. Prick the bottom all over with a fork. Wrap the whole pie pan in plastic wrap and refrigerate for about 1 hour.

Preheat the oven to 375°F.

Remove the plastic wrap and bake the crust for about 20 minutes or until lightly browned. While the dough bakes, make the filling.

To make the filling: Heat the oil in a heavy pot over high heat. Add the onion and sauté until translucent, about 3 minutes. Reduce the heat to low. Add the flour and whisk until golden brown, about 2 minutes. Turn the heat back up to high. Add the milk and sherry gradually, whisking constantly until the mixture thickens, a minute or two.

Pour the milk mixture into a bowl and add the spinach, eggs, cheese, nutmeg, and salt and pepper to taste. Mix thoroughly and pour the filling into the partially baked pie shell. Bake for 30 minutes or until the quiche looks set but not firm. Cut into wedges and serve hot.

FARFALLE WITH BROCCOLI AND SALMON

1 pound farfalle (bow ties)

1½ pounds skinless salmon fillet, cut into 1-inch cubes

1 bunch broccoli, cut into small florets

FOR THE SAUCE

⅓ cup extra virgin olive oil

1 large onion, chopped

3 tablespoons flour

1 cup milk

⅓ cup vodka

⅔ cup goat cheese (about 5 ounces), cut into small cubes

¼ cup good red or yellow caviar

Salt and freshly ground pepper

MAKES 8 SERVINGS

The list of ingredients sounds odd, but the finished dish is so delicious, I take my chances every time. The robust flavors of broccoli, vodka, goat cheese, salmon, and caviar all come together in this luxurious dish. Skip the caviar if you cannot find an excellent brand (sushi restaurants will part with a little jar, for a price).

Half-fill a large pot equipped with a pasta insert with water, and bring it to a boil. Add the pasta and cook until just tender. Remove the insert and transfer the pasta to a platter.

Replace the insert in the pot, add the salmon and broccoli, and cook for about 4 minutes. Remove the insert and transfer the salmon and broccoli to the pasta platter. Keep the platter warm.

Meanwhile, make the sauce. Heat the oil in a skillet over high heat. Add the onion and sauté until translucent, about 3 minutes. Reduce the heat to medium-low. Add the flour and cook, whisking, until the mixture is golden brown, 1 to 2 minutes. Turn the heat back up to high. Very slowly add the milk and the vodka, whisking constantly, about 2 minutes. The mixture will thicken. Add the cheese and let it melt for just a few seconds. Add the sauce to the pasta platter. Add the caviar, and salt and pepper to taste, and toss. Serve hot.

ARTICHOKE, TOMATO, AND CHEDDAR BREAD PUDDING

3 cups milk

6 eggs

2 stale baguettes, or 1 loaf stale Italian bread, cut into 1-inch cubes

⅓ cup olive oil

1 medium onion, chopped

4 large cloves garlic, minced

3 large tomatoes, peeled, seeded, and diced

½ cup basil leaves, packed, cut into ribbons

Two 10-ounce boxes frozen artichoke hearts, coarsely chopped

Salt and pepper

1¼ cups grated cheddar cheese

¼ cup fresh bread crumbs

1 tablespoon softened butter

MAKES 8–10 SERVINGS

Bread puddings, sweet or savory, are so versatile and can be so elegant, that we forget how they came into being in the first place—a clever recycling of stale bread and other modest leftover ingredients, transformed into a new dish and creating endless variety. Puddings remain a favorite comfort food, long after the days of penury. You can also be creative with bread puddings. This is one of my favorite inventions. I prefer crusty bread to square soft bread in this dish, but then I prefer it in general. Stale is better simply because it won't get soggy. No need for fresh artichokes here: Frozen are perfectly fine.

Preheat the oven to 375°F.

In a bowl, beat the milk and eggs together. Add the bread cubes, mix, then set aside.

Heat the oil in a skillet over high heat. Add the onion and garlic and sauté until translucent, about 3 minutes. Add the tomatoes and basil and sauté until most of the liquid has evaporated, about 3 minutes. Stir in the artichoke hearts and salt and pepper to taste.

Grease a 9 x 13-inch lasagna pan. Pour half of the bread mixture into the pan, packing it tightly. Top with half of the tomato mixture, and sprinkle half of the cheese on top. Repeat with the second half of the bread mixture, the second half of the tomato mixture and the second half of the cheese.

In a small bowl, toss the bread crumbs and the butter together; sprinkle on top of the casserole. Bake for about 45 minutes or until the top of the bread pudding is golden brown. Serve hot.

POLENTA-VEGETABLE CASSEROLE

FOR THE POLENTA

9 cups water

3 cups coarse cornmeal

1 cup grated Parmesan cheese

Salt and pepper

FOR THE FILLING

¼ cup olive oil

1 medium onion, chopped

6 large cloves garlic, minced

1 medium eggplant, peeled and cut into ½-inch cubes

2 medium zucchini, cut into ½-inch cubes

1 red bell pepper, cut into ½-inch cubes

3 cups canned crushed tomatoes

⅓ cup packed basil leaves, chopped

1 tablespoon dried oregano

Salt and pepper

Makes 8–10 servings

Polenta is easy to prepare, and so delicious you can serve plain wedges as a side dish with grilled fish and a salad. Don't be tempted to buy the ready-made rolls of polenta you see at some grocery stores—homemade leaves them in the dust. Make sure you buy coarse cornmeal, as fine will not have enough texture. Don't let eggplant boss you around, here or anywhere. Because its texture is so porous, it absorbs oil so readily it seems as though it will never be saturated. But you don't need to add any oil, as it resurfaces when the eggplant starts getting very hot.

Preheat the oven to 375°F.

To make the polenta: Bring the water to a boil in a large pot. Add the cornmeal and stir until thick. This should take only a few minutes. Stir in the cheese and salt and pepper to taste. Pour the mixture onto a greased cookie sheet, in a layer no thicker than ½ inch. You might need an additional cookie sheet (you will fill only half of it). Let the polenta cool.

To make the filling: Heat the oil in a large skillet over high heat. Add the onion and garlic and sauté until translucent, about 3 minutes. Add the eggplant, zucchini, and bell pepper and sauté for 2 to 3 more minutes. Add the tomatoes, basil, oregano, and salt and pepper to taste, and cook for 2 minutes.

Grease a 9 x 13-inch lasagna pan. Line the bottom of the pan with a layer of polenta, making sure you leave no blank spaces. Add half of the vegetable mixture. Repeat with another layer of polenta and the rest of the vegetable mixture. Bake for about 30 minutes or until bubbly. Let the casserole cool slightly before cutting it into squares. Serve warm.

RICOTTA FRITTERS

Vegetable oil for frying

4 eggs

3 cups low-fat ricotta cheese

1½ cups flour

¼ cup golden raisins

1 teaspoon cinnamon

1 teaspoon grated lemon zest

¼ cup sugar

Dash of salt

Makes 24 fritters;
6–8 servings

These may be nothing more than dressed-up cheese latkes, but they are so light and fragrant you might even consider serving them for dessert, with a scoop of vanilla ice cream: latkes à la mode. (For my advice on frying and reheating, see page 125.)

Heat ⅓ inch of oil in a heavy pot over high heat. Combine the eggs and ricotta in a food processor and process until smooth. Add the flour and process for just a few seconds until the batter is smooth.

Transfer the batter to a bowl and add the raisins, cinnamon, lemon zest, sugar, and salt. Mix until thoroughly combined. Form the batter into small patties or drop by heaping tablespoons and cook in the hot oil. Fry until golden, about 3 minutes on each side. Drain on paper towels. Serve hot or warm.

CHEESE LOGS

FOR THE CHEESE MIXTURE

FOR THE CHEESE MIXTURE

8 ounces cream cheese, at room temperature

8 ounces sharp cheddar cheese, cut into cubes, at room temperature

½ cup grated Parmesan or crumbled Roquefort cheese, at room temperature

½ cup (1 stick) butter, at room temperature

¼ cup dry sherry

1 tablespoon black walnut extract

FOR THE GARNISH

½ cup chopped toasted walnuts (see Toasting Nuts, page 33)

Paprika

Coarsely ground pepper

MAKES 15 SERVINGS

These are great fun to make and will greatly enhance any brunch table. You can display these logs on those colored paper leaves sold at specialty kitchen and stationery stores. I offer three different presentations for the basic recipe. Black walnut extract goes beautifully with cheese and is easy to find at gourmet and health food stores.

To make the cheese mixture: Combine all the ingredients in a food processor and process to form a smooth paste. Divide the mixture into three portions, and form each portion into the desired shape.

For a log: Roll the mixture into a log 2 inches in diameter. Roll the log in the walnuts, pressing hard so the walnuts adhere. Wrap the log in plastic wrap, and refrigerate until firm, about 1 hour.

For a loaf: Form the mixture into a square loaf. Roll the loaf in paprika on all sides. Wrap in plastic wrap and refrigerate.

For a triangle: Form the mixture into a triangle. Roll in coarsely ground pepper on all sides. Wrap in plastic wrap and refrigerate.

Remove the logs from the refrigerator about 1 hour before serving to bring to room temperature. Serve with a basket of bread or crackers, or on slices of cocktail bread as canapés.

APRICOT BUTTER

½ cup dried apricots, packed

2 tablespoons apricot brandy, such as Leroux or Hiram Walker

1 cup (2 sticks) unsalted butter, at room temperature

MAKES ABOUT 1½ CUPS

Serve this delicious spread with scones, muffins, or toast.

Soak the apricots in boiling water for a few minutes and drain them.

Place the apricots in a food processor and process until smooth. Add the brandy and butter and process again until smooth. This butter will keep in the refrigerator for up to two weeks.

Breads
and Flatbreads

Who said we were too old to have fun at the playground? Just as children build castles out of sand and water, we build bread out of flour, water, and yeast. Perhaps this is why we don't feel quite the same wonder and awe about any other food that we feel about bread. We Orthodox Jews are not allowed to throw any of it away, and we reserve a special blessing for it at every Shabbos meal, holiday, and celebration. When preparing a large batch of dough, we are required to take out a small portion and burn it, in commemoration of the gift of bread made to the high priests, or Kohanim, who were assigned major duties in the Holy Temple.

To think that something so marvelous can be obtained from so little! An old French song goes: "Nothing moves me more than a woman's hands in the dough." What is it about making bread that strikes such a primeval chord in all of us? Is it the mystery of the yeast-and-water encounter; the delight at seeing it come alive and bubble and overflow exuberantly; the soothing, sensuous pleasure of kneading the dough, then watching it grow in all directions and take on different whimsical shapes; or the haunting redolence of the golden baked loaves that invades our homes? Bread-baking therapy, I highly recommend it!

There are four important secrets of successful bread baking:

WATCH THE TEMPERATURE. Hot and cold temperatures and drafts kill the action of yeast and inhibit the rising of the dough. So make sure the water you mix with the yeast is warm, and that you let the dough rise, covered, in a draft-free area.

NOT TOO MUCH SALT, PLEASE! Remember you are going to eat this bread with other foods, which are often salty, such as cheese, lox, and various spreads.

Opposite, clockwise from center: Skillet Cornbread, Challah, Paratha, and Khobz (Moroccan Bread)

DO NOT BE TEMPTED TO ADD MORE FLOUR. The gluten in flour expands during the rising process and absorbs the liquids in the recipe, eliminating stickiness and yielding a light dough.

CHECK FOR DONENESS. A well-baked bread sounds hollow when tapped on its bottom. Turn the loaves upside down to cool, to avoid having moisture condense on the bottom crust, making it soggy. Wrap the cooled loaves tightly in plastic wrap. If you are not serving the bread on the day you are making it, freeze the wrapped loaves.

BASIC WHITE BREAD

1½ tablespoons active dry yeast

1½ cups warm water

1 tablespoon sugar

4 cups flour

1¼ teaspoons salt

2 tablespoons olive oil

MAKES 3–4 LONG THIN
LOAVES OR 2 MEDIUM LOAVES

My son Yakov can't live without this bread: A loaf a day is the very least he is satisfied with. "This bread rules, this bread rocks," he always says with delight. He tells me, "If everyone could have as much of your bread as I do, and you sold it, you would be a millionaire." Still, I wouldn't charge him! Yakov is spending this year in faraway Sydney, Australia, and I pray he keeps safe and finds good bread there.

Consider this the "mother recipe." You will be amazed to see how many variations you can make. If you want to make a larger batch of bread and freeze it, this recipe can be easily doubled.

Mix the yeast, ½ cup of the warm water, and the sugar in a big bowl. Let the mixture bubble for about 5 minutes. Add the flour, salt, oil, and the remaining 1 cup of warm water. Mix by hand until just combined.

Turn the dough out onto a lightly floured flat working surface and knead for 10 minutes, turning the dough a quarter turn every 2 to 3 minutes and punching it down often to eliminate any air pockets. (Alternatively, transfer the dough to the bowl of an electric dough mixer and set for 5 minutes kneading.) Transfer the kneaded dough to a large mixing bowl (remember, the dough will expand). Let it rise in a warm draft-free area for about 3 hours.

Preheat the oven to 400°F.

Shape the bread into 3 to 4 long skinny loaves. (If you like your bread to have less crust and more crumb, shape the dough into 2 medium loaves. If you want a loaf with no crust and all crumb, place the dough in 2 lightly greased loaf pans.) Place the loaves on a foil-covered cookie sheet about 2 inches apart. Slash each loaf on the diagonal in several places with a very sharp knife.

Bake for about 40 minutes (a little longer for the larger loaves) or until the bread sounds hollow when tapped on the bottom.

Variations

◆ *Oat bread:* Substitute ¾ cup rolled oats for ¾ cup flour in every 4 cups of flour (so use 3¼ cups flour plus ¾ cup oats instead of 4 cups flour). Do not substitute more than ¾ cup of oats for every 4 cups of flour—oats have no gluten, and your bread won't rise. You can also substitute semolina, fine cornmeal, or buckwheat flour in the same proportions. Bake as for Basic White Bread.

◆ *Whole wheat bread:* Substitute whole wheat pastry flour (available at health food stores) for white flour in equal parts. Make sure you use pastry flour, as it is very fine and will yield just about as light a bread as white flour. Bake as for Basic White Bread.

◆ *Herb and cheese bread:* Add to the dough ½ cup plain yogurt, ¼ cup chopped dill, and ½ cup grated cheddar cheese. Knead all the additions into the dough thoroughly before letting it rise. Place the risen dough in two loaf pans. Bake as for Basic White Bread.

◆ *Caraway or poppy seed bread:* Knead ¼ cup caraway or poppy seeds into the dough thoroughly before letting it rise. Bake as for Basic White Bread.

◆ *Walnut-raisin bread:* Add to the dough ¾ cup dark raisins, ½ cup chopped walnuts, and 2 tablespoons dark molasses. Knead all additions into the dough thoroughly before letting it rise. Shape into a thick loaf or 2 smaller loaves. Bake as for Basic White Bread.

◆ *Zaatar bread:* Roll out some of the risen dough into a very thin rectangle or round (about ½ inch thick). Brush lightly with olive oil and sprinkle generously with *zaatar* (a delicious Israeli mixture of sesame seeds, oregano, and sumac). Bake at 375°F for only 15 to 20 minutes. Do not let the dough get crisp or it will harden.

◆ *Focaccia:* Roll the risen dough into a 1-inch-thick oblong or round. Poke it all over with a skewer. Brush with olive oil and add toppings such as crushed tomatoes, oregano, and ground pepper; finely chopped onion; grated cheese; chopped fresh herbs (thyme, rosemary, and sage). Bake in a preheated 350°F oven for about 40 minutes.

ON KNEADING

When I was growing up, we had a rich cousin who had a masseuse come to her house twice a week to help reduce her unsightly bulges. Once her intrigued maid asked her, "What is it that this lady does to you each time she comes?" To which my cousin answered, "You know, if you massage a fat area, you end up reducing it." The maid looked horrified and said vehemently, "Oh, no, Madame! When you knead the dough, it grows, and grows, and grows!"

KHOBZ (MOROCCAN BREAD)

1¼ tablespoons active dry yeast

1½ cups warm water

1½ teaspoons sugar

4½ cups flour, or a combination of regular and whole wheat pastry flour

1 teaspoon salt

1 tablespoon fennel seeds or anise seeds

2 tablespoons sesame seeds

MAKES 2 LOAVES; 8 AMPLE SERVINGS

In Morocco, bread is not just the outside of a sandwich; it is sustenance itself. Every single morning, Moroccans make bread. They mix the dough, shape the loaves, let them rise, and wait for the young boy who will take them to the municipal oven, then back to the house just in time for lunch. No wonder the city streets are so fragrant and the local children so well coordinated, they're always racing around barefoot with huge trays balanced on their heads! You will not even find instructions for baking in most Moroccan bread recipes. They simply end with, "Let the loaves rise and send them to the oven."

Here then, is a recipe for my native bread, baked right at home. You can substitute 1 cup semolina for an equal amount of flour, or use equal parts of whole wheat and white flour, for a coarser texture.

Dissolve the yeast in ½ cup of the warm water. Add the sugar and let the mixture "proof" for a few minutes; the yeast mixture will bubble, "proof" that it is active. In a mixing bowl, combine the flour, the yeast mixture, the remaining 1 cup warm water, salt, fennel seeds, and sesame seeds. Stir lightly.

Turn the dough out onto a lightly floured flat working surface and knead it for about 15 minutes. Make sure you work on every part of the dough, punching it down regularly to expel any air bubbles, until you have a firm but pliable dough.

(Alternatively, place the dough in the bowl of a dough mixer and knead for about 5 minutes.)

Divide the dough into 2 pieces. Shape each piece into a flat circular loaf, about 9 inches in diameter. Arrange the loaves far enough apart on a cookie sheet to give them room to rise. Let rise for about 2 hours in a warm draft-free place, covered with a clean cloth.

Preheat the oven to 375°F.

Prick the tops of the loaves all over with a fork. Bake for about 35 minutes, until the bread is nicely browned.

WRAPPING THE BREAD

In Morocco, no one bothers to wrap the bread. What for? There won't be a crumb left, and anyway, a fresh batch will be made the next day. Bread is stored for the day on flat wicker platters topped with dome covers called *tbikas,* to protect it from dust and humidity. But I am not about to bake bread every day, so I make a big recipe and freeze it. Every time my mother sees me take out my bread loaves and unwrap them, she tells me: "Your bread looks like it just came out of the operating room!"

CHALLAH

2 tablespoons active dry yeast

2 cups warm water

¼ cup honey or sugar

2 eggs

¼ cup vegetable oil

½ tablespoon salt

6 cups flour

1 egg, beaten with ¼ cup water

Sesame or poppy seeds, optional

MAKES 2 LOAVES

This is the traditional braided Jewish bread served on Shabbos and for holiday celebrations. Personally, I don't like bread that tastes like cake, so my recipe contains just enough oil and eggs to enrich it and make it festive yet retain a bread texture.

Mix the yeast, water, and honey in a big bowl and let the mixture bubble for about 5 minutes. Add the eggs, oil, and salt, and beat. Add the flour and mix thoroughly by hand.

Turn the dough onto a lightly floured flat working surface and knead for about 10 minutes. Turn the dough a quarter turn every 2 to 3 minutes and punch it down often to eliminate any air pockets. (Alternatively, transfer the dough to the bowl of a dough mixer and set for 5 minutes of kneading). Transfer the kneaded dough to a big mixing bowl (remember, it will expand). Let the dough rise for 3 hours in a warm draft-free area, covered with a cloth.

Preheat the oven to 350°F.

To shape the challah: Divide the dough into 2 pieces. Divide each piece into thirds and roll each third into a long thin rope. Pinch the 3 ropes together at one end to hold them in place. Braid the ropes, and place the braid on a foil-covered cookie sheet. Repeat with the remaining pieces of dough. Place the loaves well apart on the cookie sheet.

Brush each loaf with the egg-and-water mixture and top with seeds if desired. Bake for 45 minutes to 1 hour, until the loaves sound hollow when tapped on the bottom.

Variations

◆ *Whole wheat challah:* Substitute whole wheat pastry flour for the white flour. Be sure to use pastry flour, as it is very fine and will yield almost as light a bread as white flour.

◆ *Raisin challah:* Served on Rosh Hashanah. Add 1 cup of raisins to the dough. Divide the dough into 2 pieces. Shape each piece into a long thin rope and roll it into a coil. You will have 2 round loaves.

PARATHA (INDIAN SKILLET FLATBREAD)

1 cup whole wheat pastry flour

1 cup flour

⅔ cup fine cornmeal

¾ teaspoon salt

1½ cups warm water

Vegetable oil, for brushing

MAKES 8 SERVINGS

There's no need to let this bread rise. It has a layered texture without a lot of oil or butter. It is best eaten warm, plain or with chutney. It can be made in advance and reheated in a 300°F oven. Do not let it get crisp or it will harden.

Mix all the dough ingredients together in a bowl. Turn the dough out onto a lightly floured work surface and knead for just a few minutes. Brush the dough with oil and let rest for a few minutes.

Divide the dough into 8 balls. Roll out each ball into a 5-inch circle and brush it lightly with oil. Fold the dough circle in half, then into a triangle, and roll it out again. Brush again lightly with oil on both sides.

Heat a nonstick skillet over high heat. Fry the flatbreads for a minute or two on each side, one at a time. The bread will get dark and blistered. Keep the bread warm in a very low oven until you finish frying the whole batch.

SKILLET CORNBREAD

¾ cup medium cornmeal

1 cup flour

1 teaspoon baking powder

1 teaspoon baking soda

½ teaspoon salt

3 tablespoons sugar

1 egg

2 tablespoons vegetable oil

1¼ cups plain yogurt

MAKES 6–8 SERVINGS

You can decide to make this bread at the drop of a hat. It doesn't need to rise, and it's always delicious. When making quick breads, the trick is to avoid overmixing the batter, or the bread will be tough. This bread is delicious as it is, but for a dairy meal you can enhance it by adding ½ cup grated cheddar cheese and 3 tablespoons chopped dill to the egg mixture before combining it with the flour mixture.

Preheat the oven to 425°F.

Grease a 9-inch round or 8-inch square pan, or an iron skillet, with oil and put it in the oven while you mix the bread.

In one bowl, combine the cornmeal, flour, baking powder, baking soda, salt, and sugar and mix thoroughly. In another bowl, mix the egg, oil, and yogurt. Pour the egg mixture into the flour mixture and stir with a wooden spoon until just combined. Immediately pour the batter into the hot pan. Bake for about 20 minutes or until the top is cracked and golden. Serve warm or at room temperature.

Variation: If you want to make this bread nondairy, mix 1¼ cups soy milk with 1½ tablespoons vinegar and let the mixture rest for about 10 minutes. (When mixed with an acid component, it will curdle, imparting the same tangy taste and soft crumb as yogurt. Such is the magic of soy milk: It behaves exactly like milk.) Substitute this mixture for the yogurt and proceed with the recipe.

Desserts

When my daughter was about ten years old, she told me: "Mommy, you are the fattest skinny person I know. Make sure you don't gain any weight, or you will become the skinniest fat person I know." Now, at eighteen, she is five foot five and weighs a hundred and six pounds, and she is a tough act to follow. Still, I am happy to report that I have never stepped out of the dread borderline my daughter set up for me. I try my hardest to come up with baked goods that are interesting, natural, and delicious without being prohibitively rich.

One of my friends calls my baking "la cuisine sans beurre." We kosher cooks, especially when it comes to baking, seem to be working with our hands tied behind our backs. You might ask how can anyone make a fantastic chocolate cake or a great batch of chocolate chip cookies, without butter? Having experimented extensively with countless recipes, the only answer I can think of is that certain limitations beget creativity. In Morocco, we couldn't find kosher ice cream, so my mother, a resourceful cook if I ever knew one, made ice cream with oil. Don't make that face—it was fabulous!

In fact, Levana's Bakery won the award for "Best Carrot Cake in the City" in *New York* magazine twenty-some-odd years ago. Back in those days, as start-up bakers, our main goal was to create simple, delicious, natural pareve (nondairy) desserts for kosher kitchens that could be served at the end of a meat meal. We were amazed by our success. Even then, the kosher public represented only a small part of our clientele. Our customers avoided dairy products for a wide variety of reasons and could never find desserts worth eating or serving guests that were butter- or milk-free, so they were delighted with our baked goods. We sold our carrot cake, chocolate cake, honey cake, chocolate chip cookies, oatmeal cookies, and many other desserts to numerous restaurants, as well as to Macy's and Zabar's.

The desserts I am sharing with you in this chapter are the culmination of many years of mad-scientist experimenting. I even remember fondly my first concoctions, which brought quizzical looks, then the indulgent smiles which, instead of telling me to give up, spurred me on. Before long my efforts brought delighted grins to everyone's face. The success we have had with our line of homemade desserts—both when Levana Restaurant was just a bakery and in all the years I have had my catering business and cooking classes—is ample proof that I didn't work hard for nothing. Only a few of the recipes, about half a dozen in all, didn't yield good results with oil and therefore contain the butter or margarine which I go to any length to avoid. What about nondairy creamer, nondairy whipping cream, and other chemical-laden artificial products? Nowhere to be found!

I want to say a quick word about chocolate. No matter what the recipe, use only the best. The difference between a chocolate cake, chocolate chip cookies, and brownies made with inferior chocolate and those made with an excellent variety cannot be overstated. I recommend Callebaut, Droste, Ghirardelli, or Hershey's. On the same note, when it comes to vanilla and other flavorings, use only the real thing, please! Artificial versions *will* affect the final product.

And finally, I mix most of the ingredients for my baked goods in a food processor. If you don't have one, a mixer will do fine. The only trick to mixing batters in the food processor is to avoid overprocessing, or the batter will lose its texture. Mixing batters with a food processor will take a little getting used to, but you will find it well worth it in the long run.

Opposite, clockwise from upper left: Chocolate Chip Cookies and Lemon Butter Cookies, Pecan Brownies, Cranberry-Hazelnut Biscotti, and Oatmeal Cookies

CHOCOLATE CAKE

1 cup soy milk

1 tablespoon lemon juice

2⅔ cups flour

1½ teaspoons baking powder

1½ teaspoons baking soda

Pinch of salt

1 cup plus 2 tablespoons best-quality cocoa powder

1¼ cups hot water

3 tablespoons instant espresso powder

3 tablespoons brandy, rum, or bourbon

1 tablespoon vanilla

3 eggs

2⅔ cups sugar

1 cup vegetable oil

MAKES 16 GENEROUS SERVINGS

Buttermilk makes chocolate cakes very tender and moist. I make a perfect nondairy substitute for buttermilk by mixing soy milk and lemon juice. I am not suggesting you enjoy this mixture as a drink on its own, but it will do wonders for your baking. I have heard from hundreds of people that this is the best chocolate cake they have ever had. Have you noticed how difficult it is to be modest about a great baked creation? It must be because a perfect cake is often the ultimate yardstick by which culinary talent is measured. This is a very large cake, so do not be alarmed by the amount of sugar used, and do not try to reduce it or the cake will taste bitter.

Preheat oven to 325°F.

In a small bowl, mix the soy milk and lemon juice and set aside. Mix the flour, baking powder, baking soda, salt, and cocoa in a bowl and set aside. Mix the hot water with the coffee, brandy, and vanilla in another bowl and set aside.

In a food processor, process the eggs and sugar until light and fluffy. Add the oil and process just until combined. Beginning and ending with the dry ingredients, add the flour mixture in thirds, alternating with the coffee mixture. Pulse 2 to 3 times after each addition, just to incorporate. Add the reserved soy milk mixture and pulse again for a few more seconds. The batter will be very runny.

Pour the batter into a greased and barely floured 10-inch springform pan. Bake for 75 minutes or until a knife inserted in the center comes out clean. Unmold the cake and invert it onto a rack to cool. Turn right side up to serve.

CARROT CAKE

1½ cups sugar

4 eggs

1 cup vegetable oil

3 cups flour

1¼ teaspoons baking soda

Pinch of salt

1 teaspoon cinnamon

½ teaspoon ground cloves

1 cup canned unsweetened crushed pineapple, undrained

3 cups grated carrots, packed

½ cup raisins

½ cup coarsely chopped walnuts

1 cup unsweetened grated coconut, optional

MAKES 12 GENEROUS SERVINGS

Here is the recipe for the aforementioned award-winning cake. My mother used to get such a kick out of this recipe. She would ask, "Why not a turnip cake or a tomato cake, while you are trying to be creative?" She didn't know she was on the right track—we also make delicious pumpkin cake and zucchini bread, and other vegetable-based baked treats. I assure you it was wrenching to have to choose only two dozen dessert recipes for this book!

Preheat the oven to 350°F.

In a food processor, process the sugar and eggs until light and creamy. Add the oil and pulse just until combined. Add the flour, baking soda, salt, cinnamon, and cloves and mix for just a few pulses. Transfer the batter to a bowl. Add the pineapple, carrots, raisins, walnuts, and coconut, if using, folding them in with a wooden spoon until just well combined.

Pour the batter into a greased 10-inch springform pan or tube pan. Bake for about 1 hour or until a knife inserted in the center of the cake comes out clean. Invert the cake onto a rack to cool. Turn right side up to serve.

HONEY CAKE

3 cups flour

2 teaspoons baking powder

2 teaspoons baking soda

Pinch of salt

1 tablespoon ground cardamom

1 tablespoon ground ginger

¼ teaspoon nutmeg

2 teaspoons cinnamon

4 eggs

1 cup dark brown sugar, packed

1 cup honey

1 cup vegetable oil

1 cup very strong warm tea (2 tea bags steeped in 1 cup hot water)

½ cup ground almonds, optional

3 tablespoons sliced almonds (add only if using the ground almonds)

MAKES 12 AMPLE SERVINGS

Although it's a traditional treat on Rosh Hashanah, the Jewish New Year, this moist and spicy cake is welcome throughout the year. Some people refrain from eating nuts during this holiday, because the Hebrew numerical value of "nut" is the same as that for "sin." If you're one of these people, don't worry: The cake is delicious without the nuts too!

Preheat the oven to 325°F.

In a bowl, mix together the flour, baking powder, baking soda, salt, cardamom, ginger, nutmeg, and cinnamon and set aside. In a food processor, process the eggs with the sugar, honey, and oil, just until combined. Beginning and ending with the dry ingredients, add the flour mixture in thirds, alternating with the tea. Pulse 2 to 3 times after each addition, just to incorporate. Add the ground almonds, if desired.

Pour the batter into a greased 10-inch springform pan or tube pan. Top with the sliced almonds, if using. Bake for 1 hour or until a knife inserted in center of the cake comes out clean. Invert the cake onto a rack to cool. Turn right side up to serve.

COFFEE CRUMB CAKE

FOR THE BATTER

3 cups flour

1 tablespoon baking powder

Pinch of salt

1½ cups plus 3 tablespoons sugar

1 tablespoon cinnamon

4 eggs

1 cup vegetable oil

1 tablespoon vanilla

1 cup unfiltered apple cider or
apricot juice

FOR THE STREUSEL

½ cup flour

2 tablespoons margarine

2 tablespoons sugar

Makes 12 generous servings

This is my son Yakov's favorite cake. "Mommy, almost as good as Entenmann's," he would say when he was a little boy. If you knew Yakov, you would understand the enormity of the compliment. The cut slices are so pretty, with a swirl of cinnamon in each, and the streusel topping provides a wonderful crunch.

Preheat the oven to 350°F.

To make the batter: Mix together the flour, baking powder, and salt in a bowl and set aside. Mix the 3 tablespoons sugar and the cinnamon in a small bowl and set aside.

In a food processor, combine the 1½ cups sugar with the eggs and process until light and fluffy. Add the oil and vanilla and process just until combined. Beginning and ending with the dry ingredients, add the flour mixture in thirds, alternating with the juice. Pulse 2 to 3 times after each addition, just to incorporate.

Pour half the batter into a greased 10-inch springform pan or tube pan.

Sprinkle the cinnamon-sugar mixture evenly on top of the batter. Pour the second half of the batter evenly over the cinnamon sugar.

To make the streusel: In a small bowl, mix the flour, margarine, and sugar lightly together until the mixture resembles coarse meal. Sprinkle this topping over the cake batter.

Bake for about 1 hour, or until a knife inserted in the center of the cake comes out clean. Invert the cake onto a rack, and turn right side up so the topping doesn't fall off.

ALMOND-WINE CAKE

2 cups flour (during Passover substitute 1½ cups potato starch)

1 tablespoon baking powder

¾ cup dry red wine

2 tablespoons orange zest

3 tablespoons brandy or rum

6 egg whites

Pinch of salt

1½ cups sugar

½ cup extra virgin olive oil

1¼ cups finely ground almonds (you can substitute hazelnuts, walnuts, or pecans)

MAKES 12 SERVINGS

This is my favorite Passover cake. As much as I would like to make my life easier by minimizing Passover preparations, I have never had the heart to buy premade desserts. The ingredients in this cake are assertive and deliciously fragrant. You will want to make it all year round.

Preheat the oven to 350°F.

Combine the flour and baking powder in a bowl and set aside. Combine the wine, orange zest, and brandy in another bowl and set aside. In a third bowl, beat the egg whites and salt until stiff but not dry and set aside.

Using an electric mixer, cream the egg yolks and sugar together until the mixture falls in ribbons from the beaters. Add the oil and mix again. Beginning and ending with the dry ingredients, add the flour mixture in thirds, alternating with the wine, mixing after each addition until just combined. Add the nuts and mix just until combined. Gently but thoroughly fold in the beaten egg whites with a wooden spoon.

Pour the batter into a greased 10-inch springform pan or tube pan. Bake for 1 hour or until the point of a knife inserted in the center comes out clean. Unmold the cake and invert it onto a rack to cool. Turn right side up to serve.

ORANGE-POPPY SEED CAKE

FOR THE CAKE

3 cups flour

1 tablespoon baking powder

Pinch of salt

2 tablespoons grated orange zest

5 eggs

1½ cups sugar

1 cup vegetable oil

1 tablespoon vanilla

¾ cup orange juice

¾ cup poppy seeds

FOR THE SYRUP

¼ cup orange juice

¼ cup sugar

3 tablespoons margarine

Makes 12 generous servings

This cake is bursting with poppy seeds and fragrant with orange zest. It soaks up the orange syrup and takes on a lovely sheen.

Preheat the oven to 350°F.

To make the cake: In a large bowl, mix together the flour, baking powder, salt, and orange zest and set aside. In a food processor, combine the eggs and sugar and process until light and fluffy. Add the oil and vanilla and process until just combined. Beginning and ending with the dry ingredients, add the flour mixture in thirds, alternating with the ¾ cup orange juice. Pulse 2 to 3 times after each addition, just to incorporate. Add the poppy seeds and pulse 2 to 3 more times.

Pour the batter into a greased 10-inch springform pan. Bake for about 1 hour, or until the point of a knife inserted in the center comes out clean.

To make the syrup: While the cake is baking, place the syrup ingredients in a small saucepan and heat until thickened, 3 to 4 minutes.

When the cake is done, immediately unmold it. Prick it all over with a skewer, and brush the syrup all over the top and sides while the cake is still hot. The cake will absorb all the syrup. Let the cake cool completely before serving.

BABKA

FOR THE BREAD

2 tablespoons active dry yeast

⅓ cup warm water

½ cup sugar

5½–6 cups flour

½ cup oil

1 cup soy milk

2 eggs

⅔ teaspoon salt

FOR THE TOPPING (OPTIONAL)

2 tablespoons margarine, at room temperature

6 tablespoons flour

6 tablespoons sugar

FOUR FILLINGS (EACH FOR 1 BABKA)

½ cup best-quality chocolate chips, melted

¼ cup sugar, ⅓ cup ground walnuts, 1 teaspoon cinnamon, mixed

¼ cup jam mixed with 2 tablespoons orange juice

Dairy filling: ½ cup ricotta cheese mixed with 1 teaspoon grated lemon zest, ¼ cup golden raisins, 2 tablespoons sugar, ¼ cup ground almonds

MAKES 2 LOAVES

Every culture calls this sweet bread something different: brioche, babka, kugelhopf, kuchen, kokosh. The recipes vary only slightly, and whatever you call it, you will be crazy about it! My version is streamlined and nondairy. The fillings are very easy to make, so try a different filling for each of the babkas.

To make the bread: Mix the yeast, water, and sugar together in a small bowl and let it bubble while you prepare the rest of the recipe.

Combine the flour (start with 5½ cups, and add the remaining ½ cup only if you need it), oil, soy milk, eggs, and salt in a bowl and stir together. Add the yeast mixture and knead for 10 minutes; the dough should be soft and elastic. (Alternatively, use an electric dough mixer, set at low speed for 5 minutes.) The dough should be softer than bread dough. Let the dough rise for 1 hour, in a warm draft-free place, covered.

To make the topping: Mix the topping ingredients together in a small bowl.

Preheat the oven to 350°F.

Divide the dough in half. On a barely floured board, roll out each piece into an 8 x 12-inch rectangle, with the short side facing you. Brush the dough lightly with oil. Spread your filling of choice on each rectangle and roll it up tightly, jelly-roll style. Transfer each roll to a loaf pan, seam-side down, and sprinkle on the topping (if you are not using topping, brush on beaten egg mixed with a little water).

Let the loaves rise in a draft-free place for about 30 minutes. Bake for 35 to 40 minutes, until golden brown. Invert the cake onto a rack to cool. Turn right side up to serve.

LEMON CAKE

FOR THE CAKE

3 cups flour

½ teaspoon baking soda

1 cup plain yogurt

2 tablespoons grated lemon zest

2 tablespoons lemon juice

1½ cups sugar

2 sticks (1 cup) butter, at room temperature

3 eggs

FOR THE SYRUP

⅓ cup lemon juice

2 tablespoons grated lemon zest

⅓ cup sugar

4 tablespoons butter

MAKES 12 GENEROUS SERVINGS

This is perfect for brunch but also for dessert, with fruit or sorbet. Don't substitute margarine for the butter; you will notice the difference. A friend of mine took a large chunk of this cake on a plane trip to Chicago and shared it with the flight attendants. One of them e-mailed me that she must have more and asked if she could have the recipe. I am used to my recipes getting a lot of mileage on the ground, but this was the first time at 30,000 feet!

Preheat the oven to 325°F.

To make the cake: Mix the flour and baking soda together in a bowl and set aside. Mix the yogurt, lemon zest, and lemon juice in another bowl and set aside.

In a food processor or mixer, beat the sugar and butter until light and fluffy. Add the eggs one at a time and pulse or mix each time until incorporated. Beginning and ending with the dry ingredients, add the flour mixture in thirds, alternating with the yogurt. Pulse 2 to 3 times after each addition (or mix briefly), just to incorporate.

Pour the batter into a greased 10-inch springform pan. Bake the cake for about 1 hour or until the point of a knife inserted in the center comes out clean.

To make the syrup: When the cake is almost done, bring all the syrup ingredients to a boil in a small saucepan. Reduce the heat to medium and cook for about 5 minutes, until slightly thickened.

Carefully unmold the cake and place it on a round tray. Using a skewer, prick holes all over the cake while it is hot and pour the hot syrup all over the cake. Cool completely before serving.

TIRAMISU

1¼ pounds store-bought sponge cake

1 pound silken tofu, thoroughly drained and dried with layers of paper towels

2 tablespoons vegetable oil

½ cup sugar

8 ounces tofu cream cheese (Tofutti brand only)

2½ tablespoons espresso powder, dissolved in ½ cup hot water

¼ cup brandy, rum, or bourbon

8 ounces best-quality semisweet chocolate, chopped

MAKES 12 GENEROUS SERVINGS

This dessert is so fabulous that I never bother to make the original dairy version. It's also healthier, thanks to my staunch ally tofu. When you serve it, don't tell anybody about the tofu until they have tasted and raved about it. In my kitchen, I have adapted the expression, "Behind every successful man, there is a surprised mother-in-law," to "Behind every delicious tofu dessert, there is a shocked and happy guest."

It is fine to use good store-bought sponge cake. Although it is not as pretty as ladyfingers, it maintains its shape better when soaked in the espresso and brandy. To chop chocolate, scrape the block vertically with a sharp knife: It will fall off in little shards or curls. The tofu cream cheese must be the Tofutti brand. I have tried other brands, and they looked and tasted like spackle! Once you have all the ingredients in place, the dessert takes only about ten minutes to assemble. Try your best to make this dessert a few hours before serving time, or even the day before, in order to give the sponge cake ample time to soak up all the flavors.

Preheat the oven to 375°F.

Cut the cake into ½-inch thick slices. Toast the slices in the oven for about 15 minutes, turning them once, until medium-brown on all sides. Let cool.

In a food processor, combine the tofu, oil, and sugar and process until perfectly smooth. Add the tofu cream cheese and process for a few more seconds. Pour the mixture into a bowl. Combine the coffee mixture and brandy in a container equipped with a spout, such as a glass measuring cup.

Grease a 1½ quart (6 cup) loaf pan and line it with plastic wrap, letting the sides overhang. Line the bottom of the pan with the cake slices, trimmed to fit tightly. Pour half of the coffee mixture evenly and carefully over the cake. Spread half of the tofu mixture evenly over the cake. Sprinkle half of the chocolate over the tofu mixture. Repeat the layers of cake, coffee, tofu mixture, and chocolate.

Fold the overhanging plastic wrap toward the center of the mold. Refrigerate for a few hours until set. To serve the tiramisu, unmold it and cut into slices.

CHOCOLATE-ESPRESSO CHEESECAKE

FOR THE CRUST

1 package (5 ounces) plain graham crackers

1 stick (4 ounces) butter, at room temperature

FOR THE BATTER

16 ounces cottage cheese

16 ounces cream cheese

16 ounces sour cream

4 eggs

1 cup sugar

¼ cup cornstarch

¼ cup lemon juice

1 tablespoon vanilla

1 stick (4 ounces) butter, at room temperature

⅔ cup chopped best-quality semisweet chocolate (or chocolate chips)

1½ tablespoons instant espresso powder

2 tablespoons brandy, rum, or bourbon

MAKES 20 SERVINGS

Another one of the signature desserts from the good old Levana Bakery days. We used to get swamped with orders before Shavouot, the traditional "dairy" holiday. This recipe appears regularly in various publications and is rich and heavenly. For variety's sake, you might decide to make an all-white cheesecake with no chocolate marbling: Simply skip the step of making the chocolate mixture, and proceed as described below.

Preheat the oven to 375°F.

To make the crust: In a food processor, process the graham crackers into fine crumbs. Add the butter and pulse to combine. Grease a 10-inch round spring-form pan and line the bottom and sides with the buttered crumbs, pressing hard to make the crust compact. Bake the crust for 15 minutes and set aside. Reduce the oven temperature to 325°F.

To make the batter: In a food processor or mixer, process or beat the cottage cheese until it is perfectly smooth. Add the cream cheese and sour cream and process again until smooth. Add the eggs, sugar, cornstarch, lemon juice, vanilla, and butter and process again until smooth.

In a small saucepan, combine the chocolate chips, espresso powder, and brandy and cook over very low heat until the chips are just melted (or use the microwave). Stir ½ cup of the batter into the chocolate mixture and set aside.

Pour the white batter on top of the crust. Drizzle on the reserved chocolate mixture and use a knife to swirl through the batter to get a marbled effect (be careful not to cut the crust).

Bake for 1 hour and 10 minutes; the cake will look barely firm and will have pulled away from the sides. Turn off the oven and leave the cake inside for 2 hours without opening (so the top won't crack). Remove the cake from the oven and let it cool completely before refrigerating overnight. Cut into slices and serve.

CHOCOLATE-HAZELNUT MOUSSE TORTE

FOR THE CAKE

1½ cups flour

¼ cup soy milk powder

1 teaspoon baking powder

1 teaspoon baking soda

Pinch of salt

⅔ cup best quality cocoa powder

1 cup hot water

1½ tablespoons instant espresso powder

2 tablespoons brandy

1 tablespoon vanilla

2 eggs

1½ cups sugar

⅔ cup oil

FOR THE CHOCOLATE MOUSSE

1½ cups best-quality semisweet chocolate chips

1 tablespoon instant coffee

2 tablespoons brandy or rum

½ cup sugar

1 pound silken tofu, thoroughly drained and dried on layers of paper towels

¼ cup vegetable oil

FOR THE HAZELNUT MOUSSE

1 pound extra-firm tofu, thoroughly drained and dried on layers of paper towels

1 cup unsweetened hazelnut butter (not a dairy product; available at health food stores)

1 cup superfine sugar

MAKES UP TO 20 SERVINGS

I have made hundreds of these for parties. A few years ago, a couple whose wedding I was catering wanted this very cake—but luxuriously decorated to their specifications—on their wedding day. I remember we helped the cake stylist they hired set up his counter, his tools, and a few sheets of the cake in the humongous walk-in refrigerator in Bridgewater's restaurant, where the wedding was taking place. It was a sweltering Sunday in July, and the heat in the kitchen was near volcanic, but the poor pastry chef looked half frozen when he resurfaced after about six hours of intense decorating! Needless to say, the cake was a masterpiece!

Preheat the oven to 325°F.

To make the cake: Mix the flour, soy milk powder, baking powder, baking soda, salt, and cocoa together in a bowl and set aside. Mix the hot water, espresso powder, brandy, and vanilla together in another bowl and set aside.

In a food processor, combine the eggs and sugar and process until light and fluffy. Add the oil and process until just combined. Beginning and ending with the dry ingredients, add the flour mixture in thirds, alternating with the coffee mixture. Pulse 2 to 3 times after each addition, just to incorporate.

Pour the batter into a greased 10-inch round springform pan. Bake the cake for 1 hour or until a knife inserted in the center comes out clean. Let the cake cool.

To make the chocolate mousse: In a saucepan, combine the chocolate chips, coffee, brandy, and sugar over very low heat just until the chips melt (or use the microwave) and set aside. In a food processor, combine the tofu and oil and process until smooth. Add the reserved chocolate mixture and process for 1 more minute. Spread the mousse on the cooled cake. Refrigerate until the chocolate mousse is set, about 2 hours, before adding the hazelnut mousse layer.

To make the hazelnut mousse: In a food processor, combine the tofu with the hazelnut butter and process until smooth. Add the sugar and process for 1 minute more. Spread the hazelnut mousse on top of the chocolate mousse layer.

Refrigerate the finished cake until set. Dust with cocoa powder before serving.

Note: You can make the chocolate and hazelnut mousses up to 2 days in advance.

Variations: The chocolate and hazelnut mousses are quite versatile. Pour either into individual parfait glasses and refrigerate until set, then top with strawberry or raspberry sauce and chopped toasted nuts, or use a dollop of mousse on chocolate or almond cake as a garnish instead of whipped cream or ice cream. Bolder yet, spread a little of either mousse as a filling between layers of cake.

APPLE-PEAR STRUDEL

FOR THE FILLING

2 firm-ripe pears, peeled and finely diced

2 Granny Smith apples, peeled, cored, and finely diced

⅓ cup raisins or currants

⅓ cup sugar

Juice and grated zest of ½ lemon

⅓ cup chopped pecans or walnuts

1 teaspoon cinnamon

¼ cup finely ground bread crumbs

FOR THE PASTRY

12 sheets phyllo dough

½ cup vegetable oil

MAKES 12 GENEROUS SERVINGS

Store-bought phyllo dough makes this dessert a snap. I have included several tips for working with phyllo (see page 31); when you get the hang of it, you will actually have fun using it and enjoy its versatility and flaky melt-in-your-mouth texture. Granny Smith is my favorite kind of apple for baking, but McIntosh will do just as well. Use fresh bread crumbs, made by grinding a slice of white bread or challah in the food processor.

Preheat the oven to 375°F.

Mix all the filling ingredients together in a bowl.

Take 1 sheet of the phyllo, place it flat on a cutting board with the short side facing you, and brush it lightly with oil. Repeat twice (3 sheets total). Place a quarter of the filling along the short end of the phyllo and roll it up tightly, jelly-roll style. Place the roll on a cookie sheet. Make 3 more rolls, using 3 sheets of phyllo and a quarter of the filling for each, and place them on the cookie sheet. Make sure the rolls fit snugly on the cookie sheet, so that the filling doesn't seep out of the open ends while baking. Fill any empty spaces with rolled-up foil "balls."

Using a sharp knife, score each roll about 5 times, making the slits 2 inches apart. Brush the rolls with oil. Bake for 30 minutes, or until the pastry is light brown and crisp. Cut along the scored lines with a sharp knife. Serve the strudel warm or at room temperature.

Note: You may make the strudel in advance and reheat it uncovered in a 300°F oven until crisp, about 15 minutes.

Variations: You might want to try some variations on the filling, such as all pear or all apple instead of half and half, or use dried cranberries, almonds, and ground ginger instead of raisins, walnuts, and cinnamon. If you decide to make the strudel with pitted fruit such as plums or peaches, add 3 tablespoons cornstarch to the filling to absorb the extra moisture.

COUSCOUS-ALMOND PUDDING

1¼ cups coconut milk

1¼ cups water

Good pinch of saffron

2 tablespoons oil

⅓ teaspoon salt

½ cup golden raisins

1⅔ cups couscous

⅔ cup sugar

1 tablespoon ground cardamom

1 tablespoon grated orange zest

1 tablespoon orange flower water

1 cup slivered almonds, toasted and coarsely ground (see Toasting Nuts, page 33)

MAKES 8 SERVINGS

Comfort food with a twist! The couscous soaks up the liquids and becomes moist and flavorful, and the seasonings work beautifully together. If you like, you can top the pudding with mint leaves and surround it with berries.

In a large pot, bring the coconut milk, water, saffron, oil, and salt to a boil. Reduce the heat to low, add the raisins, and cook for 5 minutes. Turn off the heat. Add the couscous, sugar, cardamom, orange zest, and orange flower water. Mix quickly with 2 forks, making sure no lumps remain. Immediately cover the pot tightly with 2 layers of aluminum foil and let the couscous rest for about 15 minutes. Uncover the pot, fluff the couscous again with 2 forks, and let it cool. Stir in the almonds.

To serve, pack a small lightly greased individual ramekin with the pudding and invert it onto a plate. Repeat with the remaining mixture.

APPLE FLAN WITH RASPBERRY SAUCE

FOR THE APPLES

3 tablespoons vegetable oil

6 McIntosh or Granny Smith apples, peeled, quartered, seeded, and cut into thick wedges

¼ cup light brown sugar, packed

1 tablespoon grated lemon zest

FOR THE CUSTARD

¾ cup plus 2 tablespoons sugar

3 large eggs

½ cup vegetable oil

1 cup flour

1 tablespoon vanilla

2 cups soy milk

3 tablespoons brandy

FOR THE SAUCE

One 12-ounce bag frozen unsweetened raspberries

1 cup cranberry juice

3 tablespoons sugar

¼ cup crème de cassis (available at liquor stores)

¼ cup lemon juice

2 tablespoons cornstarch, mixed with a little water until dissolved

MAKES 8–10 SERVINGS;
ABOUT 3 CUPS SAUCE

The combination of apples and custard is very French; you will love it! French flan differs from the Latin flan in that it is thickened with a little flour before baking. You may be surprised to learn that soy milk makes custard just as well as regular milk.

This raspberry sauce is delicious and can be served with many other desserts, including chocolate cake, lemon cake, cheesecake, and almond cake. If you happen to own one of those baker's (crème brûlée) torches, you can go over the whole top of the finished flan instead of putting it under the broiler.

Preheat the oven to 350°F.

To prepare the apples: In a heavy skillet, heat the oil over high heat. Add the apples and sauté for 2 to 3 minutes; do not let them get mushy. Stir in the brown sugar and lemon zest, cooking until the apples are caramelized, 2 to 3 more minutes. Grease a 9 x 13-inch pan. Spread the apple mixture in the bottom of the pan and set aside.

To make the custard: In a food processor, combine the ¾ cup sugar and the eggs and process until light and lemon-colored. Add the oil and process until just combined. Add the flour and pulse until just combined. Add the vanilla, soy milk, and brandy and pulse until just combined. Pour the custard over the apples.

Bake the flan for about 25 minutes, or until the top is very lightly browned and the custard is barely set. Turn the oven to broil. Sprinkle the 2 tablespoons of sugar on top of the flan and broil for a few seconds until lightly browned (watch it carefully, it burns easily).

To make the sauce: In a small saucepan, bring the raspberries, cranberry juice, sugar, crème de cassis, and lemon juice to a boil. Reduce the heat to medium and add the cornstarch mixture. Cook, stirring, until the mixture is just thickened and no longer looks cloudy, about 1 minute. Transfer the mixture to a food processor or blender and process until smooth. Strain the sauce. Cool completely before serving. The sauce can be made up to 2 days in advance and refrigerated.

Serve the flan warm or at room temperature, plain or with the sauce or a scoop of sorbet.

Variation: You can make an equally delicious sauce with frozen strawberries, and you won't need to strain it.

CHOCOLATE CHIP COOKIES

2 eggs

¾ cup sugar

¾ cup dark brown sugar, packed

¾ cup plus 2 tablespoons vegetable oil

1 tablespoon vanilla

2½ cups flour

¾ teaspoon baking powder

¾ teaspoon baking soda

⅛ teaspoon salt

1½ cups best-quality chocolate chips, the smaller the better

Makes about 4 dozen cookies

I always make sure I have a box filled with homemade goodies on hand for the children. So it seemed natural that, the first time my daughter Bella went away to summer camp, I would make her a batch of chocolate chip cookies for the road. Her roommates loved them, she reported, so would I mind bringing some more on visiting day? I set out to make a quadruple recipe, filled a huge canister with chocolate chip cookies, and brought it along to camp. She called me the very next day, gushing: "Thank you so much, Mommy. Everyone loved your cookies. Even the driver had some. They are all gone. The whole camp agrees: Your cookies rule!" My daughter couldn't have known that, right there and then, she had become inadvertently responsible for something very important in my summer life: The abolition of the care-package custom.

Besides high-quality ingredients, the secret of good chocolate chip cookies is a soft and chewy texture, achieved by baking them only until they are are just cooked. A good cookie sheet makes a difference too: the heavier the better, as a heavy sheet will distribute the heat evenly and gradually. They freeze well and will also keep fresh for several weeks in a sealed container.

Preheat the oven to 375°F.

Using an electric mixer, beat the eggs and sugars together until light and fluffy. Add the oil and vanilla and mix in thoroughly. Add the flour, baking powder, baking soda, and salt and mix at low speed. Fold in the chips by hand.

Drop the dough by heaping teaspoonfuls 1 inch apart onto cookie sheets lined with foil. Bake only one tray at a time. If your cookie sheets are the professional heavy-gauge type, bake the cookies for 10 minutes. If they are lighter, bake for 8 minutes. The cookies will firm up as they cool, so do not be tempted to bake them longer or they will harden.

Store the cookies in tin boxes, separating each layer with foil or wax paper so they don't stick together.

OATMEAL COOKIES

2 eggs

½ cup sugar

¾ cup brown sugar

¾ cup vegetable oil

1 tablespoon vanilla

Pinch of salt

1 cup flour, or whole wheat pastry flour

1 tablespoon baking soda

1 tablespoon baking powder

1 teaspoon cinnamon

1½ teaspoons allspice

Pinch of nutmeg

½ cup chopped walnuts

½ cup raisins, optional

3 cups old-fashioned oats

MAKES ABOUT 50 COOKIES

I am purposely putting this recipe back-to-back with the chocolate chip cookie recipe to illustrate the differences between a soft, chewy cookie and a crisp, crunchy one. These are almost as dangerous as the chocolate chip cookies, so my advice is to double the recipe: These freeze perfectly too! My son Maimon, a nutrition nut, meticulously computed the calories in these cookies and discovered that they're much less caloric than granola, which he adores. So now he crumbles oatmeal cookies on top of his yogurt instead. Try it, you might like it too! I find that old-fashioned oats work best in this recipe.

Preheat the oven to 375°F.

Using an electric mixer, beat the eggs and sugars together until light and fluffy. Add the oil and beat again. Add the vanilla, salt, flour, baking soda, baking powder, cinnamon, allspice, and nutmeg, and mix at low speed until well combined. Stir in the walnuts, raisins, if using, and oats.

Drop the dough by heaping teaspoonfuls 1 inch apart onto cookie sheets lined with foil. Bake for about 16 minutes, or a little longer, until the cookies are light brown and crisp. Let cool completely on a rack before storing in a tightly sealed container.

CRISPING COOKIES

If your cookies or biscotti need crisping and freshening, preheat your oven to 375°F for about 20 minutes. When it is good and hot, turn the oven off and put your cookies in (no space necessary between the cookies) until the oven cools.

LEMON BUTTER COOKIES

2 sticks (8 ounces) butter, at room temperature

¾ cup sugar

1 teaspoon vanilla

1 egg

¼ cup lemon juice

2 tablespoons grated lemon zest

1 teaspoon baking powder

Pinch of salt

2 cups flour

1 cup cornstarch

1 egg, beaten with a little water

Confectioners' sugar

Makes about 40 cookies

These cookies will be at their most heavenly made with butter, but if you are making them for a nondairy meal, go ahead and substitute margarine. The cornstarch makes these cookies meltingly tender.

Using an electric mixer, beat the butter and sugar together until light and fluffy. Add the vanilla and egg and beat again. Add the lemon juice, lemon zest, baking powder, salt, flour, and cornstarch (gradually) and beat at low speed until thoroughly mixed.

Shape the dough into logs about 6 inches long, 2 inches wide and 2 inches thick. Wrap each log in plastic and refrigerate for about an hour until firm enough to slice (you can also freeze and slice just before baking).

Preheat the oven to 325°F.

Using a serrated knife, cut each log into ⅛-inch thick slices, placing each on a cookie sheet lined with foil as you go. Make sure the cookies are at least ½ inch apart on the sheet. Brush the tops of the cookies with the egg wash and sprinkle on a light coating of confectioners' sugar.

Bake the cookies for about 20 minutes, until golden (do not let them get dark, or they will taste burnt). Cool completely before storing in a tightly sealed container.

CRANBERRY-HAZELNUT BISCOTTI

3 eggs

1 cup sugar

1 cup vegetable oil

2 tablespoons orange juice or soy milk

3 cups flour

1 tablespoon baking powder

¼ teaspoon salt

1 tablespoon ground cardamom

2 tablespoons orange zest

¾ cup dried cranberries

1½ cups coarsely chopped hazelnuts

1 egg mixed with 3 tablespoons water

MAKES ABOUT 60 BISCOTTI

Here's a wonderful gift for your out-of-town friends. These biscotti do not need refrigeration and are sturdy enough to withstand the rigors of shipping. They will last for about three months in a tightly sealed tin. Dried cranberries are readily available and provide tang without unwanted moisture.

Preheat the oven to 400°F.

Using an electric mixer, beat the eggs and sugar together until the mixture falls in ribbons from the beaters. Add the oil, and mix just until combined. Add the juice or soy milk, flour, baking powder, salt, cardamom, and orange zest, and mix just until the mixture turns into a smooth dough. Transfer the dough to a mixing bowl and stir in the cranberries and hazelnuts, until just evenly incorporated.

Divide the dough into 5 pieces. On a very lightly floured board, roll each piece into a 12-inch cylinder. Transfer each cylinder onto a cookie sheet lined with foil and flatten it into a log about 2½ inches wide and ½ inch thick. Make sure the shaped logs are at least 1 inch apart. Brush the logs with the egg wash.

Bake the logs for 20 minutes. Reduce the oven temperature to 325°F. When the logs are cool enough to handle, carefully transfer them to a cutting board. Using a sharp knife, cut each log into ½-inch-thick slices. Put the slices back on the cookie sheet, cut-side down, and bake for 20 more minutes or until the biscotti are golden brown and crisp.

PECAN BROWNIES

8 ounces best-quality chocolate, chopped, or 2 cups semisweet chocolate chips

2 sticks (8 ounces) margarine

4 eggs

1 cup sugar

½ cup flour (during Passover, use ½ cup potato starch)

1 tablespoon vanilla

¾ cup toasted pecans, broken into pieces, optional

MAKES 24 BROWNIES

I used to think that a brownie was just a brownie, until I made a batch with the best-quality imported chocolate. I like to bake these brownies in a round, shallow fluted pan and serve them in wedges like a tart. If you like nuts, see my tips for toasting them on page 33. If you don't like nuts, omit them and proceed with the recipe.

Preheat the oven to 375°F.

Melt the chocolate and margarine in a small saucepan over very low heat, or microwave in a bowl for about 1 minute. Using a food processor or an electric mixer, beat the eggs and sugar until light and fluffy. Add the chocolate mixture, flour, and vanilla, and pulse or mix until just combined. Fold in the nuts, if desired, by hand.

Pour the batter into a greased 11-inch round springform tart pan. Bake the brownies for 35 minutes, until the top is barely firm; they will set completely with the residual heat sticking to the pan. Let cool before cutting.

ALMOND-APRICOT TART

FOR THE CRUST

2 eggs

2 teaspoons baking powder

⅓ cup vegetable oil

½ cup sugar

2 tablespoons orange flower water

1 tablespoon vanilla

2 cups flour

FOR THE FILLING

1 cup apricot jam

4 egg whites

Dash of salt or cream of tartar

⅔ cup sugar

2 tablespoons cornstarch

1 cup finely ground almonds

MAKES 12 SERVINGS

Almonds and apricots are an ideal match, and this tart is a model of understated elegance. The crust is crumbly, cookie-like, and fragrant. My mother gets the credit for this creation.

Preheat the oven to 375°F.

To make the crust: Using a food processor or a mixer, pulse all the crust ingredients until just combined. Spread the dough in the bottom and sides of an 11-inch springform tart pan.

To make the filling: Spread the jam on top of the dough. In a bowl, beat the egg whites and salt together until they form soft peaks. Add the sugar and cornstarch gradually and beat until firm and glossy. Gently fold in the almonds by hand. Pour the egg white mixture into the pan.

Bake the tart for about 40 minutes or until the top is set and golden. Serve at room temperature.

LEMON CURD TART

FOR THE CRUST

1 stick (4 ounces) plus
1 tablespoon margarine

½ cup sugar

Pinch of salt

2 eggs

2 teaspoons vanilla

1 tablespoon grated lemon zest

2 cups flour

FOR THE LEMON CURD

2 tablespoons grated lemon zest

½ cup lemon juice, strained

1 cup sugar

3 eggs, beaten

1 stick (4 ounces) margarine
❖
Berries, for garnish

MAKES 8–10 SERVINGS;
ABOUT 2½ CUPS LEMON CURD

The crust for this tart is like a cookie dough, so you can bake it up to two days in advance. You can make the lemon curd up to a week in advance, then fill the baked crust with the curd just before serving. Tart and refreshing, lemon curd is also delicious spread on toast or muffins. You might want to double the recipe so you have an extra jar on hand.

Preheat the oven to 350°F.

To make the crust: In a food processor, combine the margarine, sugar, and salt and process until light and fluffy. Add the eggs one at a time and pulse each time until just incorporated. Add the vanilla, lemon zest, and flour and pulse for just a few more seconds. Spread the dough in an 11-inch springform tart pan and prick it all over with a fork.

Bake the crust for 30 minutes or until golden brown. Let cool completely before filling.

To make the lemon curd: Bring a small pot of water to a boil, then turn the heat to low. In a bowl set on top of the water, whisk together the lemon zest, lemon juice, and sugar. When the mixture is hot, add the eggs, whisking constantly until thick, about 7 to 8 minutes. Add the margarine and whisk until it is incorporated and the mixture looks smooth. Cool completely.

To assemble the tart, spoon the lemon curd into the cooled crust. Garnish with berries, if desired.

POACHED PEARS
WITH CHOCOLATE SAUCE

FOR THE PEARS

4 whole cloves

One 1-inch piece ginger, cut in half lengthwise

1 cinnamon stick

8 black peppercorns

16 Seckel pears, stems on

½ cup apple cider

½ cup dry red wine

½ cup sugar, or less to taste

1½ lemons, thinly sliced

FOR THE SAUCE

1 cup soy milk

¼ cup soy milk powder

¼ cup corn syrup, light or dark

8 ounces best-quality bittersweet or semisweet chocolate, chopped

4 tablespoons (½ stick) margarine, at room temperature

Pinch of salt

MAKES 8 SERVINGS;
ABOUT 2 CUPS SAUCE

Here is a dessert that is much more luxurious than the sum of its modest parts, although the pears are also delicious served just with their poaching liquid. Choose barely ripe pears. If Seckel pears are not in season, substitute medium-sized pears such as Forelli. The chocolate sauce is very versatile and can be used with cakes, puddings, and crêpes.

To poach the pears: Tie the cloves, ginger, cinnamon stick, and peppercorns in a piece of cheesecloth and set aside. Starting about ½ inch down from the stems, peel the pears. Put the cider, wine, sugar, lemon slices, cheesecloth bundle (making sure it is submerged), and pears in a pot just big enough to contain the pears, so they remain in an upright position. Bring the liquid to a boil. Reduce the heat to medium and cook, covered, for 10 minutes. Insert a knife into the fruit; it should feel barely tender. If you have to force the knife, it means that the pears should cook for a few more minutes. Cool completely.

To make the sauce: In a small saucepan, stir the soy milk, soy powder, and corn syrup together over medium heat, until it is hot but not boiling. Reduce the heat to low and add the chocolate, whisking until smooth. Turn off the heat and add the margarine and salt, whisking until the sauce is smooth and glossy. Let the sauce cool.

To serve, dip the pears in the chocolate sauce and stand them on individual plates. Spoon the poaching liquid around the pears.

MARZIPAN-STUFFED DRIED FRUIT AND NUTS

FOR THE MARZIPAN

3 cups blanched almonds (4 cups ground)

2 cups confectioners' sugar

2 egg whites

2 tablespoons orange flower water

Dash of almond extract, optional

FOR THE FRUIT AND NUTS

36 plump pitted dried dates, prunes, and/or apricots; or 72 walnut halves

MAKES ABOUT 3 DOZEN

Dried fruit stuffed with almond paste is originally a French confection, but it has been part of Moroccan cuisine for generations. My family is so fond of dried fruit and nuts that any addition to the repertoire is always welcome.

My version of almond paste is not too sweet, quite delicious, and simple to make—it puts its commercial counterpart to shame. It also freezes very well. You can buy the almonds blanched, or blanch them yourself (see box).

To make the marzipan: In a food processor, process the almonds into a very fine powder. Add the sugar, egg whites, orange flower water, and almond extract, if using. Process again, until you get a very smooth paste. Refrigerate for ½ hour before using.

To stuff the fruit: Shape little logs of almond paste and place them snugly in the center of the fruit. Make 3 oblique decorative slits in the almond paste with the back of a knife blade. If desired, place the stuffed fruit in decorative paper cases.

To stuff the nuts: Shape little balls with the almond paste, about 1½ inches in diameter. Stick a perfect toasted walnut half on opposite sides of the ball. If desired, place the stuffed nuts in decorative paper cases.

BLANCHING ALMONDS

When I was growing up, this job was entrusted to us kids. We ate one almond for every four or five we blanched, stifling our laughter at my mother's sighs as she observed how slowly the pile grew.

To blanch almonds, drop them in boiling water for a few seconds, and the skins will come right off. Be sure to dry the almonds thoroughly before proceeding with the recipe.

Ground blanched almonds can be found at some specialty food stores and are labeled "almond flour." They are perfect for the job, but smell them before using and make sure there is no trace of rancidity.

APRICOT MOUSSE

3 cups dried apricots, packed

1 pound silken tofu, thoroughly drained and dried on paper towels

¼ cup vegetable oil

¼ cup apricot brandy

Juice of 1 lemon

1 tablespoon lemon zest

4 egg whites

¼ cup sugar

MAKES 8 SERVINGS

I am always giving cooking demonstrations on making desserts with tofu. Each time I feel like an explorer who has struck gold. I can't tell you how many people I have converted—to think that you can get such elegant, delicious results from such an unlikely ingredient!

In a bowl, soak the apricots in just enough hot water to cover for ½ hour. Drain and thoroughly dry them.

In a food processor, process the apricots until perfectly smooth. With the motor running, add the tofu and oil and process until very smooth. Add the apricot brandy and lemon juice and zest and process again until smooth. Transfer the mixture to a bowl and set aside.

In another bowl, beat the egg whites with the sugar until stiff peaks form. Fold the egg whites into the reserved apricot mixture gently but thoroughly. Pour the mousse into dessert glasses, or leave it in the bowl, and refrigerate until set, 4 to 6 hours.

BAKLAVA

FOR THE FILLING

1½ pounds walnuts, ground medium-fine

½ cup sugar

2 tablespoons cinnamon

1 tablespoon ground ginger

1 teaspoon ground cloves

3 tablespoons orange flower water

2 tablespoons lemon extract
❊
1 pound phyllo sheets (see Working with Phyllo, page 31)

¾ cup vegetable oil (you might not need it all)

2 cups honey

¼ cup toasted sesame seeds

MAKES 48 PIECES

I know that many cookbooks offer a recipe for this Mediterranean classic, but I couldn't resist sharing my discovery with you: When you pour plain honey on hot baklava, it absorbs it completely, ending all the sticky mess syrup tends to make. Just use honey straight from the jar!

Preheat the oven to 375°F.

To make the filling: Mix all the filling ingredients together thoroughly in a bowl.

Stack the phyllo sheets on a cutting board. Cut through the whole stack crosswise. Make a new pile by stacking the two piles: The sheets should now be the same dimensions as the pan you are using. If they are a little bigger, trim them to fit. If they are a little smaller, overlap the leaves to fill the blank spaces.

Brush a 9 x 13-inch pan with oil. Working very quickly, place 3 sheets of phyllo neatly in the pan and brush them lightly with oil. Repeat this process four more times (you will use 15 phyllo leaves). Spread half the filling evenly on top of the phyllo. Repeat this process with 15 more phyllo leaves (and oil), and spread the remaining filling evenly on top of the phyllo. Repeat the process with the remaining 15 phyllo leaves (and oil).

Using a serrated knife, cut through the top set of leaves (this is called scoring): 3 times lengthwise, 5 times crosswise, then diagonally across each rectangle to make 48 pieces. Brush the top of the baklava with oil.

Bake for 35 minutes or until the baklava is golden brown and crisp. Remove the pan from the oven and immediately pour the honey evenly over the top. Sprinkle on the sesame seeds. Watch the honey disappear through all the hot layers. Cool the baklava completely. To serve, cut all the way through the scored lines to make individual pieces.

STRAWBERRY-WINE MOLDS

3 cups cranberry juice

2 cups dry red wine (Burgundy or Bordeaux)

Juice of 2 lemons

6 cups frozen strawberries (about three 12-ounce packages)

½ teaspoon allspice

One 12-ounce jar red currant jelly

3 tablespoons crème de cassis (available at liquor stores)

¼ cup sugar

⅔ cup cornstarch, dissolved in a little cold water (during Passover, substitute potato starch)

FOR THE GARNISH

Sliced strawberries

Mint sprigs

Whipped cream

MAKES 8 SERVINGS

Here's the Jell-O of your childhood revisited. These are tart, spicy, and refreshing. You will love the brilliant color and luxurious texture.

In a medium pot, combine the cranberry juice, wine, lemon juice, strawberries, allspice, jelly, cassis, and sugar. Bring to a boil. Reduce the heat to low and cook for about 5 minutes. Add the cornstarch mixture and cook 10 more minutes, until thickened.

Transfer the mixture to a food processor and process until perfectly smooth.

Pour into individual serving glasses or ramekins and refrigerate until set, about 8 hours. Top each serving with a sliced strawberry and a sprig of mint, if desired. (If you are serving this dessert with a dairy meal, top each serving with whipped cream.)

Favorites from Levana Restaurant

The restaurant business is in our blood. When my daughter Bella was just a little girl, she wrote, "The Little Red Riding Hood got lost in the woods. She was terrified, she started crying for her mommy, she was exhausted. And then she got hungry and went to a restaurant." I am sorry I didn't keep a diary of our early days at Levana Restaurant, but I remember a few gems, which I would like to share with you.

When we were still a bakery, a gentleman came every day and settled at a table for several hours, ordering only a cookie and a cup of coffee that he had refilled, free of charge, a dozen times. His tip? "I left you *The New York Times*," he would say with a big-spender wink.

The super of the restaurant's building, a colossus of a man, would come charging in every day during lunchtime and boom, "Give me a roll with a hole in the middle, whatever the hell you call it!" For years he refused with a vengeance to call it a bagel. "That's Jewish talk, not for me," he would say each time.

A customer once came for dinner and ordered the very best dishes and wines on our menu. We marveled at his bottomless appetite, as he ate unhurriedly and with great gusto. When he was finally presented with the bill, he reached for his breast pocket and produced . . . a dollar bill, which he majestically handed to the stunned waiter. I still remember my irate mother-in-law yelling after him in the street, with a formidable Russian accent: "I hope you choke on it!"

During one of our first annual wine-pairing dinners, we were served quail. If you have ever eaten quail, you probably know that the color of its needle-thin bones is identical to that of its flesh. And that's how I found myself with a bone stuck in my throat. Torn between panic and good manners, I mouthed the words "Call Hatzalah!" (our local,

dedicated volunteer ambulance service) to my husband Maurice, and a moment later we quietly rushed out to the ambulance, leaving our stunned guests to finish their dinner. In the emergency room at Roosevelt Hospital, we were met by an eager but green young medical student, who proceeded to read about choking from a huge medical dictionary. I had to wait for the medical staff to arrive in the morning and was given a heavy bucket of janitor's supplies to hold in each hand, causing my shoulder-line to drop and reveal an X-ray of the bone! I remember the frenzy that set in as I was wheeled into the operating room, with a team of plastic surgeons working on me. The bone became famous, and the doctors fought to keep it. Well, I thought, they can have it! I don't even care that I choked in style: It would have been a chic but stupid way to go!

Here are some of our favorite dishes. I have purged the recipes of their impenetrable chef's jargon and streamlined them considerably in order to make them accessible—but every bit as delicious—for you in your home kitchen. Remember, I am in the home cook's corner!

Specialty butcher shops will be happy to secure fancy cuts of meat for you, provided you give them a couple of days' notice. You can have all cuts of meat trimmed and ground as needed.

Opposite: Parsley-Crusted Baby Rack of Lamb

PARSLEY-CRUSTED BABY RACK OF LAMB

¼ cup flat-leaf parsley, leaves and stems

1 large clove garlic

1 tablespoon Dijon mustard

1 tablespoon olive oil

1½ teaspoons coarsely ground pepper

¾ teaspoon cumin

¾ teaspoon ground coriander

1 whole baby rack of lamb, bones completely trimmed and left long

MAKES 2 SERVINGS

Do you still get misty-eyed when your wedding anniversary rolls around? If you can't take your spouse to Levana Restaurant to celebrate, the next best thing will be this baby rack of lamb (see photo, page 184), ready in a snap and served at home. One rack feeds two people: That's you! Serve with mashed potatoes and steamed baby vegetables drizzled with a little olive oil and sea salt.

Preheat the oven to 500°F.

Combine the parsley, garlic, mustard, olive oil, pepper, cumin, and coriander in a food processor and process until smooth.

Place the lamb meat-side up in a baking pan. Cover the meatless part of the bones with foil. Spread the parsley mixture evenly on the meat, using up all of it. Bake 20 to 25 minutes for medium rare.

To serve, slice between the chops with a sharp knife. Allow 4 chops per person.

PORCINI-CRUSTED BLACK SEA BASS
WITH MINT SAUCE

FOR THE SAUCE

½ cup fresh mint leaves, packed

1 cup boiling water

¾ cup dry vermouth

1½ tablespoons olive oil

1½ medium shallots, quartered

½ cup domestic mushrooms

1½ tablespoons flour

2 tablespoons soy milk

Salt and pepper

FOR THE FISH

1½ tablespoons porcini powder

1 tablespoon instant organic potato flakes (available at health food stores)

2 tablespoons flour

1½ tablespoons olive oil

4 fillets of black sea bass (about 6 ounces each), skin on, patted dry

Salt and pepper

1 tablespoon Dijon mustard, mixed with a few drops of water

MAKES 4 SERVINGS;
ABOUT ¾ CUP SAUCE

Moi, use potato flakes? The organic kind is all natural and, paired with the porcini powder, provides an ethereal crunch. Porcini powder is available at specialty food stores, or make your own by grinding dried porcini into powder in a food processor.

To make the sauce: In a large bowl, combine the mint and boiling water, cover, and steep for at least 15 minutes. Strain and transfer liquid to a small saucepan. Add the vermouth and cook over high heat until reduced to about ½ cup, about 5 to 7 minutes.

Heat the oil in a skillet over high heat. Combine the shallots and mushrooms in a food processor and pulse until coarsely chopped. Add this mixture to the skillet and sauté until all the liquid evaporates, 4 to 5 minutes. Reduce the heat to low and whisk in the flour. Turn the heat up to medium and whisk in the hot vermouth mixture in a slow stream. Whisk in the

soy milk and salt and pepper to taste and simmer for another 3 minutes. Strain the sauce.

To prepare the fish: Combine the porcini powder, potato flakes, and flour on a plate and set aside. Heat the oil in a large skillet over high heat. Season the fillets with salt and pepper to taste, dip them in the mustard, then roll them in the porcini powder mixture. Place the fillets in the skillet, skin-side down, and cook for about 3 minutes, or until the skin looks crisp. Turn the fillets over and cook for 2 more minutes.

Serve hot, with the sauce drizzled over the fish.

SALMON MEDALLIONS WITH CHARDONNAY-CELERY ROOT SAUCE

FOR THE FISH

1 side salmon, about 3 pounds, tail cut off, skin and bones removed

Juice of 1 lime or lemon

2 tablespoons olive oil

Salt and pepper

FOR THE SAUCE

2 cups Chardonnay

2 tablespoons olive oil

2 tablespoons green peppercorns in brine, lightly crushed

4 boneless anchovies, rinsed well

1 small celery root, peeled and cut into ½-inch cubes

4 shallots, thinly sliced

2 sprigs fresh thyme, leaves only

2 sprigs tarragon, leaves only

1 cup water

4 chives, thinly sliced

Freshly ground pepper

MAKES 6 SERVINGS;
1½ CUPS SAUCE

You will love the neat, rounded shape of these medallions. The sauce is thickened naturally by the light starch of the celery root.

To prepare the fish: Cut off the flat opaque strip that runs the whole length of the salmon side and discard. Cut the salmon into 6 slices about 1½ inches thick. Next cut through each of these slices, stopping before the end so each slice remains in one piece; you will have 6 very thin, long rectangles. Roll each rectangle tightly to create 6 medallions. Secure each medallion with 2 short skewers stuck into the fish at right angles.

Rub the medallions with the lemon juice, oil, and salt and pepper to taste. Place the medallions in a foil-lined pan just large enough to hold them. Bake for 20 minutes.

To make the sauce: Combine the wine, olive oil, peppercorns, anchovies, celery root, shallots, thyme, tarragon, and water in a saucepan and bring to a boil. Cook for about 20 minutes, until the liquid is reduced to about 1½ cups. Puree the sauce until smooth in a food processor or blender, then strain through a medium strainer. Stir in the chives and pepper to taste.

To serve, pour the sauce over the salmon medallions and serve hot.

CHICKEN AND DUCK LIVER SALAD WITH WARM RED WINE VINAIGRETTE

FOR THE LIVERS

½ pound chicken livers

½ pound duck livers

3 tablespoons duck fat

FOR THE VINAIGRETTE

4 large cloves garlic, thinly sliced

2 medium shallots, thinly sliced

¼ cup dry white wine

¼ cup red wine vinegar

2 sprigs thyme, leaves only

Salt and freshly ground pepper

❈

6 cups frisée or romaine lettuce leaves, torn into bite-sized pieces

Makes 6 servings

Because of their high blood content, livers undergo a separate koshering process. They are not soaked and salted as are poultry and meat, but must be broiled to draw out excess blood. This is the reason why they are always packed and sealed separately. Although chicken livers are easily obtainable, duck livers must be ordered as a specialty item. Likewise, duck fat is available only upon request. What a treat!

Preheat the broiler.

To prepare the livers: Broil the livers on all sides just until they are no longer pink, about 3 minutes on each side. When the livers are cool, slice them about ¼-inch thick and set aside. Heat the duck fat in a skillet over high heat. Add the liver slices and sauté for 1 minute. Remove the livers with a slotted spoon.

To make the vinaigrette: Add the garlic and shallots to the skillet the livers were cooked in and sauté until translucent, about 3 minutes. Add the wine, vinegar, thyme, and salt and pepper to taste and cook for 2 to 3 more minutes.

To serve, toss the lettuce leaves with the warm vinaigrette on a platter and top with the livers.

ROAST DUCKLING
WITH MAPLE-ORANGE SAUCE

FOR THE DUCKS

2 ducks, about 5 pounds each

1 large onion, coarsely chopped

1 large carrot, coarsely chopped

3 ribs celery, coarsely chopped

FOR THE SAUCE

1 large orange, unpeeled, cut into 1-inch cubes

1 lemon, unpeeled, cut into 1-inch cubes

1 Granny Smith apple, unpeeled, cut into 1-inch cubes

½ cup maple syrup

1 cup strong Lapsang souchong tea (2 tea bags steeped in 1 cup boiling water for 10 minutes)

1 cup dry red wine

10 juniper berries, lightly crushed with a rolling pin

2 sprigs thyme, leaves only

2 sprigs sage, leaves only

Freshly ground pepper

MAKES 6–8 SERVINGS;
1½ CUPS SAUCE

The combination of Lapsang souchong tea and maple syrup provides a marvelous mahogany glaze and a smoky flavor. The duck is delicious served with cooked tiny green lentils and roasted root vegetables.

Duck skin is very thick and releases enormous amounts of fat during the roasting process. The trick is to drain all that fat thoroughly, but don't discard it! Store it in a glass jar in the refrigerator. You can also save cooked duck skin for other uses—heat it in a skillet until very crisp and dark, and crumble it, you will get delicious duck cracklings. Add the cracklings and a dollop of duck fat to mashed potatoes or noodles; it doesn't get better than this!

Preheat the oven to 500°F.

To prepare the ducks: Tie the ducks' feet together with string and pierce the skin with a knife in several places to let the fat escape during roasting, taking care not to pierce the flesh. Place the ducks breast-side down in a roasting pan. Scatter the onion, carrot, and celery around the ducks.

Roast for 45 minutes. Lower the oven temperature to 375°F and roast for another 20 minutes. Remove the fat from the pan (reserve for other uses) and turn the ducks over. Transfer the vegetables and any cooking juices to a saucepan and set aside. Return the ducks to the oven, turn the temperature back up to 500°F, and roast for 15 more minutes.

To make the sauce: Add the orange, lemon, apple, maple syrup, tea, wine, juniper, thyme, sage, and pepper to taste to the saucepan with the reserved vegetables and juices. Bring the mixture to a boil. Reduce the heat to medium-high and cook for about 15 minutes or until the sauce is thickened and reduced to about 1½ cups. Strain the sauce, pressing on the solids to extract flavors.

When the ducks are done, transfer them to a cutting board and let rest for a few minutes. Carve the ducks and transfer the meat to a serving platter. Pour the sauce over the ducks before serving.

ROAST GOOSE WITH MUSHROOM GRAVY AND WILD RICE-CHESTNUT STUFFING

FOR THE STUFFING

7 cups water

2½ cups wild rice, rinsed and drained

¼ cup olive oil

1 large onion, quartered

3 shallots

4 ribs celery, peeled and halved

1 large bunch flat-leaf parsley

1 pound fresh chestnuts, boiled, peeled, and coarsely chopped (see page 114), or 1 cup dried chestnuts, boiled, drained, and chopped

Salt and pepper

FOR THE GOOSE AND GRAVY

1 goose, 12 to 14 pounds

1 bottle dry white wine

2 medium onions, sliced paper-thin in a food processor

6 bay leaves

2 tablespoons juniper berries, lightly crushed with a rolling pin

2 tablespoons coarsely ground black pepper

3 sprigs fresh rosemary, coarsely chopped, or 2 tablespoons dry rosemary

1 tablespoon dry sage

1½ pounds mixed wild mushrooms such as shiitake, morels, and chanterelles, sliced (discard shiitake stems)

Makes 12 servings

You will create quite a sensation with this dish—food doesn't get more luxurious than this. But goose doesn't come cheap, so don't waste any of it. Save the liver for broiling, and slice it into the gravy. Save the fat that accumulates during roasting, store it in a glass jar in the refrigerator, and use it for flavoring rice, pasta, or mashed potatoes. The bones and scraps make a fabulous broth.

To make the stuffing: Bring the water to a boil in a large pot. Add the rice and cook until the grains just begin to open, about 35 minutes.

Meanwhile, heat the oil in a heavy skillet over high heat. Combine the onion, shallot, celery, and parsley in food processor and pulse until coarsely chopped. Add this mixture to the skillet and sauté until the vegetables are translucent, about 3 minutes. Stir in the chestnuts and salt and pepper to taste.

Preheat the oven to 450°F.

To prepare the goose and the gravy: Wash and dry the goose thoroughly, removing the neck, giblets, and liver, saving them for another use. Prick the skin all over with a fork to let the fat escape during the roasting. Stuff the goose loosely with the prepared stuffing. Place the goose breast-side down in a heavy roasting pan, just large enough to accommodate the bird. Cover the goose with a triple layer of cheesecloth.

In a bowl, combine the wine, onions, bay leaves, juniper berries, pepper, rosemary, and sage. Pour this mixture over the goose, making sure to thoroughly soak the cheesecloth.

Roast the goose for about 45 minutes. Reduce the oven temperature to 325°F and bake for 2½ more hours, basting every 30 minutes (make sure the cheesecloth gets soaked each time you baste). Remove the cheesecloth and turn the goose over, breast-side up. Bake for 1 hour, or until the juices run clear. Transfer the goose to a carving board and let it stand for 15 minutes before carving.

While the goose is standing, make the gravy. Remove the fat from the cooking liquids and reserve for another use. Strain the remaining cooking liquids into a saucepan and add the mushrooms. Cook, uncovered, over high heat, until the gravy is reduced to 4 cups, 5 to 8 minutes.

To serve, remove the stuffing from the goose cavity and transfer it to a bowl. Carve the goose, arrange it on a platter, and serve with the gravy and stuffing.

VENISON TERRINE

¾ pound chicken or duck livers

1½ pounds venison shoulder,
ground medium coarse

½ pound smoked turkey breast,
cut into ⅓-inch cubes

1 black truffle, fresh or canned,
minced

1 cup pistachios, toasted
(see Toasting Nuts, page 33)

4 medium shallots, minced

¼ cup minced flat-leaf parsley

1 tablespoon dried rosemary

1½ teaspoons dried sage

1½ teaspoons allspice

1½ teaspoons white pepper

3 tablespoons green peppercorns
in brine

½ cup flour

2 eggs

¼ cup dry sherry

¼ cup brandy or bourbon

⅓ cup extra virgin olive oil
❈
Dijon mustard, for serving

Gherkin pickles, for serving

Makes 12–14 first-course
servings

Rather than wax apologetic for the outrageous list of ingredients in this recipe, I urge you to make it for a special occasion and enjoy it with special friends. (You can substitute ground chicken or turkey for the venison when you are in a more modest mood.)

Preheat the broiler.

Broil the livers just until they are no longer pink, about 3 minutes per side. Cut the livers into ⅓-inch cubes. Reduce the oven temperature to 375°F.

Combine the livers and the rest of the ingredients in a large bowl, mixing thoroughly. If the mixture seems too loose, add a little flour. Pour the mixture into a greased 6- to 8-cup mold, packing it tightly. Cover the mold with foil, place it in a baking pan, and fill the pan with enough hot water to come about two thirds up the sides of the mold.

Bake the terrine for 1½ hours. Bring the mold to room temperature, top it evenly with weights (bricks or heavy cans), and chill.

To serve, pour off any liquids that have accumulated on the terrine, then unmold it. Cut into slices, ⅓-inch thick if serving as a first course, or ½-inch thick if serving as a main course. Serve the terrine with Dijon mustard and gherkins.

VENISON LOIN WITH RED CURRANT-WINE SAUCE AND CHESTNUT-SWEET POTATO PUREE

FOR THE SAUCE

2–3 pounds venison bones and scraps

1 medium onion, cut into ½-inch cubes

1 large carrot, cut into ½-inch cubes

2 ribs celery, peeled and diced

2 quarts (8 cups) water

2 cups dry red wine

2 sprigs thyme, leaves only

3 bay leaves

1 tablespoon juniper berries, lightly crushed with a rolling pin

Coarsely ground pepper

¼ cup red currant preserves

FOR THE PUREE

1 pound dried chestnuts (available at specialty and health food stores)

4 medium sweet potatoes, peeled and cut into 1-inch cubes

8 medium shallots, peeled and quartered

¼ cup olive oil

Pinch of nutmeg

Salt and pepper

6 cups water

FOR THE VENISON

3 tablespoons olive oil

1 venison loin (about 3 pounds), cut into 12 one-inch-thick slices

Makes 6 servings; 1¼ cups sauce

The venison loin is a strip about 12 inches long and 2 to 3 inches in diameter. When buying the loin, ask your butcher for venison bones and scraps, which will make the base of your sauce.

My son Yakov loves to hang around in the kitchen when he finds me cooking, declaiming, "The day will come when the sweet potato and the turnip will bow down to the potato, when the avocado will bow down to the cucumber." Yet he can down this puree in no time. That's because I call all mushes mashed potatoes when he's around. So what's in a name?

Preheat the oven to 450°F.

To make the sauce: Place the bones and scraps, onion, carrot, and celery on a baking sheet and roast for about 20 minutes. Transfer the mixture to a large pot, add the water, and bring to a boil over high heat. Cook, covered, for about 45 minutes.

Add the wine, thyme, bay leaves, juniper berries, and pepper to taste, and cook for another 15 minutes or until the liquid is reduced to 1½ cups. Add the preserves and cook for 1 minute more. Strain the sauce, pressing on the solids to extract maximum flavor. Keep the sauce warm while you cook the meat.

To make the puree: Place all the puree ingredients in a large pot and bring to a boil. Reduce the heat to medium and cook, covered, for 40 minutes or until the chestnuts are tender. The mixture must look dry. If any liquid remains in the pot, reduce it over high heat. Mash the mixture with a potato masher. Keep the puree warm while you cook the meat.

To prepare the venison: Heat the oil in a skillet over high heat. Add the venison slices and sear to the desired degree of doneness, about 2 minutes on each side for medium rare.

To serve, allow 2 slices per guest. Drizzle the sauce over the meat and the puree, and around the plate.

BISON BURGERS WITH VIDALIA ONIONS AND CHIPOTLE SAUCE

FOR THE SAUCE

2 canned chipotle peppers, with 2 tablespoons of the liquid

½ cup ketchup

4 large cloves garlic

6 sprigs cilantro

Salt

FOR THE ONIONS AND BURGERS

3 tablespoons olive oil

2 large Vidalia onions, thinly sliced

2 pounds ground bison

Freshly ground pepper

6 hamburger buns, split

2 beefsteak tomatoes, thinly sliced

MAKES 6 SERVINGS;
ABOUT 1 CUP SAUCE

Bison is also known as buffalo. The good news about this expensive treat is that in addition to being succulent, bison meat is very lean and low in cholesterol, placing it head and shoulders above all other kinds of meat. Chipotles are smoked chilis and are most commonly found canned. Use them sparingly; they're hot, hot, hot! You might want to make a large batch of the sauce, as it keeps very well. Try your best to find Vidalia onions, as they are sweet and delicious and will offset the other robust flavors of the dish beautifully.

To make the sauce: Combine all the sauce ingredients in a food processor and process until smooth. Store in a glass jar in the refrigerator.

To prepare the onions and burgers: Heat the oil in a skillet over medium heat. Add the onions and cook, covered, until brown, about 20 minutes. Set aside.

Preheat the broiler or grill.

Mix together the meat and pepper to taste. Form 6 patties about 1 inch thick. Broil the patties for about 3 minutes on each side for medium-rare.

Toast the buns in the broiler for about 1 minute.

To serve, spread some of the onions on each bun and top with a burger, tomatoes, and a dab of the sauce.

CHESTNUT-CHOCOLATE TRUFFLES

2 cups dried chestnuts

2 sticks (8 ounces) unsalted margarine

2 cups best-quality semisweet chocolate chips

1 cup sugar

¼ cup brandy

2 cups chopped toasted hazelnuts (see Toasting Nuts, page 33)

MAKES ABOUT 3 DOZEN TRUFFLES

Luscious and intriguing—and so easy! Chestnuts and chocolate have a natural affinity and team up with crunchy toasted hazelnuts to produce these luxurious treats. Thanks to the availability of dried chestnuts, you can enjoy these truffles anytime.

In a saucepan, boil the chestnuts in water to cover for about 40 minutes, until tender. Drain thoroughly.

In a saucepan, combine the margarine, chocolate chips, sugar, and brandy over very low heat until just melted (or microwave for 2 minutes). In a food processor, process the chestnuts until smooth. Add the chocolate mixture and process for a few more seconds. Transfer

the mixture to a bowl and stir in the hazelnuts.

Grease a 1½-quart rectangle mold or loaf pan and line it with plastic, letting the sides overhang. Pour in the batter, and fold the plastic toward the center of the mold. Refrigerate until set, 3 to 4 hours. Unmold the loaf and cut it into 1¼-inch cubes. The truffles will keep in the refrigerator for up to 3 weeks.

FROZEN HALVAH-PECAN TERRINE WITH MAPLE-RUM SAUCE AND PECAN LACE COOKIES

FOR THE TERRINE

½ cup soy milk powder

2 tablespoons cornstarch

½ cup cold water

1 cup sugar

4 eggs

1 cup boiling water

1 pound extra-firm tofu

2 pounds vanilla halvah

1 teaspoon maple extract

1 tablespoon vanilla

1 cup pecans, toasted and coarsely chopped (see Toasting Nuts, page 33)

FOR THE SAUCE

½ cup maple syrup

¼ cup dark corn syrup

¼ cup soy milk powder mixed with ½ cup cold water

¼ cup rum

FOR THE COOKIES

⅓ cup dark corn syrup

¼ teaspoon cream of tartar

½ stick (4 tablespoons) unsalted margarine

⅓ cup brown sugar

½ cup toasted pecans, chopped

½ cup flour

3 tablespoons quick oats

Pinch of salt

1½ teaspoons vanilla

MAKES 12 OR MORE SERVINGS; ABOUT
1 CUPS SAUCE; 3 DOZEN COOKIES

Crumbled halvah and toasted pecans add a delightful crunch to this unusual frozen treat. In order to make unmolding easier, use a springform pan. The sauce is very versatile. Make a big recipe and serve it with crêpes, flan, ice cream, and more. The same goes for the cookies the recipe makes three dozen, so you'll have plenty of leftovers.

To make the terrine: In a small bowl, mix the soy milk powder and cornstarch with the water and set aside. Bring a few inches of water to a boil in a double boiler. Reduce the heat to low, keeping the water at a simmer. Combine the sugar, eggs, reserved soy milk mixture, and boiling water in the top of the double boiler, whisking constantly until thickened, 3 to 4 minutes. Let the mixture cool slightly.

Drain the tofu and pat it dry; crumble 1 pound of the halvah and leave the other pound whole. Combine the tofu, maple extract, vanilla, and whole halvah in a food processor and process for a full 3 minutes. Add the egg mixture and process for a few more seconds. Transfer the mixture to a bowl and stir in the crumbled halvah and pecans. Pour the mixture into a spring-form 1½-quart rectangle mold or loaf pan, greased and lined with plastic. Freeze the terrine for 6 to 8 hours.

To make the sauce: Bring all the sauce ingredients to a boil in a small saucepan.

Reduce the heat to medium and cook for about 5 minutes. Let the sauce cool before storing in a glass jar.

To make the cookies: Preheat the oven to 375°F.

In a saucepan, heat the corn syrup, cream of tartar, margarine, and sugar over low heat until just melted. Turn off the heat and add the pecans, flour, oats, salt, and vanilla. Mix until well combined.

Drop by half-teaspoonfuls 2 inches apart onto cookie sheets lined with foil (the cookies expand greatly). Bake for 8 minutes. If the cookies are not perfectly crisp 1 minute after they come out of the oven, put them back in for 1 to 2 minutes. Let cool and store in an airtight container. Do not refrigerate.

To serve, take the terrine out of the freezer a few minutes before serving. Unmold it and cut it into thin slices. Drizzle some sauce over each slice and stand a cookie in the center of the slice.

MENUS

Here are twenty menus for all occasions. These are only suggestions of course, but I composed these menus with the main guidelines in mind—budget, texture, color, and preparation times.

A MOROCCAN BANQUET
Moroccan Fish Cakes in Lemon Sauce
Chicken Couscous
Moroccan Tomato Salad
Roasted Beet and Swiss Chard Salad
Marzipan-Stuffed Dried Fruit and Nuts

AN ASIAN DINNER
Miso, Shiitake, and Swiss Chard Soup
Salmon Teriyaki
Grilled Marinated Steak with Green Peppercorn Sauce
Vegetable Fried Rice
Chinese Pickled Cabbage

A FRENCH DINNER
Wild Mushroom Soup
Baked Striped Bass Niçoise
Herbed Sautéed New Potatoes
Celery Root and Cabbage Salad with Rémoulade
Apple Flan with Raspberry Sauce

AN ITALIAN DINNER
Cream of Broccoli and Watercress Soup
Marinated Tomato Salad
Farfalle with Broccoli and Salmon
Wild Mushroom, Asparagus, and Tomato Ragout
Tiramisu

AN INDIAN DINNER
Curried Butternut Squash Soup
Lamb and Eggplant Curry
Basmati Rice
Paratha (Indian Skillet Flatbread)
Couscous-Almond Pudding

A LATIN DINNER
Herb-Marinated Olives
Potato-Leek Frittata
Chili Sans Carne
Tuna Burgers with Watercress-Wasabi Sauce

Fresh Corn Salad
Almond-Wine Cake

A WEEKDAY DINNER
Tricolor Ribbon Salad with Cider-Shallot Dressing
Chicken Breasts in Garlic-Lemon Sauce
Herbed Sautéed New Potatoes
Sautéed Spinach
Chocolate Chip Cookies

A VEGETARIAN DINNER
Mushroom-Chestnut Pâté with Green Goddess Sauce
Stir-Fried Tofu and Vegetables on Soba Noodles
Salad of Mesclun and Avocado with Basil-Honey Dressing
Carrot Cake

A SALAD DINNER
Wild Rice Salad on Sautéed Watercress
Fresh Corn Salad
Chinese Beef Salad
Minted Tabbouleh Salad
Tricolor Ribbon Salad with Cider-Shallot Dressing

A SHABBOS DINNER
Cold Poached Salmon with Horseradish-Dill Sauce
Spinach, Cranberry, and Mango Salad with Curried
    Mango Dressing
Pot-au-Feu
Almond-Apricot Tart

A PURIM BUFFET
Blackened Tuna with Black Bean Salsa
Moroccan Tomato Salad
Beef Chunks with Lemon-Oregano Sauce
Chicken Tagine with Prunes and Almonds
Champagne Risotto with Arugula, Peas, and Asparagus
Mashed Potatoes
Chocolate Cake
Frozen Halvah-Pecan Terrine with Maple-Rum Sauce and
    Pecan Lace Cookies

Opposite: An Indian dinner

A PASSOVER DINNER

Trout Stuffed with Gefilte Fish in Jellied Broth

Matzoh Ball Soup

Brisket in Sweet-and-Sour Sauce

Cider-Roasted Turkey with Dried Fruit Stuffing

Artichokes and Carrots in Lemon Sauce

Potato Kugel (see Potato Latkes)

Almond-Wine Cake

Poached Pears with Chocolate Sauce

A SHAVOUOT DINNER

Onion Soup

Salad of Mesclun and Avocado with Basil-Honey
    Dressing

Sea Bass Stew

Linguine with Wild Mushrooms

Chocolate-Espresso Cheesecake

A THANKSGIVING DINNER

Venison Terrine

Cider-Roasted Turkey with Dried Fruit Stuffing

Hot and Sweet Parsnips

Braised Red Cabbage and Apples

Chocolate-Hazelnut Mousse Torte

A CELEBRATION DINNER FOR TWO

Wild Mushroom Soup

Arugula, Pear, and Walnut Salad with Walnut
    Vinaigrette

Parsley-Crusted Baby Rack of Lamb

Steamed Baby Vegetables

Wild Rice

Flambé Apple Crêpes with Maple-Rum Sauce

"GOING ALL OUT" DINNER FOR TWELVE

Salmon Medallions with Chardonnay-Celery Root Sauce

Chicken and Duck Liver Salad with Warm Red Wine
    Vinaigrette

Roast Goose with Mushroom Gravy and Wild Rice-
    Chestnut Stuffing

Asparagus and *Haricots Verts*

Apple-Pear Strudel

Chocolate-Hazelnut Parfait (see Chocolate-Hazelnut
    Mousse Torte)

CELEBRATING ON A BUDGET

Chili sans Carne with Guacamole and Corn Chips

Chicken Paella

Hot and Sweet Parsnips

Grilled Minted Beef Kabobs

Kasha with Mushrooms and Onions

Chocolate Chip Cookies

Orange-Poppy Seed Cake

JUST FINGER FOODS FOR A CROWD

Salmon Tartare

Nori-Wrapped Fish Sausages with Watercress-Wasabi Sauce

Herb-Marinated Olives

Chinese Pickled Cabbage

Liver Pâté with Brandy and Green Peppercorns

Individual Pastillas

Curried Chicken Salad in Tiny Crêpes

Vegetable Latkes (see Potato Latkes)

Herb Focaccia (see Basic White Bread)

Cranberry-Hazelnut Biscotti

Chestnut-Chocolate Truffles

Marzipan-Stuffed Dried Fruit and Nuts

A COLD SUMMER LUNCH

Cold Fruit Soup

Salade Niçoise with Grilled Tuna

Mixed Roasted Vegetables

Pecan Brownies

BRUNCH

Arugula, Pear, and Walnut Salad with Walnut Vinaigrette

Spinach-Ricotta Pie

Gravlax

Cheese Logs

Skillet Cornbread

Lemon Cake

KOSHER WINES

The vindication of kosher dining as a genuine gourmet experience is no small part of the culinary revolution of our era. Contemporary chefs have stopped characterizing kosher meals as overcooked, heavy, and dull. Gifted kosher chefs have inaugurated a style that is simultaneously kosher and internationally sophisticated. Not surprisingly, the wine industry has followed suit, battling popular misconceptions that were fixated on the sweet ritual wines associated with Shabbos and other festive meals. Today's kosher wines include crisp whites and mellow reds that are beginning to win medals in international competitions. They provide the perfect accompaniment to elegant kosher meals.

Kosher laws governing wine apply only to the method of handling the grapes. The equipment must be exclusively reserved for the kosher product; only Shabbos-observant Jews may process the grapes (unless the wines are *mevushal*—see below); yeasts and other substances used in the process must be kosher; and no artificial substances or preservatives may be introduced.

The apparent mystery of mevushal is equally straightforward. Because mevushal indicated a process similar to pasteurization, early critics recoiled from the notion of "boiling" wine—and perhaps in those days the objection was legitimate. Today, mevushal means that the crushed grape juice is flash-heated to approximately 85°C for mere seconds before immediate cooling; it is *never boiled*. The final product enjoys several advantages: handling by non-orthodox personnel will not affect kashrut and, on the plus side, the process has been shown to enhance the aroma of white wine and the shelf stability of all varieties, and certain flavors are actually improved.

Terroir, the defining factor that controls the quality of all fine wines, is a matter of geography, climate, and harvest conditions—the rules of kashrut exert no effect whatever on terroir. The most significant determinant of wine quality, in tandem with expert vinification, is the nature of the grape, as determined by the local terroir. The reason that the first kosher wines were so dauntingly sweet is that in New York, the only grapes available were acidic Concords, which required massive infusions of sugar to be merely palatable. When an elite, haute-kosher population discovered the pleasures of wine with food, kosher-conscious grape-growing frontiers opened up in California (Baron Herzog and Hagafen), in Europe (Italy's Bartenura and France's Château Giscours in the famous Bordeaux region), and nonsectarian Korbel has even launched a fine kosher sparkling wine. Most notably, a kosher Israeli wine industry is thriving and earning an international reputation. Thanks to the stimulation of European and Californian vintners and an exciting microclimate, Israeli wines are no longer about sweet Manischewitz, or even about the initially mediocre Carmel

products, which started sweet but are making sophisticated strides. Globally respected labels bear the names of Golan, Tishbi, Dalton, Katzrin, Yarden, Segal, Benyamina, and there are more to come. They honor any table, kosher and otherwise, eliciting a loud *L'Chaim* to the marriage of kosher food and kosher wine.

Here is a list of kosher wines I would recommend. Although it is extensive, it is by no means exhaustive, and most good liquor stores will be able to recommend many more excellent choices.

SPARKLING WINES
Champagne, Kedem (New York)
Blanc de Blancs, Bartenura (Italy)
Asti Spumanti, Rashi (Italy)
Asti Spumanti, Bartenura (Italy)
Brut, Baron Herzog (California)
Brut de Blancs Royale (France)
Brut Cuvée, Hagafen (California)
Cremant d'Alsace, Abarbanel (France)

LIQUEURS AND BRANDIES
Bartenura liqueurs (etrog, lime, mandarin, lemon)
Leroux liqueurs (crème de cassis, applejack, triple sec,
    curaçao, peppermint, apricot)
Sherry Royale, Kedem (New York)
Sweet Vermouth, Kedem (New York)
Dry Vermouth, Kedem (New York)
Partom 10-year-old Port, Carmel (Israel)
Montaigne Cognac (France)
Montaigne Cognac Napoleon (France)
Louis Royer X.O. Cognac (France)
Grappa, Givon (Israel)
Grappa, Givon special reserve (Israel)

FRENCH WHITES
White Merlot, Abarbanel
Chardonnay, Herzog selection
Bordeaux, Demi, Châteauneuf

Bordeaux, Demi-Sec, Château Peroudier Bergerac
Minervois, Château La Reze White
Macon-Villages, Bokobsa
Sancerre, Le Plessis
Vouvray Moelleux
Chablis Premier Cru
Gewürztraminer, Alsace, Abarbanel
Riesling, Alsace, Abarbanel

FRENCH REDS
Valflore, Herzog selection
Merlot, Herzog selection
Syrah, Abarbanel
Cabernet Sauvignon, Abarbanel
Cabernet Sauvignon, Baron Herzog
Minervois, Château La Reze
Bordeaux, Delagrave
Bordeaux Superieur, Château Bel-Air
Minervois, Château De Paraza,
Côtes du Rhône, Cuvée du Centenaire
Chinon, Moulin des Sablons
Morgon, Cru du Beaujolais
Brouilly, Cru du Beaujolais
Haut-Médoc, Barons de Rothschild
Margaux, Château Giscours

ISRAELI WHITES
Sauvignon Blanc, Golan
Chardonnay Galil, Carmel
Chardonnay, Golan
Gewürztraminer, Gan Eden
Sauvignon Blanc, Gamla
Chardonnay, Yarden
White Riesling, Yarden

ISRAELI REDS
Emerald Hill Cabernet, Gamla
Shiraz, Carmel
Merlot, Galil, Carmel
Cabernet Sauvignon, Galil, Carmel
Cabernet Sauvignon, Golan
Merlot, Yarden

ITALIAN WINES
Pinot Grigio Bartenura (white)
Soave Bartenura (white)
Barbera d'Asti, Bartenura (red)
Chianti Classico, Bartenura (red)
Nebbiolo Langhe, Batasiolo (red)
Merlot Bartenura (red)

AUSTRALIAN WINES
Chardonnay, Teal Lake (white)
Semillon, Beckett's flat (white)
Shiraz, Beckett's flat (red)
Shiraz, Teal Lake (red)
Pinot Noir, Teal Lake (red)

CALIFORNIA WHITES
Chenin Blanc, Baron Herzog
White Zinfandel, Baron Herzog
Contour, Weinstock
Sauvignon Blanc, Weinstock
Sauvignon Blanc, Hagafen
Johannisberg Riesling, Baron Herzog
Chardonnay, Baron Herzog
Chardonnay "C'est Bouilli," Gan Eden
Chardonnay, Hagafen
Chardonnay, Russian River, Baron Herzog

CALIFORNIA REDS
Pinot Noir, Hagafen
Syrah, Hagafen
Gamay, Baron Herzog
Red Zinfandel, Baron Herzog
Cuvée "Les Trois Canards," Gan Eden
Merlot, Paso Robles, Baron Herzog
Merlot, Hagafen
Cabernet Sauvignon, Baron Herzog
Cabernet Sauvignon, Baron Herzog, Alexander Valley
Cabernet Sauvignon, Baron Herzog, Napa Valley

CONVERSION CHART

Weight Equivalents

The metric weights given in this chart are not exact equivalents, but have been rounded up or down slightly to make measuring easier.

Avoirdupois	Metric
¼ oz	7 g
½ oz	15 g
1 oz	30 g
2 oz	60 g
3 oz	90 g
4 oz	115 g
5 oz	150 g
6 oz	175 g
7 oz	200 g
8 oz (½ lb)	225 g
9 oz	250 g
10 oz	300 g
11 oz	325 g
12 oz	350 g
13 oz	375 g
14 oz	400 g
15 oz	425 g
16 oz (1 lb)	450 g
1½ lb	750 g
2 lb	900 g
2¼ lb	1 kg
3 lb	1.4 kg
4 lb	1.8 kg

Volume Equivalents

These are not exact equivalents for American cups and spoons, but have been rounded up or down slightly to make measuring easier.

American	Metric	Imperial
¼ t	1.2 ml	
½ t	2.5 ml	
1 t	5.0 ml	
½ T (1.5 t)	7.5 ml	
1 T (3 t)	15 ml	
¼ cup (4 T)	60 ml	2 fl oz
⅓ cup (5 T)	75 ml	2½ fl oz
½ cup (8 T)	125 ml	4 fl oz
⅔ cup (10 T)	150 ml	5 fl oz
¾ cup (12 T)	175 ml	6 fl oz
1 cup (16 T)	250 ml	8 fl oz
1¼ cups	300 ml	10 fl oz (½ pt)
1½ cups	350 ml	12 fl oz
2 cups (1 pint)	500 ml	16 fl oz
2½ cups	625 ml	20 fl oz (1 pint)
1 quart	1 liter	32 fl oz

Oven Temperature Equivalents

Oven Mark	F	C	Gas
Very cool	250–275	130–140	½–1
Cool	300	150	2
Warm	325	170	3
Moderate	350	180	4
Moderately hot	375	190	5
	400	200	6
Hot	425	220	7
	450	230	8
Very hot	475	250	9

INDEX (page numbers in *italics* refer to photographs)